HOW LAW KNOWS

The Amherst Series in Law, Jurisprudence, and Social Thought

EDITED BY

Austin Sarat, Lawrence Douglas, and Martha Merrill Umphrey

How Law Knows

Edited by

AUSTIN SARAT,

LAWRENCE DOUGLAS, AND

MARTHA MERRILL UMPHREY

STANFORD UNIVERSITY PRESS

Stanford, California, 2007

Stanford University Press
Stanford, California

Printed in the United States of America on acid-free, archival-quality paper

Library of Congress Cataloging-in-Publication Data

How law knows / Edited by Austin Sarat, Lawrence Douglas, and Martha Merrill Umphrey.
p. cm.—(Amherst series in law, jurisprudence, and social thought)
Includes bibliographical references and index.
ISBN-13: 978-0-8047-5525-2 (cloth : alk. paper)
1. Law—Methodology. 2. Jurisprudence. 3. Legal certainty. 4. Law and fact. I. Sarat, Austin. II. Douglas, Lawrence. III. Umphrey, Martha Merrill. IV. Series.

K230.H69H69 2006
340—dc22 2006004575

Typeset by G&S Production Services in 10/14.5 Minion

To B., my pride and joy (AS)

Acknowledgments

The chapters in this book were originally prepared for and presented as a lecture series at Amherst College during the 2004–2005 academic year. We are grateful to our Amherst College colleagues David Delaney and Nasser Hussain for their enthusiastic and helpful participation in that series. We thank our students in Amherst College's Department of Law, Jurisprudence & Social Thought for their interest in the issues addressed in this book. We are especially grateful for Conor Clarke's invaluable assistance in the preparation of our introductory essay. Finally, we would like to express our appreciation for generous financial support provided by the College's Charles Hamilton Houston Forum on Law and Social Change and to Amherst's Dean of the Faculty, Greg Call, for his interest and support.

Contents

ACKNOWLEDGMENTS *vii*

CONTRIBUTORS *xi*

Complexity, Contingency, and Change in Law's Knowledge Practices: An Introduction *1*
AUSTIN SARAT, LAWRENCE DOUGLAS, AND MARTHA MERRILL UMPHREY, WITH CONOR CLARKE

"Fact" and the Proof of Fact in Anglo-American Law (c. 1500–1850) *25*
BARBARA J. SHAPIRO

Theoretical and Methodological Issues in the Study of Legal Knowledge Practices *72*
MARIANA VALVERDE

Legal Realism as Psychological and Cultural (Not Political) Realism *93*
DONALD BRAMAN AND DAN M. KAHAN

How Law Knows in the American Trial Court *126*
ROBERT P. BURNS

Fact-Finding in Constitutional Cases *156*
DAVID L. FAIGMAN

INDEX *199*

Contributors

DONALD BRAMAN is a JD student at Yale Law School.

ROBERT P. BURNS is Professor at Northwestern University School of Law.

CONOR CLARKE is a student at Amherst College.

LAWRENCE DOUGLAS is Professor of Law, Jurisprudence & Social Thought at Amherst College.

DAVID L. FAIGMAN is Professor of Law at the Hastings College of Law.

DAN M. KAHAN is Elizabeth K. Dollard Professor at Yale Law School.

AUSTIN SARAT is the William Nelson Cromwell Professor of Jurisprudence & Political Science and Professor of Law, Jurisprudence & Social Thought at Amherst College and Five College Fortieth Anniversary Professor.

BARBARA J. SHAPIRO is Professor Emeritus in the Rhetoric Department, University of California, Berkeley.

MARTHA MERRILL UMPHREY is Associate Professor of Law, Jurisprudence & Social Thought at Amherst College.

MARIANA VALVERDE is Professor at the Centre of Criminology, University of Toronto.

HOW LAW KNOWS

Complexity, Contingency, and Change in Law's Knowledge Practices: An Introduction

AUSTIN SARAT, LAWRENCE DOUGLAS,
AND MARTHA MERRILL UMPHREY,
with CONOR CLARKE

While theology has often served as a public arena for the playing out of disputes about how and where to seek the truth, in the present day and especially in secular societies, law has become a privileged site in which people either seek the truth themselves or comment on the truth-seeking efforts of others. This dimension of law is not always acknowledged. . . . But if power works through knowledge, it should prove useful to undertake an examination of some legal events and processes that highlights the knowledge dimension.

—Mariana Valverde, *Law's Dream of a Common Knowledge*

Reflecting on the production of evidence in court cases, we recognize that legal practitioners, no less than scientists, are professional fact-makers, who weave objects, images, and rhetoric into narratives designed to compel assent from their intended audiences.

—Sheila Jasanoff, "The Eye of Everyman: Witnessing DNA in the Simpson Trial"

When citizens think about law's ways of knowing and about how legal officials gather information, assess factual claims, and judge people and situations, they are often befuddled, confused by the seemingly arcane and constrained quality of the information-gathering, fact-evaluating procedures that legal officials employ or impose.[1] Yet law's ways of knowing are as varied as are the institutions and officials who populate any legal system. And relatively few of them are highly ritualized and rule bound.[2] Most of the others are embedded in a distinctive bureaucratic culture or are entirely idiosyncratic and personal. Few are specialized and esoteric; most are rather ordinary.

All of law's ways of knowing are historically specific, evolving in response to developments both internal and external to law itself.[3] In some contexts, those procedures seem odd, artificial, and divorced from cultural common sense. In others, the ways law knows seem all too common, too reliant on quotidian assumptions and cultural stereotypes. With respect to the former, we often want law's ways of knowing to be less distant, less artificial, and more grounded in the familiar; with respect to the latter, we worry that law's ways of knowing are insufficiently removed from prevailing assumptions. We can get an initial picture of the variability of law's ways of knowing and of our reactions to them by comparing the rules of evidence in a criminal trial with racial profiling by the police.

Rules of Evidence in a Criminal Trial

Anyone who has ever served on a jury or watched a trial on television can no doubt attest that inside the courtroom, law's ways of knowing seem strange, out of touch, disconnected from the usual ways in which people acquire information or make decisions.[4] Criminal trials follow a specialized set of rules and conventions governing the admissibility of evidence, the testimony of witnesses, and what counts as a proven fact.[5] These rules and conventions are designed to keep from the jury information that is not relevant to a material fact in the case, information that, while relevant, is more prejudicial than probative, is deemed unreliable, or might distract the jury from the case at hand.

Prohibitions on hearsay and on character evidence, for example, are intended to seal off the trial from ways of knowing that people depend on to make sense of the world beyond the courtroom.[6] The former serve to exclude allegedly unreliable information, information that cannot be subject to cross-examination;[7] the latter keeps out of court knowledge that might lead the jury to make false inferences.[8] Hearsay is defined as "'second-hand' information. It occurs when a witness testifies not about something they personally saw or heard, but testifies about something someone else told them or said they saw. Hearsay usually involves an attempt to get some crucial fact entered into evidence that cannot be admitted by any other means. The constitutional due process danger that this represents is that it deprives the other side of an opportunity to confront and cross-examine the 'real' witness who originally saw or heard something."[9]

Another trial procedure forbids the use of evidence of other crimes, wrongs, or acts "to prove the character of a person in order to show action in conformity therewith."[10] Thus, in a sexual assault trial, this rule generally forbids the admission of evidence of prior assaults by the same defendant to prove that he committed the offense for which he is currently being tried.[11] What in our ordinary lives would be a plausible inference is, in the distinctive world of the trial, forbidden.

For jurors, these prohibitions and this sealing off of the trial from conventions may seem artificial and be quite frustrating. Reflecting on his experience of having served on a criminal jury, William Finnegan says, "Serving on the jury had been gratifying in its way, but it had also been profoundly irritating. I wanted to learn more about the real story, the fuller, truer tale that we jurors, with a man's freedom hanging on our judgment, had been forced to guess at lamely."[12]

Moreover, the effort to seal off the criminal trial, to constrain what jurors hear and the ways jurors obtain information, is only partially successful at best. Jurors bring to their service a full stock of folk knowledge. By folk knowledge, we mean the everyday, taken-for-granted understandings that shape people's perceptions, thinking, actions, and reactions to events and situations. As de Certeau remarks, citizens often make of "rituals, representations and laws imposed on them something quite different from what their . . . [originators] had in mind."[13] Thus, folk knowledge sometimes pushes against, as it pushes into, the domain of state law. It domesticates the arcane rules that police what can be said and known in trials. It is itself integral to state law, both constitutive and sometimes critical of it.[14]

When rules of evidence or trial procedure conflict with folk knowledge or belief, the former generally bend to the latter. Reporting on the way the jury on which he served interpreted and dealt with the trial judge's instructions, Finnegan writes, "We started discussing the alibi and were soon busily contravening Judge Berman's instruction that we 'must not, under any circumstance, indulge in speculation or guesswork, nor are you to consider anything outside the evidence.' We guessed and speculated about the lives and motives of the alibi witnesses, trying to put 'the evidence' into some narrative context that made sense. . . . Meanwhile the impossibility of considering only 'the evidence' was so obvious it was hardly mentioned."[15]

Racial Profiling by the Police

If the rules of evidence governing criminal trials are specific to law, frustrate convention, and defy folk knowledge, the world of policing seems to embrace convention and folk knowledge. Despite the requirements of the rules of criminal procedure, police depend on and deploy ways of knowing that bridge the gap between official and social worlds.[16] They depend on a set of social assumptions built up and transmitted through their own organizations and responsive to the distinctive demands of their work.[17] Reporting on his participant-observation study of police, Jerome Skolnick argues that officers organize their knowledge practices in such a way as to highlight situations of threat or danger.[18] "The policeman," Skolnick notes, "because his work requires him to be occupied continually with potential violence, develops a perceptual shorthand to identify certain kinds of people as symbolic assailants, that is, as persons who use gesture, language, and attire that the policeman has come to recognize as a prelude to violence."[19] Police, Skolnick argues, "respond to the vague indication of danger suggested by appearance. . . . [A] young man may suggest the threat of violence to the policeman by his manner of walking or 'strutting,' the insolence in the demeanor being registered by the policeman as a possible preamble to later attack."[20]

In constructing "symbolic assailants," race plays a key role. Thus, Skolnick found a high level of racial prejudice among the police he studied as well as a "broader pattern of racial and ethnic stereotyping."[21] Such stereotypes are information-gathering techniques, or rather ways in which police organize their perceptions of the world in the absence of detailed, individualized information. "They are called on in many aspects of their work," Skolnick says, "to make 'hunch' judgments, based on loose correlations."[22] Ethnic stereotypes play a substantial role in their "armory of investigation."[23]

Seen in this light, recent controversies about racial profiling may be reframed as controversies about law's knowledge practices.[24] Those who defend profiling do so on the grounds that, in some limited contexts, race is a reasonable predictor of criminal conduct and that attending to race is a rational way to gather and assess information.[25] And many of those who criticize it do so on the grounds that race is a poor surrogate for criminality; thus, the use of race in law enforcement is irrational.[26]

The term *racial profiling* has been applied to a spectrum of different police practices in which police rely on race, to one degree or another, to make inferences about criminality.[27] As Gross and Livingston define it,

> "racial profiling" occurs whenever a law enforcement officer questions, stops, arrests, searches, or otherwise investigates a person because the officer believes that members of that person's racial or ethnic group are more likely than the population at large to commit the sort of crime the officer is investigating. The essence of racial profiling is a global judgment that the targeted group—before September 11, usually African Americans or Hispanics—is more prone to commit crime in general, or to commit a particular type of

> crime, than other racial or ethnic groups. If the officer's conduct is based at least in part on such a general racial or ethnic judgment, it does not matter if she uses other criteria as well in deciding on her course of action. It is racial profiling to target young black men on the basis of a belief that they are more likely than others to commit crimes, even though black women and older black men are not directly affected.[28]

As Gross and Livingston point out,

> The range of things the government can do on the basis of racial or ethnic information is enormous. If mass imprisonment defines the high end (short of torture or execution), paying close attention may define the low end. After September 11, nobody could seriously complain about the FBI paying more attention to reports of suspicious behavior by Saudi men than to similar reports about Hungarian women—even though as a consequence many more Saudi men will set off false alarms. In between there are infinite gradations, as the government's conduct becomes increasingly intrusive, disruptive, frightening, and humiliating.[29]

In 1976, the United States Supreme Court confronted the question of the constitutionality of racial profiling in a case alleging that a Border Patrol agent investigating illegal immigration sixty-six miles inside the Mexico–United States border relied largely on ethnicity in making referrals to a secondary inspection area.[30] Ultimately, the Court found the practice constitutional.[31] Writing for the majority, Justice Powell described the governmental interest as follows: "Large numbers of aliens seek illegally to enter or to remain in the United States . . . Interdicting the flow of illegal entrants from Mexico poses formidable law enforcement problems," and argued that "the consequent intrusion on Fourth Amendment interests is quite limited. . . . It involves only a brief detention of travelers during which 'all that is required of the vehicle's occupants is a response to a brief question or two and possibly the production of a document evidencing a right to be in the United States.' "[32]

Justice Powell upheld the practice of racial profiling by saying, "Even if it be assumed that such referrals are made largely on the basis of apparent Mexican ancestry, we perceive no constitutional violation."[33] He linked racial profiling to law's knowledge practices and found race relevant to the work of the Border Patrol. As he put it, "To the extent that the Border Patrol relies on apparent Mexican ancestry at this checkpoint . . . that reliance clearly is relevant to the law enforcement need to be served."[34]

"Trade" Knowledge

Here law's knowledge practices hardly seem governed by a set of special conventions and arcane rules. Instead, common-sense inferences, broad associations, and cultural stereotypes provide the frame within which legal officials come to know the world. Indeed, a substantial scholarly literature has analyzed the ways in which various legal officials develop what Levi and Valverde call "'trade' knowledge, knowledge learned on the job and focusing on the enforcement of particular codes in particular settings."[35]

To take but a few examples from this literature, in the case of the police, Trish Oberweis and Michael Musheno argue that such trade knowledge can take a variety of forms, almost all of which are "richly normative and contingent rather than narrowly rule driven and fixed."[36] As is the case with racial profiling, police engage in "raw forms of division": classifying citizens according to racial, gender, and age-based standards, associating weakness and innocence with women, dangerousness with minorities, and so on. What this often leads to, the authors contend, is the use of "crude notions of 'badness' in combination with broad categorizations, denying the uniqueness of individuals, and enfolding them into social categories already marked for exclusion and the invocation of coercion."[37]

But the process of knowledge acquisition deployed by police is, they contend, more complex than the usual discussion of stereotyping and profiling captures. As they put it, "the identity process works in both directions . . . Due, in part, to the many ways they identify themselves, cops connect with people as unique individuals and sometimes defy the simple coercive politics of stereotyping whole groups as 'bad.'"[38] In other words, one of the rules of the trade that governs police work is that officers bring knowledge of themselves to bear in their interactions with citizens: An officer's own racial, religious, or socioeconomic experience often influences his or her interactions with citizens of a similar stripe. This in turn is one of the reasons "cops are not uniform in the norms and primary values they use to render judgment about citizens and fellow officers."[39] The knowledge processes they employ vary with their own identities, the identities of the citizens they encounter, and the web of institutional norms in which they are embedded.

The informality and variability described by Oberweis and Musheno have, in other contexts, produced a reaction, an effort to ensure greater uniformity and predictability in law's knowledge practices. Thus, Eugene Bardach and Robert Kagan observe that, within the contemporary regulatory state, there has been a drive to "reduce the variations" in regulation "by developing common interpretations of the rules and a unified philosophy of enforcement."[40] What this has produced, the authors suggest, is a loss of discretion: Under this new regulatory philosophy, regulators "must conduct inspections with an eye toward what is legally proper," not toward what personal experience or even commonsense might dictate. "In the most significant regulatory areas," they write, the law has been deliberately structured "to program inspectors to apply regulations strictly, to pressure enforcement officials to apply formal penalties to violations, and to adopt a more legalistic and deterrence-oriented stance vis-à-vis regulated enterprises."[41]

In this view, regulators increasingly come to acquire and employ legal knowledge in a rigid, formal way: They are "quick to apply legal sanctions against deviations from the law—but less able and willing to adapt the law to the situation."[42] Inspectors are expected to "detect, document and prosecute violations, rather than engage in an open-ended search for 'problems.'"[43] Unlike the police described by Oberweis and Musheno, their knowledge of legal problems is usually derived from a predetermined set of lapses that are enumerated in the regulations; case-specific knowledge that could be gained on a particular regulated site is rarely, if ever, used.

Turning from police and regulators to public defenders, research documents the distinctive ways they acquire trade knowledge. For example, according to David Sudnow, after a certain amount of time on the job, a public defender (PD) acquires a sense of what constitutes a "normal crime"—and thus, a normal criminal. "In the course of routinely encountering persons charged with 'petty theft,' 'burglary,' 'assault with a deadly weapon,' 'rape,' 'possession of marijuana,' etc.," the PD gains knowledge of the typical manner in which offenses of given classes are committed, the social characteristics of the persons who regularly commit them, the features of the settings in which they occur, the types of victims often involved, and the like. He learns to speak knowledgeably of "burglars," "petty thieves," "drunks," "rapists," "narcos," and so on and to attribute to them personal biographies, modes of usual criminal activity, criminal histories, psychological characteristics, and social backgrounds.

Public defenders and similar legal actors employ a rigid categorization system—the "classificatory schema" for criminal acts—that can serve as a "description of a population of defendants."[44] The PD, in short, becomes a veritable storehouse of information, informally collecting and organizing a host of information to apply to (and acquire knowledge of) future crimes and criminals.[45] Indeed, Sudnow suggests, the "achievement of competence as a PD is signaled by the gradual acquisition of professional command not simply of local penal code peculiarities and courtroom folklore, but, as importantly, of relevant features of the social structure and criminological wisdom."[46] This is a knowledge learned on the job, a knowledge situated somewhere between the arcane rules of evidence that govern what can be talked about in a criminal trial and the stereotypes that Skolnick describes.

In these knowledge determinations, Richard Ericson and Patricia Baranek argue that the "accused can play little or no part"; he is, in their words, "at the bottom of the 'hierarchy of credibility' and the very fact that he has committed a crime makes what he has to say discreditable, and sometimes incredible."[47] Indeed, the authors continue, the accused are almost completely dependent on other legal actors for legal knowledge; deprived of all but what his lawyer gives him, "the accused has no option but to act on faith."[48] As a "one-shot" or occasional player in the legal machine, such people do not have the time or experience to learn the intricacies of the legal process (the "recipe" knowledge that lawyers and other full-time legal actors have). This makes an accused individual especially susceptible to the procedures of lawyers and the police, who, taking advantage of the accused's helplessness, often employ tactics that would, if full knowledge were available to the accused, be recognized as illegal.

Law's Dependence on Outside Expertise

The tactics of knowledge and control described by Sudnow, Bardach and Kagan, and Oberweis and Musheno may be in the process of undergoing substantial transformation or being supplemented by new tactics and technologies. From advanced classification systems to computerized databases to drug tests, Jonathan Simon argues that knowledge strategies are ever evolving to fit a new model of "risk management" that dominates the criminal legal system.[49] Some of these methods, like drug testing, require "little in the way of discourse, communication, or explanation"; thus, unlike previous procedures we have seen, they are "part of a self-contained 'truth'-producing system that does not require interpretation of social life in the community."[50] Such a system is, in other words, disconnected from the particulars of a situation and is less dependent on the kind of trade knowledge that Valverde highlights.[51]

What this and other such penal and regulatory procedures reflect is, for Simon, the rise of mass surveillance. Almost all contemporary knowledge-acquiring methods "make use of computers and automated record analysis systems to stay on top of a large number of individuals"; almost all "seek to attain greater predictive efficiency in knowing where to target control efforts"; and almost all "seek technical contact points that permit information to accumulate on a regular and easily assimilable basis."[52] These methods "operate by identifying categories of individuals based on their capacity for self-management and permitting individuals variable access to resources and power depending on their risk group status."[53] Like drug testing, these methods provide "standardized information" that "may be of predictive value."[54]

Simon's discussion of risk management and its knowledge-gathering protocols serves as a reminder that, in its knowledge practices, law is as often dependent as it is autonomous.[55] Law borrows; it uses knowledge, information, and expertise generated elsewhere. In various contexts—legislative, regulatory, adjudicative—legal officials seek out or depend on knowledge practices developed in other social institutions.[56] This dependence sometimes facilitates legal decision making but at other times complicates it. In some contexts, legal officials develop distinctive rules governing the receipt of such specialized knowledge.[57] In others, the penetration is seamless, easy, and virtually unnoticed. And of course, law's knowledge practices radiate beyond law's boundaries, influencing the knowledge practices of the culture in which they are embedded, certifying and credentializing, lending weight to, or undermining knowledge claims made elsewhere.[58]

From the rules of evidence to the technologies of risk management, from the practices of racial profiling to the development of trade knowledge, from the generation of independent knowledge practices to law's dependence on outside expertise, even a brief survey shows that law knows in many different ways, that its knowledge practices are contingent, responsive to context, and that they change over time.[59] The chapters assembled in *How Law Knows* provide a small sample of that diversity, that responsiveness, and the influence that law's knowledge practices have on legal outcomes and on the world beyond law.

Overview of the Chapters

The next chapter by Barbara J. Shapiro places the concept of legal "fact" in historical context, examining its evolving meaning and influence over more than three centuries. Contrary to its most common contemporary use—to denote "an indisputable or demonstrable statement of truth"—Shapiro argues that the notion of fact in the period she studied was a complex idea born of diverse influences.

Indeed, she concludes that fact in early Anglo-American law "did not carry an intrinsic connotation of truth but was rather a matter whose truth was in contestation." In this understanding, legal institutions did not aim to know some concrete and incontrovertible reality but rather sought knowledge that would "yield a satisfied conscience or understanding, or its later equivalents, moral certainty and belief 'beyond reasonable doubt.'"

Since Shapiro maintains that the concept of fact (as it applies to the activity of the courts) is "conditioned, though not entirely determined, by the general views of what passes for knowledge in the society in which the legal proceedings are embedded," she also insists that fully understanding the Anglo-American approach to fact-finding requires a "look at some of the intellectual traditions that help to shape its evidentiary practices." In tracing this evolution, Shapiro looks well beyond Anglo-American legal history; indeed, she finds the roots of legal fact in the persuasive techniques of ancient Rome's rhetorical tradition, in the influence of Scripture on witness and circumstantial evidence rules, and in the medieval approach to proof and guilt determination. After examining the ancient roots of Anglo-American fact-finding, Shapiro turns to the development of fact in two of the most prominent Anglo-American legal institutions: the jury trial and witness testimony. In a discussion of changing evidentiary standards, Shapiro considers the role of oath, witness credibility, juror conscience, and circumstantial evidence—a method of proof that was, by the eighteenth century, "widely accepted as sufficient to prove [a] fact."

But besides tracing the history of the legal fact, Shapiro describes the *influence* of legal knowledge and fact-finding methodology on other discourses, including philosophy, history, religion, and science. Her conclusions in this vein may once again seem contrary to the contemporary understanding of what constitutes fact (since she argues that "fact and methods of establishing facts were first developed in the legal setting and only later adopted by other disciplines and intellectual endeavors"). But, Shapiro contends, such conclusions are of the utmost importance: "Lack of attention to the role of law in the development of the concept fact has obscured the importance of law in traditions of knowledge-making and the legitimizing of empirical approaches to knowledge."

When it comes to philosophy, she notes that "legal traditions of fact-finding influenced philosophical exploration at the same time that legal writers began to insist that legal approaches to evidence rested on sound epistemological and logical foundations." In addition, Shapiro sees an easy link between legal fact-finding and historical scholarship because facts "for the historian as for the lawyer had to be supported by convincing evidence." The concept of fact was also useful for the religious writers of the seventeenth and eighteenth centuries because, as Shapiro notes, it provided "rational grounds" for belief in Christian scripture and other theological doctrines. Finally, legal fact-finding methodology had perhaps the greatest impact on natural science. Shapiro contends that after Francis Bacon, "[c]arefully witnessed facts by credible witnesses . . . became as central to empirical investigation of nature as they did to legitimate decisions in the courtroom." Indeed, like "legal facts, scientific facts were to be evaluated on the basis of credible witnesses who had the opportunity to observe and possessed the requisite ability, probity, skill, fidelity, status, experience, and reputation." And it is on this note—stressing the role that legal concepts of fact played in "shaping modern empirical thought"—that Shapiro ends her chapter.

The next chapter, "Theoretical and Methodological Issues in the Study of Legal Knowledge Practices," by Mariana Valverde, presents another kind of historical analysis set in the Anglo-American world: an examination of the lineage and influence of pragmatist legal theory. From Oliver Wendell Holmes to Roscoe Pound to Stanley Fish, Valverde traces some of the more important shifts and developments in law's pragmatic tradition. Although these writers differ in important respects, Valverde maintains that it is possible to "sweep those differences under the rug and speak of a pragmatist temperament or habitus that runs throughout English-language legal theorizing and that is compatible with a number of philosophical models and with a variety of political stances."

Although contemporary English and American law may not be "essentially" pragmatic, Valverde argues that there is a kind of "silent dialectic" between pragmatism and antipragmatism at work in recent legal decisions. This pragmatic habitus, as she calls it, is not easily defined "but is easily described": "It is a stance that is concerned more with effects than with formal elegance and coherence. It is also one that takes law as an ever-changing formation that is deeply embedded in a complex world that can never be adequately captured in static theoretical models."

Valverde has no general objection to pragmatism, but she argues that it "does not take us very far at all." Just how, she asks, "are we then to document the very striking differences that quickly arise when legal actors . . . go on to actually examine and count the relevant effects?" Valverde contends that pragmatism doesn't offer a compelling answer to this question, and for her, this is an important point of difference between legal pragmatists and sociolegal scholars—a difference that lies in what Valverde calls "the scope of the inquiry." Valverde argues that the former set of writers "share an a priori knowledge move, a move that excludes anyone other than legislators and judges from the lawmaking function and that therefore confines pragmatic inquiries into effects to investigations of the formal legal system of discourse." Sociolegal scholars, on the other hand, "have for a long time now stressed that lawmaking has deep roots in social struggles and in economic conflicts." Too often, she believes, the "society" part of "law and society" is much more rigorously researched than the "law" part. And although it is not selectivity that is the problem, Valverde claims that an unreflective selectivity that is driven by nothing more than one's own training or one's institutional location does present problems for sociolegal research. For Valverde, the relationship between law and knowledge is broad and complex, and she is interested in avoiding the pigeonholing quality of either the pragmatic or sociolegal account.

A tendency for what she calls "sociological reductionism" leads Valverde to call for new kinds of analysis of law's knowledge practices—"new studies that resist the temptation of waving the flag of 'society' as against 'law.'" In searching for a possible means by which to conduct these studies, she turns to the actor network theory (ANT) and science and technology studies (STS) of scholars such as Bruno Latour. A key insight of Latour and others, Valverde contends, is the methodological decision that "much is to be gained by treating one's research site as if the distinction between human and nonhuman could be bracketed."

It is exactly such binary distinctions that Valverde wants to avoid: distinctions between things and people, between animate and inanimate, between legal text and lawyer, and so on. ANT and STS provide means for doing so in a new concept of "actor," which is "always relational" and has "little or no link with the sociological concept of 'agency.'" In this view, almost anything—including "persons, devices, rules, laboratory animals, chemical reagents, and knowledge bits"—can be designated as an actor as long as it is involved in a relational network of claims and interests. By operating under a theory that displaces, to some extent, "human actors," Valverde argues that the use of ANT and STS analysis diminishes the reductionism that tends to mark sociological work as a whole. Such an approach, when applied to law, would have a certain satisfying and original unity at the level of theory/method. It would show that certain features of the legal power/knowledge systems are visible in different and new ways if one sets aside the distinction between things and people and between the textual and the social.

After providing a broad outline ANT/STS analysis, Valverde moves on to explore, in broad outline, particular legal "knowledge moves" to which it might be applied. She examines several moves, the first of which she designates "anonymous allusion," a procedure in which general references are favored over specific citations: "studies show . . ."; "expert evidence supports . . ."; and so forth. The second knowledge move used by legal actors is "exemplary excerpting," in which cited passages are pulled out of their original context to add weight to a particular position. A third knowledge move is "epistemological sidelining," in which studies relevant to a particular work are marginalized "rather than accepted or rejected or distinguished." Additional moves include what Valverde calls "transmuting jurisdiction into knowledge" and "responsibilization through imputed knowledge."

Valverde concludes by suggesting that legal jurisdiction is frequently transmuted into a knowledge claim (city councilors, for example, might be presumed to "know" the city streets), and by exploring how legal officials often "impute" knowledge to hypothetical persons (Mr. X should have known), relationships of responsibility are created between actors. By no means exhaustive, Valverde's discussions are offered in "the spirit of experimentation and dialogue" and in the hopes that they might foment new and creative methodologies for conducting sociolegal research. Because legal knowledge is created by a multiplicity of sources and methods, Valverde wants to begin the search for a descriptive methodology that can do justice to complexity, contingency, and change in how law knows.

Next, in Donald Braman and Dan M. Kahan's "Legal Realism as Psychological and Cultural (Not Political) Realism," the emphasis shifts to more general questions of law and epistemology, as the authors explore how legal decision makers, like judges and jurors, come to know the law and the facts in the cases they decide. Their chapter rejects "mainstream accounts [that] cast jurors and judges either as strategic political actors or as faithful and politically inert servants of legal authority wielded by others." In their view, neither realism nor formalism provides an adequate account of how legal actors know. They argue for an account of legal knowledge that is "grounded in the social and cognitive mechanisms that we know guide human belief formation and decision making more generally."

These mechanisms are found in what they call "cultural cognition," or cultural commitments that are prior "to factual beliefs on highly charged political issues." Culture is prior to fact, Braman and Kahan argue, in "the cognitive sense that what citizens believe about the empirical consequences" of policies "*derives* from their cultural worldviews." As a result, "even citizens who earnestly consider empirical policy issues in an open-minded and wholly instrumental way will align themselves into warring cultural factions."

Drawing on the anthropological work of Mary Douglas, Braman and Kahan go on to substantiate this claim with empirical evidence of their own: "Modern sensibilities and perceptions of danger" ("it is dirty and dangerous to leave shoes on the table"), for example, "are artifacts of our commitment to distinctive cultural orderings" ("shoes are not an item traditionally associated with tables"). But unlike Douglas, Braman and Kahan proceed to ask a further question: *Why* is this the case? Their answer lies in "several overlapping psychological mechanisms" that undergird and shore up the culturally cognitive biases. By combining this social psychology with the anthropological work of Douglas, Braman and Kahan come to the broad conclusion that "various mechanisms of belief formation identified by contemporary social psychology are likely to generate risk perceptions skewed along cultural lines."

What does this mean for the relationship between law and knowledge? First and foremost, Braman and Kahan argue that "law knows in the same way that ordinary democratic citizens know." For legal officials and citizens, cultural values provide a framework within which facts are apprehended. Those values orient judges and jurors "in determining what outcome is dictated by the law and evidence at hand." Because the "most important cultural norms are structured along predictable dimensions," legal decisions themselves can appear to be quite predictable as can the lines of conflict which produce those decisions and which those decisions engender. Individuals "don't mechanically accept new information; rather, they evaluate each new piece of evidence based on its conformity with prior beliefs." Because seemingly empirical debates over all manner of public policy will be guided be the invisible hands of conflicting cultural worldviews, knowledge of legal effects is linked to culture prior to considerations of rightness and wrongness or desirability and undesirability. Moreover, Braman and Kahan maintain, cultural cognition can be used to show why framing legal debates in consequentialist terms so often fails: Because citizens disagree about what the consequences of a given policy actually are, it makes little sense to talk only about what consequences are good or bad, right or wrong.

After outlining cultural cognition and its application to legal knowledge in general, Braman and Kahan apply it to the two dominant positions in the academic debate over cultural conflict: the "culture war thesis" and the "end of ideology thesis."

Both positions, they conclude, are fatally flawed—the former for not doing justice to the influence of culture in shaping beliefs and the latter for giving too much credence to the relationship between culture and belief. Indeed, Braman and Kahan's point is not that cultural values *motivate* particular political opinions; rather, they "merely *orient* it through a complex set of interrelated social and cognitive mechanisms." The effect is filtering, not controlling.

Throughout their chapter, Braman and Kahan seek to take up the challenge of providing an empirically accurate and verifiable account of the knowledge practices of judges and jurors that will do the work that legal realism once set out to do, but do it without the flaws of the realist accounts. Realist accounts fail because they do not attend to "the subtle orientation of the mind to facts and arguments that cohere with the 'background and philosophy'" of the judge or juror. Attending to these orientations of the mind suggests that the decisions of courts are seldom likely to "resolve the controversy over norms that brought the case to court in the first place."

In "How Law Knows in the American Trial Court," Robert P. Burns emphasizes the contingency of law's knowledge practices and again focuses on questions of knowledge in particular legal institutions. Following Valverde's advice to avoid the announcement of the arrival of a postmodern legal regime, one without unified metanarratives, and concentrate our efforts, at least for now, on finely grained descriptions of what we actually do in a range of legal contexts, Burns offers descriptions of knowledge practices in the trial court in the United States. He starts by asking how decision makers at the trial level know the rules governing the case—a question that he thinks begs another question: *Who* knows the rules in the court?—Burns's preliminary answer is fairly simple: lawyers and judges.

For lawyers, knowing the rules involves following a "shifting and informal set logic based on the semantic meaning of the legal rules and the ways in which the situation may be fairly given a description and the relationship between them, supplemented by notions of the 'purposes' of various enactments." And for judges, there is another set of "professionally prescribed ways" through which knowledge is obtained. In particular, this is done through a "set of legally authoritative commonplaces available to judges for the interpretation of constitutions, statutes, and case law"—a set of "canonical justifications that can be offered more or less artfully to justify a particular subsumption of the facts." And although there is a "continuum" in how these justifications are used, Burns still finds restraint in the "screening function" played by the norms embedded in legal rules.

Matters get more complicated when the relationship between legal knowledge and the jury is considered because, Burns maintains, the jury cannot know the law in the same way that judges and lawyers can. Juror instructions might seem to indicate some kind of professionalized knowledge, but Burns argues, social scientific studies show that "juror comprehension of jury instructions is quite low." As Finnegan's description of his own jury service shows, what juries have, instead of a formalized legal understanding, is an "approach to evidence" that is "equitable" rather than "rule-based": "they are insensitive to many of the distinctions the law makes; their life-world values affect even the fact-finding process; the norms implicit in the narrative structure of the trial are of greater significance than the rules embedded in the instruction." And the jury's eclectic approach to legal knowledge, Burns says, influences knowledge moves in the trial as a whole: Lawyers, for example, are likely to construct cases with a "double helix" of norms—some from "within the practices of the jurors' life world" and others from within what is implicit in the legal rules of which the lawyer must at least be wary.

Depending on one's perspective, this eclecticism has its advantages and disadvantages, but no matter what position one takes, Burns argues that it connects trial court procedure with another important element of the story of how law knows: narrative. For Burns, narrative pervades the trial court, most notably, perhaps, in a lawyer's opening statement: an evaluative, fully characterized narrative of the kind the jury is asked to decide between. Narrative is present elsewhere as well, including evidentiary proceedings; after all, all kinds of stories can be told that are fair to the facts and stretch out toward human purposes. But, Burns argues, the trial is not only about deft storytelling. Indeed, much of the trial is wrapped up with "never completely resolved tensions" that it creates: tensions between varieties of narrative and tensions between narrative substances (legal, moral). This analysis leads Burns to the conclusion that trial court juries "know" by "relying on different levels of *constrained* narrative to build the latter toward their understanding of the case." Narrative is important for the construction of legal knowledge during the trial, but it is not without its complexities. "All of the narrative, rhetorical, and dramatic devices of the trial tend to invite a response of the whole personality to the trial itself."

After laying out this framework, Burns takes a step back to ask how we "*know* when the trial really knows." Context might seem like one possibility, but Burns has trouble with the idea of placing the trial in a "broader context of practices" for two reasons: He doesn't think there is any generalizable standard by which one can select the practices that *compose* the context; and more fundamentally, he doesn't think such an account can be given in a language that is "as rich as the language of the trial"—a language, in other words, that would do justice to it. In contrast to Valverde's push for new and more expansive ways of examining legal institutions, Burns argues that because a question of *how* law knows necessarily involves a normative consideration of when law "*succeeds* in *knowing*," a different kind of account is needed—an account that illuminates how the trial "can succeed and the forms of understanding germane to that success." For Burns, the knowledge produced in a legal trial is distinctive and, as such, deserves a unique examination. For him, the trial functions in much the way as does a work of art. It allows us to see something that could not be seen any other way.

In "Fact-Finding in Constitutional Cases," David L. Faigman shifts gears from the trial court to the Supreme Court to examine the relationship between legal doctrine and fact-finding in a constitutional setting. Since the earliest days of constitutional law, Faigman reminds us, "the Supreme Court has consistently relied on facts to inform its constitutional jurisprudence." But there is, Faigman notes, a danger in using facts to set constitutional norms: Facts are "highly indeterminate and they inevitably destabilize the sought-after stability of fundamental constitutional values." This tension, a tension between the generally dynamic quality associated with fact-finding and the allegedly stable character of constitutional doctrine, is the focus of Faigman's chapter. It is a tension, he argues, that reveals a need for balance because courts must develop a constitutional jurisprudence that allows doctrine to evolve in light of contemporary circumstances but which remains faithful to settled constitutional norms.

Faigman suggests that the Supreme Court has never developed an intelligible constitutional fact jurisprudence: It is, in his words, "one of the great silences in constitutional law." Moreover, this silence extends to more than just one constitutional realm because, he argues, fact-finding "is an essential component of both constitutional interpretation and constitutional adjudication." But Faigman notes that writers like Ronald Dworkin have attempted to avoid the malleable, indefinite character of constitutional fact jurisprudence through the idea of "interpretive facts"—facts that don't (or no longer) require empirical substantiation and can simply be applied in legal interpretation. Dworkin's argument is not without its problems, but interpretive facts do, Faigman says, play a "steadying role" in constitutional jurisprudence. This is because factual premises, in Faigman's words, "petrify" when they become repeatedly upheld as acceptable precedent. Over time, actually proving a factual predicate of a particular decision ceases to be important: It is simply accepted as law independent of its actual empirical merits. Thus, because "constitutional facts are 'interpreted' and not 'found,' justices can employ them with little fear that future researchers might call into question the premises of their handiwork."

Faigman then moves on to "set forth a proposed taxonomy of constitutional facts that furnishes the foundation on which a coherent jurisprudence of constitutional facts might be built." Drawing from the work of Kenneth Culp Davis, he identifies two main varieties: "legislative facts," which "do not usually concern the immediate parties but are general facts that help the tribunal decide questions of law and policy and discretion," and "adjudicative facts," which are "facts particular to the dispute." A key difference between them, Faigman argues, is "the level of decision making at which the asserted facts are relevant": the former are broad and recurring; the latter are limited and specific. But legislative and adjudicative facts are not, Faigman contends, the only kinds, and so he also explores another distinction in constitutional facts: "constitutional rule-facts" versus "constitutional review-facts." The former, he says, are advanced to substantiate a particular interpretation of the Constitution, whereas the latter are used to meet the pertinent constitutional rule. Faigman's intentions at this point are descriptive, not normative, and although he concedes that the lines between these categories are often haphazard and blurry, he believes the categories are nonetheless useful for examining the court's knowledge-gathering efforts.

The *process* by which the court decides on the facts—the process by which it defines "the kinds of facts that are relevant"—raises a number of "procedural issues"; most centrally, it raises the issue of deference. Since courts are not the only institutions determining the facts, they must decide how much deference they owe to another institution's, or to another court's, constitutional fact-finding. This in turn brings Faigman to a difficult question: "When, if ever, can a lower court distinguish (and thereby decline to follow) higher court precedent on the basis that the facts supporting that precedent have changed or that our knowledge of them has changed?" Faigman's answer is that it depends on the kind of fact involved. For Faigman, the really contentious cases involve "constitutional review-facts," a group that includes, among other things, factual questions such as when the fetus becomes viable and the effects of segregation on black children.

But, he continues, lower courts should have the ability to reevaluate the factual premises used, even here, for a number of reasons. First, Faigman contends that such reevaluations will enhance legitimacy by keeping the Court "in line with contemporary knowledge of the facts underlying constitutional decisions." Second, he argues that lower court review will lead the Supreme Court to use facts more carefully because "the knowledge that lower courts might revisit factual premises for their holdings should lead the justices to be more careful in explaining the reasons for their decisions." Third, Faigman believes factual reevaluations will benefit the legal system more broadly because they will "facilitate the introduction of new information into the law." Finally, Faigman stresses that such reevaluations would be used sparingly because they would require "enough empirical ammunition to overwhelm the opposing precedent." Constitutional law depends on facts, and facts, Faigman stresses, should be taken seriously. But calling attention to the dynamism and complexity of law's knowledge practices, he concludes, should not leave facts free from review; employing facts well depends on their occasional reevaluation.

Whether offering a historical examination of legal fact or a broad philosophical account of how legal knowledge practices can or should be studied, whether describing the social-psychological mechanisms through which any set of legal actors know the world or the knowledge-gathering techniques of particular legal institutions, taken together the chapters in *How Law Knows* emphasize complexity, contingency, and change. Doing so reminds us that law knows in many ways—some strange, others familiar, some highly ritualized and formal, others informal and grounded in social practice. Broadening the agenda of legal scholarship to compare the varieties of its knowledge practices allows us to understand law as an arena in which knowledge is both acquired and produced, in which knowledge is both absorbed from, but also radiated back into, the social and cultural world in which law is embedded. It allows us to understand mechanisms through which law seeks to maintain its autonomy and through which it sacrifices its autonomy. Examining law's various ways of knowing over time and in response to different philosophical traditions allows us to see how the work of law plays out in the social and cultural worlds in which law is made and remade. Today, we can no longer adequately understand that work (if we ever could) unless we undertake more of the kind of careful, contextually sensitive analyses of how law knows of the kind presented in the chapters that follow.

Notes

1. See, for example, Sally Merry, *Getting Justice and Getting Even: Legal Consciousness Among Working-Class Americans* (Chicago: University of Chicago Press, 1990), 142.

2. See Mariana Valverde, *Law's Dream of a Common Knowledge* (Princeton, NJ: Princeton University Press, 2003).

3. See Barbara J. Shapiro, *A Culture of Fact: England, 1550–1720* (Ithaca, NY: Cornell University Press, 2000). On the historical contingency of fact in another context, see Mary Poovey, *A History of the Modern Fact: Problems of Knowledge in the Sciences of Wealth and Society* (Chicago: University of Chicago Press, 1998).

4. As Ewick and Silbey note, "People often experience the law as a space outside of everyday life. Law and everyday life are seen in juxtaposition and possibly opposition rather than connected and entwined. The distance between law and everyday life is a chasm through which mundane and personal matters pass and become transfigured in awesome but also costly ways." See Patricia Ewick and Susan Silbey, *The Common Place of Law: Stories from Everyday Life* (Chicago: University of Chicago Press, 1998), 76. Also D. Graham Burnett, *A Trial by Jury* (New York: Knopf, 2001).

5. As Robert Burns puts it, "The American trial is a highly rule-bound form of rhetorical practice. . . . The law of evidence provides the 'grammar' of the trial. Only those truths that can be said 'grammatically' can become part of the legal world." See Robert Burns, *A Theory of the Trial* (Princeton, NJ: Princeton University Press, 1999), 74, 86. As Burns notes, in what he calls "The Received View" of the trial, "the law of evidence seeks to ensure that the material from which the jury builds up its value-free narrative of what occurred is reliable," p. 19.

6. Burns correctly points out that recently there has been a strong shift "toward admissibility in the law of evidence." *A Theory of the Trial*, 31.

7. For a discussion of the importance of cross-examination in ensuring reliability, see *California v. Green*, 399 U.S. 149, 158 (1970).

8. See Sherry F. Colb, "'Whodunit' Versus 'What Was Done': When to Admit Character Evidence in Criminal Cases," 79 *North Carolina Law Review* (2001), 939, 946. As Colb explains, "Supporters of the character rule argue that, notwithstanding its relevance, we should exclude character evidence because jurors tend to give it undue weight. Such jurors might convict on a flimsy factual record because of a defendant's prior criminal history." See also Edward J. Imwinkelried, "A Small Contribution to the Debate over the Proposed Legislation Abolishing the Character Evidence Prohibition in Sex Offense Prosecutions," 44 *Syracuse Law Review* (1993), 1125, 1138: "In sum, there is a risk that the lay jurors will overestimate the probative value of character as a predictor of conduct."

9. See "The Hearsay Rule and Its Exceptions," http://72.14.207.104/search?q=cache:_CsVmo3VrKoJ:faculty.ncwc.edu/toconnor/405/405lect11.htm+hearsay&hl=en. "At common law, there were five well-established exceptions to the hearsay rule, and these exceptions have been a part of the hearsay rule from the beginning. Today, there are almost three

times as many exceptions (10–20 depending upon how you do the counting), and it's not that hearsay exceptions are a growing area of evidence law, but only that more practical reasons exist making it necessary to add more exceptions. The hearsay rule, its exceptions, and hearsay evidence are some of the most defining features of Anglo-American criminal justice."

10. Under this rule, evidence of prior bad acts or crimes is generally not admissible "unless it is substantially relevant for some purpose other than to point out the defendant's criminal character and thus to show the probability that he acted in conformity therewith." *State v. Biby*, 366 N.W.2d 460, 463 (N.D. 1985). The rule acknowledges the inherent prejudicial effect prior bad act evidence may have on the trier of fact. *State v. Micko*, 393 N.W.2d 741, 744 (N.D. 1986). The rule does not authorize automatic admission merely because the proponent advances a proper purpose for the evidence; instead, the relevance and probative value of the evidence must be demonstrated. *Dahlen v. Landis*, 314 N.W.2d 63, 70 (N.D. 1981). Such evidence "may be admissible for other purposes, such as proof of motive, opportunity, intent, preparation, plan, knowledge, identity, or absence of mistake or accident, provided that the prosecution in a criminal case shall provide reasonable notice in advance of trial, or during trial if the court excuses pretrial notice on good cause shown, of the general nature of any such evidence it intends to introduce at trial." See *State v. Osier*, 1997 N.D. 170, 171 (1997).

11. Andrew E. Taslitz, *Rape and the Culture of the Courtroom* (New York: New York University Press, 1999), 129. See also, Joan L. Larsen, "Of Propensity, Prejudice, and Plain Meaning: The Accused's Use of Exculpatory Specific Acts Evidence and the Need to Amend Rule 404(b)," 87 *Northwestern University Law Review* (1993), 651.

12. William Finnegan, "A Reporter at Large: Doubt." *The New Yorker* (January 31, 1994), 56.

13. Michel de Certeau, *The Practice of Everyday Life*, trans. Stephen Rendell (Berkeley: University of California Press, 1984), xiii.

14. Folk knowledge, however, is not all of a piece, not strictly uniform in its articulation or in its presence. In the first instance, it may take the form of general beliefs people hold as a matter of cultural intuitions and sensibilities or the form of specific cultural "facts" or realizations that make up its concrete "truths." Additionally, there will be variations in the prevalence or consensus on such beliefs or factual claims. Some general beliefs or specific claims may be broadly held throughout society, while others are confined to distinct subgroups, and still others are dispersed among a less identifiable or socially concentrated minority in society.

15. Finnegan, "A Reporter at Large," 51. On the importance of interpreting facts in appellate courts, see Kim Lane Scheppele, "Facing Facts in Legal Interpretation," 30 *Representations* (1990), 42.

16. See, for example, Edward Conlon's description of policing in *Blue Blood* (New York: Riverhead Books, 2004).

17. William Muir, *Police: Streetcorner Politicians* (Chicago: University of Chicago Press, 1977).

18. Jerome Skolnick, *Justice Without Trial: Law Enforcement in Democratic Society*, 2nd ed. (New York: John Wiley, 1975), chap. 3.

19. Ibid., 45.

20. Ibid., 46.

21. Ibid., 82.

22. Ibid., 83.

23. Ibid.

24. See Frederick Schauer, *Profiles, Probabilities, and Stereotypes* (Cambridge, MA: Harvard University Press, 2003). Also Bernard E. Harcourt, "Rethinking Racial Profiling: A Critique of the Economics, Civil Liberties, and Constitutional Literature, and of Criminal Profiling More Generally," 71 *University of Chicago Law Review* (2004), 1275, 1279. According to Harcourt, "The specific conditions under which race can legitimately and constitutionally be considered in policing can be specified as follows: racial profiling for purposes of police searches is a narrowly tailored policing technique that promotes the traditional law enforcement interest in fighting crime if (1) racial profiling reduces the amount of profiled crime while (2) maintaining or increasing the efficient allocation of police resources, without (3) producing a 'ratchet effect' on the profiled population. A ratchet effect occurs when racial profiling produces a supervised population disproportionate to the distribution of offending by racial group." See also Chet K. W. Pager, "Lies, Damned Lies, Statistics and Racial Profiling," 13 *Kansas Journal of Law & Public Policy* (2004), 515; Nelson Lund, "The Conservative Case Against Racial Profiling in the War on Terrorism," 66 *Albany Law Review* (2003), 329; and Michelle Malkin, *In Defense of Internment: The Case for Racial Profiling in World War II and the War on Terror* (New York: Regnery Publishing, 2004).

25. Heather MacDonald, "The Myth of Racial Profiling," *City Journal* (Spring 2001). Found at http://www.city-journal.org/html/11_2_the_myth.html. See also Schauer, *Profiles, Probabilities, and Stereotypes.*

26. See, for example, Brandon Garrett, "Remedying Racial Profiling," 33 *Columbia Human Rights Law Review* (2001), 41.

27. See Samuel R. Gross and Debra Livingston, "Racial Profiling Under Attack," 102 *Columbia Law Review* (2002), 1413.

28. Ibid., 1415.

29. Ibid., 1426.

30. *United States v. Martinez-Fuerte,* 428 U.S. 543 (1976). Recent decisions on racial profiling are discussed by Kathryn R. Urbonya, "Rhetorically Reasonable Police Practices: Viewing the Supreme Court's Multiple Discourse Paths," 40 *American Criminal Law Review* (2003), 1387.

31. For defenses of this decision, see Anthony C. Thompson, "Stopping the Usual Suspects: Race and the Fourth Amendment," 74 *New York University Law Review* (1999), 956,

1006–1007; and Ronald J. Sievert, "Meeting the Twenty-First Century Terrorist Threat Within the Scope of Twentieth-Century Constitutional Law," 37 *Houston Law Review* (2000), 1421, 1453–1456.

32. *United States v. Martinez-Fuerte*, 557–558.

33. Ibid., 563.

34. Ibid., 564, n. 17. The Court reiterated its ruling of a year earlier in *United States v. Brignoni-Ponce*, 422 U.S. 873 (1975). Although Latino ethnicity could not itself create the reasonable suspicion required for a roving patrol stop, "the likelihood that any given person of Mexican ancestry is an alien is high enough [in an area near the Mexican–U.S. border] to make Mexican appearance a relevant factor." Ibid., 886–887.

35. Ron Levi and Mariana Valverde, "Knowledge on Tap: Police Science and Common Knowledge in the Legal Regulation of Drunkenness," 26 *Law & Social Inquiry* (2001), 819, 821. The significance of such trade knowledge has been recognized in many official decisions and pronouncements. See, for example, *People v. Ojeda*, 225 Cal. App. 3d 404, 406 (1990). In this case, the court said, "It is hardly surprising that police officers who deal daily with intoxicated persons become expert at recognizing the physical effects of intoxication, and that they learn to perceive effects somewhat more subtle than those apparent to the amateur."

36. Trish Oberweis and Michael Musheno, "Policing Identities: Cop Decision Making and the Construction of Citizens," 24 *Law & Social Inquiry* (1999), 898.

37. Ibid., 918.

38. Ibid.

39. Ibid.

40. Eugene Bardach and Robert Kagan, *Going by the Book: The Problem of Regulatory Unreasonableness* (Philadelphia: Temple University Press, 1982), 31.

41. Ibid., 57.

42. Ibid., 72.

43. Ibid., 102.

44. David Sudnow, "Normal Crimes: Sociological Features of the Penal Code in a Public Defender's Office," 12 *Social Problems* (1965), 255, 259.

45. As Andrew Green notes, "Knowledge contained in criminal cases is produced by the exercise of power which encounters and overcomes resistance, thus revealing facts that could not be known in any other way." See Andrew Green, "How the Criminal Justice System Knows," 6 *Social & Legal Studies* (1997), 6.

46. Sudnow, "Normal Crimes," 261–262. What this amounts to is, in the author's words, a set of "unstated recipes" for dealing with criminals; a PD dealing with a burglar might, for example, employ "his conception of typical burglars against which the character of the present defendant is assessed." Ibid., 266.

47. Richard Ericson and Patricia Baranek, *The Ordering of Justice: A Study of Accused Persons as Defendants in the Criminal Process* (Toronto: University of Toronto Press, 1992), 22.

48. Ibid., 77.

49. Jonathan Simon, *Poor Discipline: Parole and the Social Control of the Underclass, 1890–1990* (Chicago: University of Chicago Press, 1993), 69–71.

50. Ibid., 189.

51. Ibid.

52. Ibid., 196.

53. Ibid.

54. Ibid., 197.

55. On the nature of legal autonomy, see Stanley Fish, "Law Wishes to Have a Formal Existence," in *The Fate of Law*, Austin Sarat and Thomas R. Kearns, eds. (Ann Arbor: University of Michigan Press, 1991).

56. See Valverde, *Law's Dream of a Common Knowledge.*

57. For one discussion of such rules, see Sheila Jasanoff, *Science at the Bar: Law, Science, and Technology in America* (Cambridge, MA: Harvard University Press, 1995). Also Edward K. Cheng and Albert H. Yoon, "Does Frye or Daubert Matter? A Study of Scientific Admissibility Standards," 91 *Virginia Law Review* (2005), 471; Sheila Jasanoff, "The Eye of Everyman: Witnessing DNA in the Simpson Trial," 28 *Social Studies of Science* (1998), 713; Tony Ward, "Law, Common Sense and the Authority of Science: Expert Witnesses and Criminal Insanity in England, ca. 1840–1940," 6 *Social & Legal Studies* (1997), 343.

58. See Jennifer Mnookin, "Scripting Expertise: The History of Handwriting Identification Evidence and the Judicial Construction of Reliability," 87 *Virginia Law Review* (2001), 1723.

59. Mariana Valverde, "Authorizing the Production of Urban Moral Order: Appellate Courts and Their Knowledge Games," 39 *Law & Society Review* (2005), 419, 452. Valverde emphasizes the blurring of categories in the way law knows, with citizens deploying highly legalistic ideas and legal officials often deploying nonlegal reasoning, and the highly dynamic quality of law's knowledge practices.

"Fact" and the Proof of Fact in Anglo-American Law (c. 1500–1850)

BARBARA J. SHAPIRO

"Fact" is such a familiar concept that its meaning and changing meaning over time have been largely unexamined. Most frequently, it is taken to mean an indisputable or demonstrable statement of truth. "We must accept the fact that John is dead." It is often treated as the opposite of something else—fact as opposed to fiction, to fancy, or lie—categories in which truth or reality is contrasted with something false, invented, or imagined. Fact and opinion, fact and interpretation, and fact and value are pairings that suggest the opposition of the objective and subjective. If we speak of historical or scientific facts, we invoke consensus among experts as to the truth of some assertion. And in common discourse, fact refers to either a human action or a natural event or phenomenon. "The fact that I arose at 6:12 A.M. yesterday can be confirmed by my wife." "The fact that the sun rose at 6:12 A.M. yesterday can be confirmed by reference to the table published by the U.S. Weather Service."

The early use of fact in legal discourse differs from common usage along a number of dimensions. As suggested by the still surviving expressions "before the fact" and "after the fact," in law fact typically referred to human actions, not natural phenomena. Indeed, in early legal discourse, fact is often reserved for a single human action, the alleged criminal act for which the defendant is being tried.

Along another dimension, lawyers referred to questions or matters of fact versus questions or matters of law. In the context of trials, matters of fact were not accepted truths but opposing or contending assertions to be pleaded to a judge and/or a jury. Lawyers could speak of false facts, meaning, of course, false allegations of fact. The distinction between matters of fact and matters of law also alerts us that over time, English legal discourse, while preserving the old usage of fact as the criminal act for which the defendant is being tried, also absorbs the modern usage of fact to refer both to human actions and natural phenomena. The meaning of the words of a statute is a matter of law. When the sun rose and whether Joe hit

Tom are both matters of fact. Although this paper focuses on the development of legal usage and its role in the evolution of the law of evidence, it also argues that the concept of fact, and the means by which legal facts were to be established, provided a model for historical, scientific, and philosophical statements of fact.

The historically oriented study of the concept of fact is a quite recent development, and given the common association of fact with science, it is not surprising that most efforts in this direction have been undertaken by historians of science. The category of fact has been of special concern to those interested in the growth of seventeenth-century English experimental and empirical science, a period in which Aristotelian natural philosophy was being challenged by a new empiricism focused on particulars. Lorraine Daston suggested that the first facts were unusual and anomalous natural events. The most influential study has been that of Steven Shapin and Simon Schaffer, social constructionists, who seek to teach the social components of intellectual phenomena. They associate the concept "matter of fact" with the interests of the gentlemanly class. They argue that the category of fact or matter of fact required credible testimony and that credibility was a concomitant of high social status. Those of lower status, they claim, were not viewed as capable of producing believable facts. Mary Poovey, a literary scholar, also has explored the concept of fact, giving special prominence to the role of the business community concerned with precision and accuracy.[1] None of these scholars seriously considered the role of legal traditions in creating the scientific fact.

The law of evidence, the legal area most closely related to the concept of fact, was initially dominated by the evidence treatises of Thayer and Wigmore. Historical studies of the jury and of eighteenth-century crime to some degree touch on evidentiary matters, and the latter is concerned with institutional resources for prosecuting crime and how heightened concerns about crime drew attention to the proof of criminal acts.[2] The revival of the history of the law of evidence has been largely stimulated by the work of John Langbein, who, focusing on late eighteenth-century lawyers practicing at the Old Bailey, takes the position that there was no law of evidence before the mid-eighteenth century.[3] Langbein and other historians focus on the "rules of evidence," such as the hearsay rule or whether or not an accused person is permitted to have counsel, typically slighting pre-eighteenth-century developments and nonlegal understandings about adequate proof as well as the evidentiary practices of legal arenas other than the jury trial. The development of the concept "beyond reasonable doubt," a concept closely linked to the proof of legal facts, has attracted surprisingly little historical attention.[4]

My treatment of fact in general and legal fact in particular examines both long-term developments from classical Rome to the mid-nineteenth century and the particular concerns of specific times and places. It treats the sixteenth-century introduction of witnesses in jury trials, late seventeenth-century treason trials, eighteenth-century modifications in the treatment of circumstantial evidence, and the increasing overlap over time between philosophical and legal treatments of fact and fact-finding. It stresses the need to examine English developments in the context of European developments, especially the Romano-canon legal traditions. It deals with both institutional contexts and textual traditions. It emphasizes the need to consider arrest and pretrial procedures as well as the jury trial. I argue that fact and the methods of establishing facts were first developed in the legal setting and only later adopted by other disciplines and intellectual endeavors. Lack of attention to the role of law in the development of the concept of fact has obscured the importance of law in traditions of knowledge-making and the legitimizing of empirical approaches to knowledge.

Fact

Courts were among the first institutions to try to answer the question of how certain one can be of allegations of fact and to develop what were thought to be appropriate methods of reaching well-grounded beliefs in past events. When historians, theologians, and empirically oriented natural philosophers were faced with the same or similar problems, they would take their lead from the courts of law.

The Latin *factum*, the French *fait*, the Spanish *hecho*, and the English *fact* are associated with human acts or deeds and did not initially refer to natural phenomena. The association with human deeds or acts makes the legal phrases "before the fact" or "after the fact" more easily understood. In the legal setting, facts are initially alleged and not assumed to be true or worthy of belief. That was something that had to be established during the course of the legal proceedings. Appropriate proof had to be brought to bear on the allegations and, only if these were deemed sufficient, was the fact treated as believable. *Belief*, however sound, was not equated with *truth* in the abstract sense because belief might be incorrect.

All criminal courts deal with fact in the sense of being required to determine to the satisfaction of those making the judgment whether an accused has or has not engaged in particular past actions that the law forbids. Many noncriminal cases turned on similar questions of who did what. In some societies, the decision is thought to be made by supernatural agents and, in others, by human agents. That determination may be made by professionals such as witchdoctors or judges or by laypeople in settings like the Anglo-American jury. If the decision is made by human beings, standards are usually established to determine whether the decision is justified. Courts are sites of knowledge-making, where a variety of participants engage in creating or determining the truth of something by a set of site-specific rules. Such knowledge-making, however, is conditioned, though not entirely determined, by the general views of what passes for knowledge in the society in which the legal proceedings are embedded. For the participants in legal proceedings come from and return to the general intellectual conventions of their societies. Not even ideally are they supposed to inhabit a litigational knowledge-making realm absolutely isolated from other realms.

Although all courts face epistemological issues relating to fact determination, our primary concern here is with the Anglo-American legal system. To understand its treatment of fact-finding, it is necessary to look at some of the intellectual traditions that help to shape its evidentiary practices.

The Rhetorical Tradition

The first of these is the classical and especially the Roman rhetorical tradition and its concern with persuasive techniques.[5] The rhetorical distinction between artificial and inartificial proofs, developed by Aristotle and elaborated by Cicero, Quintilian, and the *Rhetorica ad herrenium*, played a significant role in the Romano-canon legal tradition and then, with the Renaissance revival of rhetoric, helped to shape important features of the English approach to proving legal facts. This rhetorical heritage can be seen in the evidentiary aspects of arrest and pretrial examination by justices of the peace, criteria for jury evaluation of witness credibility, and the concept of circumstantial evidence.

Ancient philosophers sought certain or demonstrative proof; rhetoricians focused on those aspects of life where only probability obtained. In the rhetorical contexts, probability was associated with likelihood, verisimilitude, and persuasiveness, not truth. The emphasis was on the presentation of a successful argument. For Aristotle and his rhetorical successors, inartificial proofs, which included witnesses, testimony elicited by torture, and contracts, were not produced by the orators but might be reinforced or countered by them. Artificial proofs were those constructed or made by the orators' art.

Cicero's *De Inventione* detailed arguments for and against those charged with crimes. He treats "the conjectural issue," sometimes translated as the "issue of fact," by exploring inference. Inferences were based on arguments "from the cause of the action, from the character of the person involved or with questions of glory, power, wealth and enmity to show motive." If other individuals had similar motives, orators must show that the accused lacked the power, opportunity, or desire to commit the act. Inferences could be drawn from "persons"—that is, personal attributes such as gender, ancestry, kinship, age, temperament, and physical constitution. Rhetors were to consider "suspicions" relating to a man's way of life, education, family, and his purposes. A person's "fortune, whether slave or free, wealthy or poor, famous or unknown, successful or a failure, a private citizen or a public official," was similarly utilized, and anything that detracted from the defendant's "honor and repute" or "interest" might be invoked. A "man's . . . , interests, deeds, accidents, speeches, purposes" all contributed to the credibility of the charges against him. Those defending an accused person were to use the same arguments to emphasize his upright character or suggest that his life, character, and past deeds were not relevant to the matter at hand. "Suspicion," which would become an important legal concept, could be derived from time, place, and occasion of the act as well as its "adjuncts" and "consequences." Visible signs, such as pallor, blood , or lust before, during, or after the act were also important. The orator was instructed to "twist" all of these categories "to best advantage."[6]

A similar treatment was provided in Quintilian's *Institutes of the Orator*, which again distinguishes between artificial and inartificial proofs and shows how witnesses, hearsay, and the products of torture could be used by prosecution and defense. He develops arguments associated with signs, tokens, indications, and vestiges that point to other things and, like Cicero, shows how "circumstances" or signs, or "indicia," as the Romano-canonist lawyers would later call them, could be used strategically. Bloodstains thus might be a sign of a murder or the result of a bloody nose. Some signs might be very powerful when used in conjunction with other proofs.[7]

The *Rhetorica ad Herennium*, a text available during the early Middle Ages, details argumentative categories useful for prosecution and defense. The text refers to "signs," which included "the Place, the Point of Time, the Duration of Time, the

Occasion, the Hope of Success, the Hope of escaping Detections," and whether the signs coincided. Signs preceded the crime, were contemporaneous with the crime, or followed the crime—in modern parlance, before the fact, during the fact, and after the fact. Some signs could be associated with innocence or guilt—for example, pallor, speaking uncertainly, or bloody clothing.[8] These signs and circumstances would play a significant role both in the Romano-canon and English notions of circumstantial evidence. Sometimes the very words of the Roman rhetoricians appear in later legal texts to assist in the evaluations of witnesses' credibility.

Scripture

Scripture provided another source for Judeo-Christian courts seeking decision-making rules. The most influential were the two or more witnesses requirement for conviction and expressions of distrust of circumstantial evidence.[9] The canon and civil law that developed in the medieval era adopted the two-witness rule and a more general uneasiness about circumstantial evidence. Ambivalence about the value of circumstantial evidence was also characteristic of the common law. The story of Susanna and the elders too would have an impact on both Romano-canon and English law and was cited to support the view that when two accusers or witnesses varied in their testimony, neither was to be credited. The Bible also highlighted the problem of false witnesses. On the whole, however, the influence of Scripture on the common law was not great. For instance, although some interregnum reformers wished to implement Old Testament legal prescriptions, they did not succeed in fundamentally altering the common law.

Medieval Developments

As Roman legal institutions and practices decayed in western Europe, they were largely eclipsed in the early medieval era by the jural practices of the Germanic tribes that intruded in and then settled in Europe and England. The era of irrational proofs, ordeals, compurgation, oaths, and oath helping, characteristic of early medieval law, needed little of what we would associate with evidence or argument. The proof of fact was thought to be largely in divine hands. As ordeals and other irrational proofs came into disrepute, they were replaced on the continent with an innovative jurisprudence, most often labeled the *inquisition process*, which dealt extensively with questions of evidence and proof. These were "rational" as opposed to "irrational" proofs and were deployed by human agents in fact determination. Canonist lawyers and northern Italian civilian jurists developed an elaborate and systematic jurisprudence that included techniques for examining witnesses, methods for discovering and verifying facts, and treatments of presumption and circumstantial evidence.

Romano-canon jurists developed a system of legal full and half proofs. Although the tradition recognized that all legal proofs were incapable of the demonstration required by philosophers, they assigned the designation of "full proof" to certain varieties and quantities of probabilistic evidence. In the area of criminal law, confession or the testimony of two unimpeachable witnesses constituted full proof of the fact. Half proofs were constructed from the testimony of those insufficiently credible or from the testimony of a single witness. If neither confession nor the testimony of two credible witnesses was available to prove a serious crime, judicial torture might be employed to elicit a confession. Torture was permissible if "signs" or "indicia" were available in sufficient quantity and quality but still insufficient to produce full proof. A learned literature dealing with the indicia developed, much of it drawn from rhetorical categories such as time, place, and the power and ability to do the act—that is, the fact.

Direct proof of the fact consisted of testimony and documents, while indirect proof included rumor, fame, suspicion, signs, conjecture, the indicia, presumptions, and circumstantial evidence, all categorized and catalogued in great detail by medieval canonists and civilians in an elaborate treatise literature. The principle that circumstantial evidence did not constitute full proof made it difficult to convict even when reasonably good evidence of guilt existed. Alternatives were developed that circumvented the required two credible witnesses or confession standard. One was the category of "manifest" or "notorious" crimes, acts so well known as not even to require an accuser. Another allowed conviction on the basis of "undoubted indicia" or "violent presumption." The frequently cited example of violent presumption—the man found holding a bloody sword standing over the body of a slain victim, which appears in both continental and English law—was already being cited in 1270. As early as the thirteenth century, William Durantis held it possible to convict in special circumstances on the basis of presumption derived from circumstantial evidence, and Thomas de Piperata permitted urban magistrates to convict on the basis of "undoubted indicia" or circumstantial evidence. Albertus Gandinus, a thirteenth-century civilian, wrote that conviction on the basis of *indicia indoubitata* was appropriate when they were so strong they compelled the conscience of the judge to believe them. In such cases, only monetary and corporeal punishments were permitted. Conviction on the basis of *indicia indoubitata* and violent presumption continued into the early modern period in the works of Aretinus, Clarus, Matthaeus, and Mascardus.[10] In some situations, then, good circumstantial evidence could result in conviction, but only nondeath penalty punishments were permitted—partial punishments for partial proof. The testimony of two or more reliable witnesses or confession remained the gold standard. However, canonists and civilians also developed the notion of the *crimen exceptum* to deal with secret or difficult to prove crimes—that is, those unlikely to produce the desired two witnesses. Circumstantial evidence in cases such as witchcraft could support the death penalty.

The *Malleus Malificarum* (1487) outlined the grades of suspicion: light, probable, and vehement. The last was sufficient to warrant conviction. The indicia and how they related to the three varieties of presumption entered the legal literature in the writings of Tancred and William Durantis. The latter distinguished presumptions as *temeraria*, or light, *probabilis*, derived from suspicion and fame, and *violenta*. Only the last merited conviction.[11]

The Romano-canon tradition distinguished between matter of fact and matter of law, both of which were determined by professional judges learned in the law. The distinction appeared in maxims as well as in the procedural manuals and is found in the law of all jurisdictions that derived all or part of their law from the civil law that developed in Italy and elsewhere during the medieval period. The French thus distinguished between *fait* and *droit*; the Spanish between *hecho* and *derecho*.[12]

Before turning to the jury and its role in fact-finding, we must briefly examine two other legal processes. Arrest and pretrial examination largely have been ignored by evidence historians, yet they are channels through which a number of evidentiary traditions would find their way into the evidentiary requirements of the jury trial.

Arrest

By the fourteenth century, arrest procedures exhibited conceptual developments that provided for notions of adequate and inadequate grounds for arrest and a procedure for suits for false arrest. The criteria used for arrest of an alleged wrongdoer for felony were the "causes of suspicion," a concept indebted to Cicero and Quintilian and the medieval canonists and civilians and outlined in

English texts by Bracton. For Bracton, rumor arising from "worthy and responsible men . . . wise and trustworthy persons" "begets suspicion." Suspicion also arose from a precedent act. From rumor and suspicion, a "strong presumption" might arise.[13] The "causes of suspicion" included the age, sex, education, parentage, character, associations, and habitual behavior of the suspect, as well as his ability to commit the act, his whereabouts at the time of the crime, the presence of witnesses and/or signs such as blood.[14]

Pretrial Examination and Renaissance Rhetoric

Similar evidentiary criteria were involved in the preliminary examination conducted by justices of the peace, an office of medieval origin, whose duties were expanded to include the examinations of those suspected and accused of serious crimes. The examination process was formally established with the Marian bail and committal statutes of 1554 and 1555 but probably existed sometime earlier. Justices were required to examine those who brought the accusation of the "fact and circumstances thereof" as well as witnesses.[15]

The justicing manuals that appeared in the late sixteenth century instructed justices to utilize the "causes of suspicion" in their examinations. These were virtually the same as the Romano-canon indicia that served to determine whether a suspect was to be examined under torture. The Renaissance revival of rhetoric helped to familiarize and legitimate the causes of suspicion. The rhetorical works of Cicero and Quintilian were widely used in the classicist curriculum of the humanist grammar schools. Erasmus's popular early sixteenth-century rhetorical textbook *De Copia* treated artificial and inartificial proofs and explained how "circumstances" relating to "things" involved cause, place, time, occasion, antecedents to the affair, collateral circumstances, consequences, opportunities, instruments, and methods. "Circumstances" related to "persons" included the familiar considerations of family, race, country, sex, age, physical appearance, inclinations, previous acts and words, passions, and so on.[16] This language would become embedded in the justicing handbooks and play an important role in the treatment of what would later be called "circumstantial evidence."

Sir Thomas Wilson's *Arte of Rhetorique* (1553), published the same time as the Marian statutes, most clearly indicates the transmission taking place from rhetorical texts to more obviously legal works. Wilson, a civil lawyer, demonstrated how parentage, sex, education, inclination, and nature might be employed by orators.

Orators were to consider whether the action was difficult or easy to accomplish and whether it was possible or impossible to perform. Considerations of "circumstances" relating to where, when, and how the deed was done were also within the purview of the orator. Wilson discusses the need to examine whether the person in question had the will or power to do the act, what his inclination and occupation were, and whether he was a gamester or frequenter of alehouses. A variety of personal characteristics, such as quarrelsomeness, were also to be treated. Alibi questions were to be addressed as well as whether the accused was bloodstained or trembling. He invoked the "places" in connection with "confirmation" so that "greate liklihoodes mai be gathered" by both sides.[17] Wilson's language, little changed, appears in the justicing handbooks.

William Lambarde's *Eirenarcha*, an early justicing handbook, included an elaborate diagram outlining the causes of suspicion to be employed by magistrates in making their examinations, noting they were "collected out of Cicero and others." The examination is treated as a "conjectural state of a cause" to be "weighed by matter," characterized as "precedent," "present," or "subsequent"—that is, before, during, or after the fact. Each of these is divided: the "precedent" into the "will to do the fact" and the "power to commit the act." The will to do the fact required consideration of the disposition of the person, which included the character and behavior of his parents, sex, and education. The justice must consider whether the accused had an idle or honest occupation, was riotous in diet or apparel, or was "brawlingly, quarrelsome, [or] lightfingered." The "causes inducing him to undertake" the act might be "forcible or impulsive," motivated by revenge, or "upon sudden offense." They might also be "persuasive"—that is, in hope of gain or out of fear. The power to commit the act called for an evaluation of the suspect's intelligence, physical capacity, and his "country," the last involving consideration of whether the accused's kindred, wealth, friends, or office might "cover" him.[18]

The "present" category involved questioning the accused's presence at the fact, taking into account the time of day, space, and location. The "occasion" must be analyzed, and if absent, "the fact could not follow." The justice then engaged in the mental operation of "comparison," which involved consideration "as none but he, or not so commodiously as he, could commit the fact."[19]

The "subsequent," or "after the fact," category included common voice and fame that he did the offense: "Witnesses that prove it, either probably or necessarily; signs which discover him, as by having blood or the goods about him; his flying away; his blushing, or change of countenance; his being in the company of other offenders; his offer of composition; the measure of his foot; the bleeding of the dead body. . . . Confession, as his doubtfully or inconstance speaking."[20]

L'office et auctoritie de justices de peace, traditionally cited as Crompton, based on Fitzherbert's earlier handbook (1583), includes a similar six-page list indicating that most of the causes of suspicion cited were to be found in Wilson's *Art of Rhetorique* (1553). Crompton notes testimony should not be accepted if part of it proves to be false and cites the story of Susanna and the elders in connection with varying testimony by accusers. The biblical reference continues in subsequent handbooks.

Crompton's manual was soon replaced by Michael Dalton's *The Country Justice* (1618), which remained the standard authority until it was gradually replaced in the mid-eighteenth century. The post-1618 editions cite "two old verses" that had appeared in Tancred:

> Conditio, sexus, aetas, discretio, fama,
> Et fortuna, fides: in testibus esta requires.[21]

Dalton's treatment of "Circumstances . . . to be considered" in examining accused felons is much the same as Lambarde's and Crompton's and exhibits the same concern for parentage, background, lifestyle, and character of the accused; his reputation in the community and his demeanor; and motives, opportunity, and capacity to commit the crime. Justices considered any direct or circumstantial evidence bearing on commission of the crime, including alibis and physical indications of guilt. He includes the Bracton material on suspicion and common fame. In 1635, Coke's brief Romano-canon definitions of the three varieties of presumption were added. Later justicing manuals repeat much of the Dalton and Crompton materials, adding statutory material and excerpts and citations from Hale and Hawkins. The same causes of suspicion would prove useful to jurors charged with evaluating testimony and considering circumstances.

The Jury Trial, Witnesses, and Witness Credibility

In England, irrational proofs were replaced by the jury trial. Despite a great deal of research, there is much that we do not know about early trial juries, which for several centuries appear to have received no instruction about evidentiary requirements. There were presentment as well as trial juries, the former existing prior to the abolition of ordeals in 1215. Trial juries composed of men of the neighborhood, which date from about 1219 to 1221, were expected to utilize their own personal knowledge of persons and events to reach their verdicts. Recent research, however, indicates that the jury was never fully self-informing. At least for a time, juries seem to have spoken informally out of court to possible informants, functioning as both information gatherers and judges of the evidence.[22]

Witnesses probably began to make their appearance in civil trials in the fifteenth century and in criminal trials during the late fifteenth or early sixteenth century. The distinction between witnesses and jurors had already been noted by Sir John Fortescue in the late fifteenth century. Since Elizabethan legislation provided for the compulsory attendance of witnesses and made perjury a crime, witnesses must by then have been a common feature of the jury trial. By the early seventeenth century, jurors ceased to deal with testimony out of court, and they were expected to testify as witnesses when providing information to fellow jurors. Jurors were now third parties who evaluated testimony about events they had not personally witnessed. Given England's growing population, increasing geographical mobility, and urbanization, it is difficult to see how juries could have continued to function if witnesses had not been incorporated into the jury trial. These and other changes in the jury trial were gradual, usually unmarked, and therefore are difficult to date with any accuracy.

Petty jurors were rather ordinary persons of "middling" social status. They were typically substantial members of their community, many with experience in local government. Independence was thought to be ensured by a property qualification and procedures for challenging potential jurors as not impartial. Contemporary writings are full of expressions of the superiority of the jury trial over all other forms of trial as well as complaints that men lacking sufficient property who were subject to improper influence were serving on juries. The same jurors often sat on both civil and criminal trials held at Quarter Sessions or when Westminster judges presided over assize (criminal) and nisi prius (civil) trials. By the very early seventeenth century, if not earlier, it was clear that English law left "both supply of testimony and the discerning and credit of testimony wholly to the juries' conscience and understanding, yea to their private knowledge."[23]

Not all persons could testify in court. Those excluded were outlined in Dalton and were similar to the Romano-canon exclusions. Felons, for example, could not testify, and the parties were excluded from civil trials. Although there was initially some confusion about the distinction between legal and credible witnesses—the former being legally competent to testify and the latter whose testimony was believable—the distinction gradually became clear.

Juries needed guidance in evaluating the testimony of the accused and witnesses. A ready-made set of criteria to assist in the evaluation of witness testimony was to be found in the Romano-canon tradition of the ecclesiastical courts, the rhetorical treatment of testimony, and especially in the instructions provided to justices of the peace for their examination of witnesses. Although John Langbein suggests that Dalton's justicing handbook erroneously conflated the law of examination with that of evidence, that conflation provides a good example of how evidentiary criteria designed for one purpose or procedure might be appropriated for another.[24] Though Dalton lists the criteria under examination, it is to be found in the "witness" portion of Chamberlain's *The Complete Justice*.[25]

By the early sixteenth century, at least some juries were told they must consider witness credibility. Jurors in the 1535 trial of John Fisher, Bishop of Rochester, were informed that the decision about witness credibility rested on their "conscience and discretion."[26] Sir Matthew Hale would praise the jury trial over all others precisely because jurors could "weigh the credibility of Witnesses, and the Force and Efficacy of their Testimonies." Observation of "the very Manner of a Witness's delivering his Testimony" might "give a probable Indication whether he speaks." "The very Quality, Carriage, Age, Condition, Education and Place of Commorance of a witness" could be best appreciated when jurors can see and hear the witnesses. These considerations allow jurors to give "the more or less Credit to their Testimony." If the jury has just cause to disbelieve what a witness swears, they are not bound to give their verdict according to the evidence or testimony of that witness. And they may sometimes give credit to one witness, though opposed by more than one. And indeed it is one of the excellencies of . . . [the jury trial]." Although the jury ought to give a great regards to witnesses and their testimony, yet they are not always bound by it; but may either upon reasonable circumstances, inducing a blemish upon their credibly, though . . . in strictness of law they are to be heard, pronounce a verdict contrary to such testimonies; the truth whereof they have just cause to suspect.[27] Jurors, who were "judges of the fact," must consider "the probability or improbability, credibility or incredibility of the witnesses and the testimony."[28]

The legal approach to fact-finding and the role of credible witnesses in that process would be given philosophical form and status by John Locke. For Locke, knowledge of fact was probable knowledge that depended on observation, experience, and "the testimony of others vouching their observations and experience." Those evaluating testimony must consider the number, integrity and skill of witnesses, consistency, and contrary testimony as well as the number and credibility of testimonies that agree or disagree. "Matter of Fact" was likely "to find more or less belief" as the "relators are more in number, and of more credit, and have no interest in speaking contrary to the truth."[29] Locke's criteria for evaluating testimony and reaching belief about facts were obviously drawn from the legal tradition.

The Number of Witnesses

Although the English were adamant about the superiority of the jury trial over the civil law trial with its two-witness rule or confession requirement and insisted that juries could convict on the basis of only one witness and sometimes on none, there were some instances in which the English either required or leaned in the direction of two witnesses. One instance was perjury, which frequently involved pitting the word of one against another and which was often identified with the biblical prohibition of false witnessing.[30]

The two-witness rule was often invoked in connection with treason. The treason law of 1537 required "two sufficient and lawful witnesses," that of 1552 "two lawful accusers," and that of 1661 "two lawful and credible witnesses." The requirement, however, sometimes wavered. When Sir Walter Raleigh, being tried for treason in 1603, appealed to the two-witness rule, the judge ruled that the treason statute had been repealed. The treason trials of the late seventeenth century also exhibited uncertainty about the number of witnesses, resulting in the 1696 treason act that permanently established the two-witness rule.[31]

During the Revolutionary period, attempts were made both in England and the colonies to extend the multiple-witness rule beyond treason as part of Puritan enthusiasm for scripturally based law.[32] Chamberlain's *The Complete Justice* (1681) lists several offenses requiring two witnesses, most of statutory origin, suggesting that Parliament may have been less suspicious of the two-witness requirement than the legal profession.[33] Although English law, with some statutory exceptions, did not require a set number of witnesses, the number of concurrent testimonies was thought to increase probability and make the evidence "more concludent."[34]

Oaths and Witness Credibility

The role of oaths in the early modern fact-finding process is something of a puzzle. Jurors from the early sixteenth century onward were expected to consider witness credibility in their determinations of fact, but such determination was complicated because neither the accused nor defense witnesses in felony trials were permitted to testify under oath. The disparity of oaths in criminal trials, George Fisher has recently argued, resulted in favoring prosecution testimony in the process of seeking to avoid a situation in which conflicting prosecution and defense testimony, both given under oath, would force jurors to become "lie detectors." According to Fisher, jurors were only very gradually allowed to choose between conflicting oath-supported testimonies. Given that witness testimony begins only in the late fifteenth century and becomes common in civil and felony trials only in the sixteenth when the gravity of oaths was already on the wane, it seems unlikely that a desperate need was then felt to shield jurors from having to make a terrible decision as to which of two oath-bound testifiers was lying.[35]

Moreover, prosecution witnesses testifying under oath might give contradictory or inconsistent testimony so that in any event jurors could not be shielded from choosing between oath takers. In the late sixteenth century, the justicing manuals noted that contradictory or inconsistent testimony was relevant to their examinations.[36] Since juries frequently heard the testimony of several prosecution witnesses testifying under oath, they too were likely to encounter contradictory or inconsistent testimony, a situation already recognized early in the sixteenth century by St. Germain. Hale noted that the ability of jurors to directly observe conflicting testimony provided "great Opportunities" to gain "the true and clear Discovery of the Truth," and in 1671, a judge pointed out that contradictions between the testimony of two witnesses "took off their whole Testimony." Judge Holt made it very clear that if jurors were "not satisfied that what the witnesses have sworn is true," they were to acquit. Locke emphasized the importance of "consistency of the parts" and "contrary testimonies" in evaluating witness testimony, and Isaac Watts, writing in 1724, referred to the necessity of considering whether those offering opposing testimony were "equally skillful and equally faithful as those who assert it." Gilbert's midcentury evidence treatise again indicates that inconsistency of a witness "removes him from all credit."[37] None of these writings suggest that once a witness had taken an oath, jurors must simply accept his testimony as true. None suggest that problems of conflicting testimony can be automatically resolved by choosing oath support over non-oath-supported testimony. None suggest that jurors should be particularly embarrassed or awe-struck by having to decide whether oath-supported testimony was true. Nor did a decision favoring one party over another, as Fisher argues, imply that the other had lied or committed perjury. They might have been mistaken or privy to more or less information than other witnesses. Juries were often directed to decide on the basis "of the whole matter," surely implying that oath-supported prosecution testimony might be outweighed by other evidence.

The ideal of the disinterested witness also affected how juries were expected to evaluate testimony. According to Hale, the testimony of disinterested witnesses was preferable to "that which is reported by persons of whose interest it is to have the thing true, or believed to be true."[38] Gilbert too insists the most credible witness was the "wholly indifferent and unconcerned" witness and that an interested witness was "a Ground for Distrust rather than belief." If jurors suspected that witnesses swore for their own safety, were friends or relations of a party, were "of a profligate or wicked temper or disposition," or thought "the bias is so strong against him, as would incline a man of his disposition, figure and rank . . . to falsify," the jury was "to disbelieve him." If he was "a man of credit and veracity, notwithstanding the bias, he might be believed."[39] Both prosecution and defense witnesses might be viewed as disinterested. Neither Hale nor Gilbert suggests that credibility was to be given only to those testifying on oath. Instead, Gilbert indicates, when a single witness testified under oath, it was essential to have "great confidence in the integrity and verity of the man." The testimony of two witnesses on oath was "higher." However, if they agreed "in every circumstance," they were either "perjured or telling the truth."[40] Jurors were free to acquit even when those giving testimony were under oath. If juries were not entitled to assess the credibility of both oath-supported and non-oath-supported testimony, there would be little reason to hear the defendant or his witnesses at all.

The "Probability of [the] Matter" was also relevant to the jury's judgment. The incredibility of the fact, according to Francis North, Chief Justice of Common Pleas, "overthrows" the testimony of a witness and "set[s] aside his credit." If the fact was contrary to experience and observation, it was "too much" to receive on the oath of a single witness.[41]

Juror consideration of circumstantial evidence also presents a problem for Fisher's argument because it might alter the oath versus non-oath balance. Many criminal trials involved both direct testimony and circumstantial evidence. As already noted, judges often charged juries to consider the "whole matter," a reference to the combination of direct and indirect evidence, only some of which was given under oath. During much of the eighteenth century, circumstantial evidence was preferred over witness testimony whether or not given under oath. The maxim "circumstances cannot lie," much cited during the eighteenth century, suggests that witnesses could and did lie.

How seriously oaths were taken is not easily resolved. Some obviously took the violation of an oath seriously. Yet we know that there were substantial numbers of acquittals in cases where the testimony of the prosecution witnesses was ignored or rejected by jurors. Verdicts against the evidence, given to reduce capital crimes to misdemeanors, were not uncommon. This practice sometimes involved the complicity of judges, and critics sometimes complained that they were often not true to their oaths. Although the oath was a powerful incentive to truth telling, contemporaries often complained that oaths were uttered in vain.[42]

By the sixteenth century, Sir Thomas More indicated that prosecution witnesses "myight swere false."[43] Perjury became a statutory crime precisely at the time when witness testimony was becoming common, suggesting that lying, even under oath, was perceived as a problem. Although it is certainly true that Gilbert indicated that the law began with the "benign and human" presumption that witnesses do "not falsify or prevaricate," that presumption, like other presumptions, might be rebutted as jurors considered the evidence before them. Character witnesses were frequently produced to enhance or diminish that presumption whether or not they had witnessed the fact in question.

Although jurors were regularly told to evaluate witness credibility, they were sometimes confused about how to assess the weight of the oath against incredible testimony. In the trial of the Earl of Strafford, several of the peers who had condemned the earl justified their position saying the witnesses had "sworn the facts" and they therefore had no choice other than to accept them. Judge North, however, angrily informed them that their behavior was "contrary to the very institution of trials." They must evaluate "the credibility of persons and things . . . which required collaction of circumstances and a right judgement . . . if you believe the witnesses find, else not."[44]

So some tension between the claims of the oath and the instruction of credibility did exist and surfaced in the Popish Plot and Exclusion trials. Prosecutors asked jurors to believe their witnesses because they were on oath while the defense insisted that they weigh the credibility of those witnesses, some of whom were accessories. Judges explained accessories were legally competent witnesses eligible to take the oath but they were to be judged as to credibility by the jurors who were "triers" of the credit of witnesses as well as "the truth of the fact."

While stressing the weight of the prosecution witnesses testifying under oath, Fisher ignores the presumably equally weighty oath taken by jurors, who swore to give "true Deliverance . . . according your Evidence as neer as God shall give your grace, so help you God."[45] Jurors swore to decide according to the evidence, not according to the oaths of prosecution witnesses. If the legal system was so deeply committed to avoiding the oath versus oath situations, the oath of the jurors must have been deeply troubling.[46] In civil trials, often heard the same day as criminal trials and sometimes by the same jurors, witnesses for both parties testified under oath, which was the situation that Fisher argues the legal system attempted to avoid at all costs. When these witnesses contradicted one another in civil cases, the legal system evidently was untroubled by the oath versus oath problem. We must also note the frequency of oath taking. Nearly every officer, from inspectors of alehouses and constables to the highest royal officials, took oaths. Tracts and assize sermons denounced the all too frequent practice of violating oaths, the commission of perjury, and careless swearing.[47] Oaths were important, but respect for and disregard of oaths were both common.

The Romano-canon treatment of oaths provides an interesting comparison because both prosecution and defense witnesses testified under oath. According to Tancred, conflicting testimony given under oaths was, if possible, to be reconciled by the judge. If that proved impossible, the judge resolved the problem by applying the maxim "Condition, sex, age, discretion, repute, And fortune, faith: these a witness must have," the same maxim later found in Dalton. In the Romano-canon system, like the common law, testimony under oath was to be disbelieved if witnesses contradicted themselves and when one witness contradicted another. The Romano-canon formulations were well known to English lawyers because they, with some modification, shaped the practice of English ecclesiastical courts and Chancery.[48] It is unclear why English judges in criminal cases should be more concerned about oaths than canon and civil lawyers. And given the English experience with the hated Star Chamber, *ex officio* oath that resulted in self-incrimination, it is not surprising that the English did not move in the direction of requiring defendants to testify under oath.[49]

Circumstances, Circumstantial Evidence, and the Jury Trial

Circumstances and circumstantial evidence also played an important role in fact-determination. It is difficult to determine when and how circumstantial evidence came to be used to establish facts. We have already noted the biblical prohibition and the Romano-canon ambivalence toward and limited use of circumstantial evidence. A similar ambivalence and somewhat reluctant use is typical of

English law, at least until the eighteenth century. "Circumstances" were related to "presumptions." The language of circumstances employed by rhetoricians found its way into the writings of pretrial examinations, which, as we have seen, drew heavily on the rhetoricians. Rhetorical writers such as Erasmus, Sherry, and Wilson explained how to reason from circumstances and how to reason from signs to cause. Circumstances sometimes implied something nonessential, inferior, or of less importance but could also mean "surrounding," having some connection to the words *circle* or *circumference*. In literary use, circumstances referred to details that surrounded the primary action. These usages sometimes appeared in legal settings as well.

Legal "evidence" was limited to documents and testimony. To the extent that circumstances might be taken into account in arriving at legal decisions about matters of fact, those circumstances must have been established by witness testimony. However, circumstances are always treated in the early writing as an entirely separate category, not included within testimony or evidence. Yet clearly, circumstances could be considered by juries in reaching verdicts. Although the scarcity of early trial accounts makes it difficult to know how early juries treated circumstances such as being found with stolen horses or other stolen goods, many convictions must have been made on inferences from circumstances. The combination of "circumstantial" with "evidence" was a late arrival. The great attention to witness testimony paid by philosophers and logicians did not include treatments of circumstances and presumptions.

"Presumptions of law" referred to rules of the court. We are concerned here only with "presumptions of fact"—that is, inferences drawn from circumstances. There is little doubt that circumstances could result in convictions. Being found in possession of stolen goods and being unable to account for them resulted in many guilty verdicts. Sir Thomas More indicated, "A man may sometimes be so suspect of felony by reason of presumptions, though no man saw hym doe it. . . . yet may be founden most often justified as necessary in connection with unlikely to be witnessed crimes such as rape, witchcraft, poisoning, some kinds of theft and some instances of treason." Circumstances and presumption were also invoked in connection with treason, both when there was uncertainty as to whether the law currently required two witnesses to prove the fact and when the government had only one witness and wished to find a surrogate for a second witness.

Legal writers took their lead from Bracton, who referred to presumption as "an ancient constitution." Bracton wrote, "Where a strong presumption lies against the appellee which does not admit of proof to the contrary, . . . as when he is arrested over the body of a dead man with his knife dripping blood; he cannot deny the death nor is further proof necessary." He warned that presumptions were not always "true." [50] The Romano-canon classifications of presumptions entered English legal literature authoritatively in Coke's *Institutes.* Coke declared that were "*probatio duplex*, witnesses and documents, but that many times juries, together with other matter, are much induced by presumptions, whereof there be three sorts—viz. violent, probable and light, or temerary. *Violenta presumption* is many times plena probatio; as if one be runne thorow the bodie with a sword in a house, whereof he instantly dieth, and a man is seen to come out of that house with a bloody sword, and no other man was at that time in the house. *Praesumptio probabilis* moveth little but *Praesumptio Levis seu temeraria* moveth not at all." [51] Nevertheless, in "cases of life," one should not "judge too hastily upon bare presumptions." [52]

Given the lack of trial records, evidence for the use of circumstances and presumptions in trials largely must be drawn from the few highly charged political procedures recorded in the sixteenth and early seventeenth centuries. Witchcraft prosecutions, where witnesses were unlikely to have observed the diabolical fact, can also shed some light on how circumstances and presumptions were employed in proving facts. Although the common law did not recognize full and half proofs, the English literature dealing with witchcraft is full of the language of signs, indicia, full and half proof, light and weighty presumptions, and the superiority of proof by two witnesses. Dalton's *Country Justice* offered a list of "signs" to assist in the "better discoverie of witches," a list that was retained in the handbooks until repeal of the statute in the mid-eighteenth century. Although Dalton's signs appear in connection with examination, printed marginalia indicate their suitability for conviction.[53]

Though trials for witchcraft waned in the early seventeenth century, this was not true for other crimes unlikely to be witnessed such as rape, poisoning, forgery, some murders, and thefts when the accused was found in possession of stolen goods. Juries often convicted on the basis of circumstances and presumption. In a 1603 treason trial, Justice Warburton indicated that horse thieves were often condemned without any witnesses at all.[54]

The use of circumstances in connection with legal proof must have been fairly well known since a character in John Webster's 1612 play *The White Devil* complains, "we have naught but circumstances to charge her with, about her husband's death." [55] In this instance, circumstances are treated as inferior to direct proof.

Another 1612 drama, however, indicates that circumstances were sufficient to convict. When the defendant in the play inquired what witnesses would testify against him, he is informed that "In case of Murder, should we never judge by circumstantial likelihoods and presumptions, no life could be secure."[56]

From the Restoration onward, we have more trial evidence. In 1663, a jury was told, "I leave the evidence to you . . . pregnant, strong and undeniable circumstances are good evidence."[57] Here we have an early indication that circumstances were becoming "evidence." In a 1679 trial, a jury was to consider the testimony of "a real positive witness, and the circumstantial evidence of a second." In 1681, jurors were instructed to consider the credit of the witnesses and to "weigh all the circumstances." In a 1681 attempted assassination case, the judge referred to "dark cases" that must be proved by circumstances. The proofs must be "very great," but jurors should not expect them to be as clear as "things done in the face of the Sun."[58] In another 1681 trial, when the defendant insisted there was no positive evidence, only insufficient "remote and conjectural Evidence," the judge responded

> In things of this nature, we are fain to retreat to such probable and conjectural Evidence as the matter will bear. I believe some of you have been of Juries at the Old Bayley, and that even for Men's Lives, you have very often, not a direct Proof of the Fact, of the Act or of the actual killing; but yet, you have such evidence by Presumption, and seems reasonable to Conscience.[59]

In a 1683 manslaughter case, jurors were to consider "the evidence and Circumstances of the Fact."[60] Judges not infrequently instructed juries to convict on the basis of "the whole" or "the whole matter"—that is, a combination of direct testimony and circumstances. In some situations, circumstances alone were sufficient to prove the fact; in others, it was the combined weight of eyewitness testimony and circumstances.

In a 1581 treason trial, the defendant, Jesuit Edmund Campion, complained there were no substantial witnesses against him. All that was laid against him was "bare circumstances." There was only "a naked presumption" against him and "nothing vehement of force." Since presumptions were only "bare and naked Probabilities," Campion asked the jury to "set circumstances aside, set presumptions apart" and "set that reason for your rule which is warranted by certainty," a rule that Anderson, the Queen's Counsel, characterized as "sufficient and manifest." A man should not "totter upon the hazard of likelihoods." Even in cases of theft, "odious circumstances" such as the fact that the companions of the accused were thieves or the accused was an "evil liver" should be considered "no necessary matter to conclude him guilty."[61] Campion was convicted. In a 1603 treason trial, Justice Warburton invoked the bloody sword example saying that condemnation was possible on the basis of presumption and circumstances, without any witnesses to the main fact.[62]

Treason trials of the late seventeenth century frequently raised the issue of whether circumstances might function as the equivalent of a second witness. In a 1679 case, for example, the jury was to consider the testimony of "a real positive witness" and the circumstantial evidence of a second. In a 1681 case, the judge advised the jury to consider both the credit of the witnesses and "weigh all the circumstances." He also informed them that it was the opinion of all judges that "substantial Circumstances joined to one positive Testimony" were held to be "sufficient Proof."[63]

By the eighteenth century, notions of circumstantial evidence and the soundness of conclusions drawn from them were widely accepted as sufficient to prove the fact. The growing acceptance and even preference for circumstantial evidence may have drawn support from the sermons and writings of natural theologians, which attempted to prove the existence of God from his effects or works. Bishop Butler, for example, stated that the weight of circumstantial evidence "was frequently as convincing as that which is the most express and direct."[64] Butler and other natural theologians were frequently cited in legal evidence treatises. Over time, the notion that evidence and circumstances were two different things eroded, as did the notion that circumstances were less reliable than witness testimony.[65]

During the course of the eighteenth century, the relative value of direct testimonial and circumstantial evidence was reversed, and it was now thought that although eyewitnesses might lie, facts could not. The maxims "circumstances cannot lie" and "facts cannot lie" were often expressed. "One of the greatest men who ever sat in a court of judicature" is reported to have said that circumstances in many cases were "of greater force, and more to be depended upon, than the testimony of living witnesses." Witnesses may be deceived or mistaken, "but circumstances, gentlemen, and presumptions, naturally and necessarily arising out of a given fact, cannot lie."[66] That the circumstances or the given facts themselves largely were established by witness testimony, and that those witnesses too might lie, as well as opposed eyewitnesses to the criminal act, does not seem to have been considered. After all, testimony that the defendant ran from the murder scene with a bloody sword might be as perjured or mistaken as the testimony that he had run the victim through. No doubt what was involved in this prioritizing of circumstances was the judgment that testimony by several witnesses as to a collection of surrounding circumstances, many of which persisted over time, was more likely to be reliable and more easily checked for plausibility than the testimony of a single witness as to the supposed criminal act itself, a particular act that occurred at a particular moment in time. Testimony that a defendant habitually consorted with thieves might appear more reliable and subject to verification than the testimony of a supposed eyewitness, who might have been frightened or distracted at the time, that he had seen the defendant commit the theft. Certainly, we have learned about the pitfalls of eyewitness testimony in more recent times.

Although the term *violent presumption* does not occur much in the Old Bailey Proceedings, our best source of eighteenth-century criminal trials, "strong presumption" makes an occasional appearance, on some occasions taken as sufficient to prove the fact. In other instances, it did not come "up to full proof."[67] Jurors in one case were asked to consider whether presumptions "do not speak stronger than a thousand witnesses."[68] In a 1716 case, King's Counsel argued that "Presumptions, when strong, and when the nature of the case will admit of no other Evidence, is good in Civil Law, Common Law, and all the law in the world."[69] In a 1741 case, we encounter, "These are all Facts which the Jury only could determine, either by positive, presumptive or circumstantial Evidence."[70] Blackstone's *Commentaries on the Law of England* referred to "circumstantial evidence" and violent and probable presumptions, suggesting that by the time Blackstone wrote, circumstances were recognized as evidence.[71]

The trial of Mary Blandy in 1752, a notorious poisoning case, elicited the mutually supporting claims that secret crimes necessarily depended on circumstantial evidence, that circumstantial evidence was more convincing than direct testimony, and that "facts cannot lie."[72] The defendant in another 1752 trial also cited the maxim. When the defendant insisted on the need for positive evidence, the prosecution responded that circumstantial evidence "is the best and surest of all kinds [of evidence] whatsoever, and the least likely to deceive and mislead." Facts collected from several individuals "point to the same center of Truth" and "can never mislead the judgment or impose upon the belief . . . and are the surest and most unerring guides to conduct the truth." The judge concurred, indicating that violent presumption was full proof and was, in his opinion, better than "one positive evidence, whose memory may be deceitful, or who may possibly be suborned; but in facts made apparent from circumstances, which are dumb, we cannot be deceived."[73] In the sensational trial of John Donellan (1781), the judge told the jurors:

> That a presumption which necessarily arises from circumstances is very often more convincing and more satisfactory than any other kind of evidence, because it is not within the reach and compass of human abilities to invent a train of circumstances which shall be so connected together as to amount to a proof of guilt, without affording opportunities of contradicting a great part, if not all of these circumstances.[74]

William Paley commented unfavorably on jurors' reluctance to convict on the basis of indirect evidence or when positive proof was lacking. "A concurrence of well authenticated circumstances" is "stronger ground of assurance than positive testimony, unconfirmed by circumstances."[75] Paley and others who preferred circumstantial evidence to witness testimony expressed their views during a period when on the one hand there was a heightened fear of crime and on the other the evidence of "thief takers" who received monetary rewards for conviction, which made the problem of perjured testimony a serious one. Nineteenth-century treatise writers such as Starkie would question the superiority of circumstantial evidence.

The treatise literature, which emerged in the eighteenth and nineteenth centuries, absorbed continental treatments of circumstantial evidence and frequently cited Romano-canon evidence texts favorably. Assimilation had become easier as continental writers placed their discussions of legal proof in a natural law setting.

Jury Certainty and Beyond Reasonable Doubt

Once juries heard the prosecution and defense testimony, they had to reach a verdict. Had the evidence for the alleged fact been sufficiently strong for conviction? How strong was sufficiently strong? Before witnesses became a routine part of the jury trial, jurors, at least in theory, reached their decision from their own knowledge. We have little or no information as to whether or not they received judicial instructions about that knowledge. After witnesses were introduced and verdicts had become largely based on evidence presented in court, we begin to encounter references to the jury's conscience and understanding.[76] At the beginning of the seventeenth century, Francis Bacon and a 1607 royal proclamation indicated that verdicts were left to the "juries' conscience and understanding."[77]

From the beginning of the jury trial, it seems that criminal juries were expected to be as sure as they could be of their verdicts. The first enunciated standard, the "satisfied conscience," was a test that over time became synonymous with rational belief, moral certainty, and "belief beyond reasonable doubt." I have traced this evolution elsewhere and give only an abbreviated account here.[78]

Reported state trials frequently included the charge to the jury. Although the recorded cases are distributed unevenly over time and typically involve politically charged trials, there is no reason to believe that judicial instructions differed in routine felony trials. From the late fifteenth century, jurors were to give their verdicts "according to your evidence and your conscience." In the early sixteenth century, the jurors, according to Thomas More, must seek "sure and certain persuasion & belief in his own conscience" that has been "induced reasonably."[79] After hearing the evidence, the jury was instructed that its verdict was to be determined "as they think in their conscience the truth of the fact is." They were to "determine what their conscience judge clearly prove concerning the Fact."[80] Hale also indicated that it was the "conscience of the jury, that must pronounce the prisoner guilty or not guilty."[81] The most common jury instructions included phrases such as "if you believe," "if you believe on the evidence," "if you believe what the witness swore," and "if the evidence is sufficient to satisfy your conscience." Late seventeenth century pamphlets insisted that jurors were to be "fully satisfied in their conscience" after examining the "credit of the Evidence," "satisfied in their particular Understanding and Conscience," "according to their Conscience and the best of their Judgment" and must not follow another's "Understanding or Reasoning." Jurors were expected to bring their reasoning faculties to bear on the evidence they heard.[82] The judgment of conscience did not mean deferring to emotion, authority, or the wishes of another individual but required reason and intellect. According to Locke, "all obligations bind conscience, and lay a bond on the mind itself, so that not fear of punishment, but a rational apprehension of what is right" obliges us to follow it.[83] Satisfactory proof of the fact required rational belief, and to go against conscience was to go against reason.

In Protestant England, moral decision making was in the hands of the individual. *Conscience* and *satisfied conscience* are the terms of casuistry. According to the casuists, moral matters were not capable of mathematical or demonstrative certainty but nevertheless might be so probable as to be morally certain. The "sure," "right," or "satisfied" conscience was characterized as having attained moral certainty. A satisfied conscience required the full persuasion achieved by means of the rational faculties. It was sufficient if the decision maker "know it upon the grounds of a convincing probability, as shall exclude all rational grounds of doubting it,"[84] a statement that links "moral certainty" with the later "beyond reasonable doubt."

The terminology of judicial charges changed little between 1700 and 1750, although there are more frequent references to the "mind," "understanding," and "judgment" of the jurors. Jurors were "rational men" who would "determine according to your consciences, whether you believe those men guilty, or not."[85] The most common directive was belief based on evidence, and jurors were instructed to take great care in weighing and examining evidence. The newer "understanding" rests on the same rational deliberation as the older "conscience." Later instructions begin to give attention to doubts that might arise in the minds of jurors. The understanding and conscience utilized the same rational deliberation.

The late eighteenth century exhibits the first use of the beyond reasonable doubt language. It appears unambiguously in the 1770 Boston Massacre trials and in a rare shorthand account of a 1777 Old Bailey trial.[86] In 1797, jurors were informed that if they had any reasonable doubt, then they must acquit, it being the "invariable direction of an English court of justice to lean to the side of mercy." Several turn of the century Irish trials combine the beyond reasonable doubt standard with notions of satisfied conscience and belief.[87] "Beyond reasonable doubt" in the mid-nineteenth century is defined as

> It is not merely possible doubt; because everything relating to human affairs, and depending on moral evidence, is open to some possible or imaginary doubt. It is that state of the case, which, after the comparison and consideration of all the evidence, leaves the mind of the jurors in that condition that they cannot say they feel an abiding conviction of moral certainty, of the truth of the charge . . . the evidence must establish the truth of the fact to a reasonable and moral certainty; a certainty that convinces and directs the understanding, and satisfies the reason and judgement. . . . This we take to be proof beyond a reasonable doubt.[88]

The language of the satisfied and doubting conscience and that of moral certainty are not currently in common parlance, but at the time, they were employed to mean "belief beyond reasonable doubt." That phrase came to define the standard of proof of a criminal fact in law.

Fact, Philosophy, and the Treatise Tradition

The new genre of the evidence treatise that developed in the mid-eighteenth century interacted with contemporary epistemological discussions. Legal traditions of fact-finding influenced philosophical exploration at the same time that legal writers began to insist that legal approaches to evidence rested on sound epistemological and logical foundations. We have already shown that Locke's treatment of testimony generalized the legal approach to fact-finding. In 1724, Isaac Watt was insisting that logic was the basis for "Inquiries after Truth" both in the natural sciences and human actions and that assent in both must be exactly proportioned to the degree of evidence. He also examined the basis for assessing the credibility of witness testimony and "concurrent circumstances."[89] Twenty-five years later, David Hartley, who was frequently cited by evidence writers, examined the nature of assent and dissent and the differences between true, doubtful, and fictitious narrations of fact. Some facts were practically "certain," and others were "liable to doubts." Fact, for Hartley, did not mean truth. George Campbell's *Philosophy of Rhetoric* treated facts in a similar way. All decisions of fact involved moral evidence, and these in turn involved degrees of certainty up to the summit of moral certainty. Campbell also discussed witness credibility and belief beyond reasonable doubt.[90]

The eighteenth-century evidence treatises, notably those of Sir Geoffrey Gilbert and John Morgan, are supported by a Lockean foundation. Later treatises would utilize Hartley, Reid, Paley, Stewart, Kirwan, Whately, and Mill. Gilbert begins his *The Law of Evidence* with a brief summary of Lockean principles. There were degrees of certainty that ran from "perfect Certainty and Demonstration" down to "Improbability and Unlikeness" as well as "Acts of the Mind proportioned to these Degrees of Evidence." These acts of the mind ran from "full Assurance and Confidence, quite down to Conjecture, Doubt, Distrust and Disbelief." Given that, the law could never obtain certain knowledge because litigation depended on transient events "retrieved by Memory and Recollection." Legal rights were "determined by Probability," which would be assessed by examining the credibility of witnesses, allowing juries to reach verdicts that they had no reason to doubt.[91]

John Morgan's *Essays upon the Law of Evidence* similarly suggests that there are degrees of knowledge and acts of the mind proportioned to the evidence. When one reached a judgment based on credible and disinterested witnesses, the mind had no choice but to "acquiesce therein" and "ought not any longer to doubt but, to be nearly if not as perfectly well-satisfied as if we of ourselves knew the fact."[92] Lawyers as well as philosophers agreed that only some facts reached the level of beyond reasonable doubt.

Thomas Reid and the Common Sense school developed an inductive philosophy in response to Hume in which well-attested facts are treated as "knowledge" rather than "probability." Their approach to fact-finding quickly found its way into the legal treatise and legal education. It is found in the legal lectures of the

American James Wilson, who taught that moral evidence could be graded from possible to probable and from conjecture to the highest degree of moral certainty. Both testimony and concurrent circumstances, when strong enough to "force belief," permitted juries to gain moral certainty about facts and events. Testimony not only provided "the greatest part" of the jury's business but was equally applicable to the works of nature, the "whole stupendous fabric of natural philosophy" being based on the same epistemology as law.[93] The legal logic of fact-finding was being generalized to a variety of human endeavors.

Richard Kirwan, a logician who considered jurors and the legal profession his primary audience, emphasized the importance of the logic of proof in countries with jury trials. Kirwan considered evidentiary topics such as "suspicion," doubt, and the "indubitable proofs productive of certainty," frequently referring to the law, legal situations, and the evidence treatises of Gilbert, Capel Lofft, Thomas Peake, and McNally.[94] Daniel McKinnon's *The Philosophy of Evidence* also provided a discussion of certainty, probability, and assent as well as the role of testimony and circumstantial evidence, referring to the epistemology of Locke, Reid, and Dugald Stewart.[95] James Gambier's *Guide to the Study of Moral Evidence, or of That Species of Reasoning Which Relates to Matters of Fact and Practice* again emphasized the importance of the rules of evidence for jurors who must be able to know when facts have been proven. He treated witness credibility and the difference between presumption and proof in matters of fact. He too indicates that evidence was capable of producing moral certainty—that is, a probability so high as to exclude all reasonable doubt.[96] References to moral certainty and beyond reasonable doubt and the need to link evidence to degrees of belief are in the philosophical literature, the evidence treatises, and in more condensed form, in jury instructions for fact-determination. Fact was now both a philosophical and a legal category.

Thomas Starkie's influential *Practical Treatise on the Law of Evidence* insists juries must rely on the general principles of belief involved in inquiry "as to the truth of any particular fact." Though the law sometimes added special requirements, such as excluding certain kinds of testimony, legal facts were no different from others. "Full proof of the fact" was established when "evidence satisfied the minds of the jury of the truth of the fact in dispute, to the entire exclusion of every reasonable doubt." This state of mind was "moral certainty," a mental state also identified with "satisfied belief" and "satisfied conscience and understanding."[97]

Simon Greenleaf's *Treatise of the Law of Evidence*, which cited logicians and epistemologists, concluded "the most, that can be affirmed" in matters of fact is "that there is no reasonable doubt concerning them. The true question . . . is whether the facts are shown by competent and satisfactory evidence." These must "satisfy the mind and conscience." Greenleaf also believed that the law shared its principles of evidence with the historian, the naturalist, the traveler, and the astronomer. From the mid-eighteenth century and for much of the nineteenth century, philosophers and legal writers insisted that the facts of nature and the facts of law were to be established by the same reasoning processes.[98]

Although the concept of fact and methods of establishing facts beyond a reasonable doubt developed in the legal arena, law was not the sole discipline to make use of that concept or its approach to evidence and proof before it became generalized in the philosophical literature.[99]

Fact and History

History, like law, deals with human acts and deeds—that is, "matters of fact"—and historians too gave a prominent role to witnesses, events, and occurrences. Many early modern historians were both English and French and were legally trained. Among the most admired English lawyer-historians were Sir Thomas More and Sir Francis Bacon. It is therefore not surprising that historians spoke of "fact" and "matter of fact" and adopted the established legal discourse for dealing with such matters. Thomas Blundeville in the late sixteenth century treated history as the "deeds" of individuals and public weals, noting that "every deed is done by some person, for some cause, tyme, and place with means and instruments," and historians must investigate the "power, skill, and industry" of the historical actors, language that echoes the justicing manuals.[100]

Early modern historians often referred to facts. For some historians, history was "bare Narration of matter of Fact" or "plain matter of fact." The faithful historian reported "nothing but fact" or promised a "true Accompt" of "Matter of Fact."[101] For Thomas Hobbes, "the register of knowledge of Fact is called History," and history was based on the testimony of witnesses.[102] For others, historians were to combine an account of the facts with discussions of the causes of the events they reported.

Historians who witnessed or participated in the events they wrote about were particularly valued, and many characterized themselves as witnesses or apologized if they were not themselves eye or ear witnesses. As in the legal setting, eyewitnesses were preferred to secondhand sources, and hearsay was distrusted. Historians, like witnesses, were required to sincerely and impartially relate historical facts. The faithful historian was as much a commonplace as the faithful witness.

Impartiality, a necessity for witness, juror, and judge, was equally necessary for the historian reporting on and making judgments on historical facts. "Verity" and "Indifference" were the "prime virtues" of the historian, and impartiality was the "Glory of Historians." Thomas Fuller, a seventeenth-century historian, wrote "if the Witnesses be suborned, the Record falsified, or the Evidence wrested, neither posterity can Judge rightly of the Actions of the present time; or this time, give a certain judgment of the Ages past." Another historian, Peter Heylyn, invoked the language of the law when he noted "in matter of fact, we put ourselves upon an ordinarie Jurie, not doubting, if the evidence prove fair, the Witnesses of faith unquestioned and the Records without suspicion of imposture, but they well doe their conscience and find for the Plaintiffe or Defendant, as the cause appears."[103] The legal language of Fuller and Heylyn was not unusual.

Among historians, truth was contrasted with slander, libel, or lying or with fiction or romance. Over time, there was increasing condemnation of intermixing fact with invented speeches, poesy, or fictions. Historical facts or feats must be real. Historians often wrote of "Evident and Visible Fact" or referred to "matter of Fact" derived from personal observations or the reliable testimony of others. It was even suggested that the historian was on "oath" to tell "the whole truth, and nothing but the truth" and to "assert the verity of all matters of Fact."[104]

Facts for the historian as for the lawyer had to be supported by convincing evidence. Thomas Sprat, writing of the "plain Matter of Fact" of the Rye House Plot, for example, insisted that evidence for matters of fact must be presented in the "clearest Light and Evident Proof." Robert Brady treated documents as "matter of Fact laid down, and warranted by such as lived in the very times when the Thing was done . . . or by sufficient Record."[105] As in law, documents as well as witnesses established past facts.

Not all historical facts, however, could be believed. Where the evidence was insufficient, historical as well as legal matters of fact might be doubted. A late seventeenth-century historian could refer to "palpable Errors in Matters of Fact," noting that "scarce anybody" was "satisfied . . . with the Truth of Matters of Fact" relating to the civil war. The historian must know the "Verity of the Facts" he recounts and was culpable if he "differ[ed] from the truth of Fact" or denied or "smother[ed] Matter of Fact." An early eighteenth-century historian wrote that some historical facts were false, grossly improbable, or no longer tenable, and historians must "reject candidly what cannot be thus established."[106]

The term "fact" or "matter of fact" was not synonymous with truth, and historians sometimes were, and sometimes were not, "furnish'd with all the necessary Assurances to know the truth of the Fact." Only some facts were "undeniable Matters of Fact." Bolingbroke defined "an historical fact" as something that did not contradict "general experience and our own observations." If supported "by the testimony of proper witnesses, it acquires all the appearances of truth, that is, it becomes really probable in the highest degree."[107] In history as in law, not all facts were treated as true. Those with insufficient proof remained dubious and might be rejected. Fact had not yet become synonymous with truth.[108]

Fact and Religion

Religious writers of the seventeenth and early eighteenth century also found the concept of fact useful.[109] Fact was used to provide rational belief that the miracles of the New Testament were true, that the Old Testament accounts of Creation and the origin of humankind were believable, and to establish the principles of natural religion. These principles would be grounded on reason, not by intuition, authority, or divine inspiration.

Efforts to establish that the facts reported in the Bible were true and could be rationally established had their origin in Hugo Grotius's widely read *The Truth of Christianity* and were elaborated in England by latitudinarians arguing against skeptics expressing doubt as to the truth of Scripture and against Roman Catholics advocating the doctrine of infallibility and the superiority of authority and the oral tradition. A great deal, therefore, hinged on the success of the theologians who based their arguments on the reasonableness of belief in scriptural accounts. The theologians, like the lawyers, distinguished rational belief in matters of fact from mathematical demonstration. They argued that it was unreasonable to question the truth of well-established matters of fact simply because they had not been personally observed. Belief in the facts related in Scripture was based on the testimony of the Apostles who were reliable eyewitnesses.

Edward Stillingfleet will serve as an example of the rationalist theologians whose language echoes legal language. Stillingfleet argued that it might be reasonable to distrust the truth of accounts conveyed by "uncertain fame and tradition." If, however, the account in question was "attested by a sufficient number of credible persons who profess themselves the eye witnesses of it, it is accounted an unreasonable thing to distrust any longer the truth of it." This was particularly true in cases where what is reported "is a thing easily and clearly perceived" and when many witnesses agreed in the same testimony. The Apostles were credible witnesses, having no motive to lie and "lacked Mean or vulgar motives." Christ's miracles were visible, and no illusion of sense was possible because many saw him raise a man from the dead and many witnessed his resurrection. When "all witnesses fully agree not only the substances, but in all material circumstances of the story, what ground or reason can there be to suspect a forgery or design in it." Since this was "the Foundation whereupon the firmest assent is built, as to any matter of fact," there was no reason to disbelieve the birth, miracles, life, death or resurrection of Jesus Christ.[110]

"Matter of Fact" was also used to show that there were rational grounds for believing in the scriptural accounts of the Creation and the Flood, a more difficult argument to make because there were no human witnesses to the Creation. The eminent judge Sir Matthew Hale attempted to prove that the biblical account of the origin of man was sound. Although he admitted he could not rely on human testimony, he cited several "instance[s] of Fact" to show that mankind had a beginning in time. He provides eight "Evidence[s] of Fact" to show that "reasonablenesse of the Divine Hypothesis touching the origination of the world and particularly of Men." Though none "singly and apart" was sufficiently weighty, the "concurrence and coincidence" of multiple evidences carried "a great weight, even as to the point of Fact."[111] The argument runs closely parallel to the standard legal arguments about circumstances and inferences or presumption.

Fact also plays a role, albeit an indirect one, in the proofs for God's existence. Fact could not play a direct role because spirit could not be observed. Natural facts, however, could be employed to infer the existence and attributes of God in much the same way that signs and circumstances were deployed to infer guilt. John Ray's popular *The Wisdom of God Manifested in the Works of Creation* employed natural facts observed by reliable witnesses to establish belief in the existence and wisdom of God. Ray insisted he utilized only "Matter[s] of Fact" and "Experiment[s]" that were "undoubtedly true" lest he "build upon a Sandy and Ruinous Foundation." Well-proved "facts" were "most effective to convince, all that deny or doubt" the existence and wisdom of the deity.[112]

Fact and Natural Science

Fact is currently so often associated with the natural sciences that it seems counterintuitive to argue that fact was a latecomer to the natural sciences. But it was only when naturalists began to emphasize the accuracy of particular observations rather than appealing to common experience that fact entered the realm of natural philosophy. Philosopher and lawyer Francis Bacon played a pivotal role in shifting the focus of natural philosophers from syllogistic argumentation, the citation of authority, and the appeal to common experience to that of particular observations of natural phenomena requiring careful firsthand observation reported by reliable witnesses. The credit of observed phenomenon was to be evaluated as "certainly true, doubtful whether true or not, certainly not true." It was necessary to ascertain whether the reporter affirmed the observation "of his own knowledge; also again whether it was a thing of which, if it really happened, there must needs have been many witnesses, and finally whether the author was a vain-speaking and light person or sober and severe; and the like points, which bear on the weight of the evidence." Carefully witnessed facts by credible witnesses thus became as central to empirical investigation of nature as they did to legitimate decisions in the courtroom.

Bacon also introduced experiments, humanly constructed events, or natural "facts" that might be observed in a variety of different conditions.[113] When the observation of natural phenomenon, whether ordinary, unusual, or experimentally created, the "facts of Nature" became central to the natural sciences. Baconian natural facts had an advantage over legal facts because repetition was often possible and there were instruments such as telescopes and microscopes to aid in observation. Thomas Hobbes, no admirer of the empirical method, treated natural observations as fact. Natural history was the "History of . . . [the] Facts, or Effects of Nature." Fact in both civil and natural history was derived from "sense and memory" and was characterized as "the knowledge required in a witness."[114]

The term *matter of fact* became central to the English scientific community. Thomas Sprat, the historian of the Royal Society, employing then standard legal terminology described the research program of the "New Philosophy" as being grounded in "matter of fact," which meant a natural and experimental history based on observation and experiment. He suggested, with considerable exaggeration, that the Royal Society "only deal[t] in matter of Fact." The society privileged its "own touch and Sight" over hearsay or secondhand experience, though sometimes, he admitted, they were "forced to trust the reports of others." Witnessing by its members gave credence to the experiment observed and the "concurring testimonies" of its members ensured that the society's "assurance" was firmly based. The society protected itself from the dangers of unfounded reports by reducing "such matters of hearsay and information, into real, and impartial Trials, perform'd by their Experiments" that were capable of "exactness, variation, and accurate repetition." Indeed Sprat specifically invokes the judicial model, asserting that because of its size, the capacity of the society for reaching moral certitude was superior to that of the courts.[115]

Robert Boyle and Robert Hooke, two prominent naturalists of the Restoration era, played an important role in publicizing the concept of matter of fact. Boyle, like Sprat, believed that natural history was the "only sure Foundation of Natural Philosophy." That foundation was matters of fact—that is, experiments and observations "faithfully made and deliver'd." Boyle noted the importance of "judicious and illustrious witnesses" and insisted that experimental "matters of fact" "ought to be brought to trial." Knowledge of fact was derived from sense and communicated to others by testimony. Reported experience might be based on an individual's sensation, the testimony of others, or in some instances, revelation. Boyle emphasized "the bulk of the matters of fact I deliver should consist of things, whereof I was myself an actor or an eye-witness." Boyle invoked "the testimony of Nature" and treated testimony as "certificates to attest Matters of fact."[116]

Social status, for Boyle, was not the sole or even the most important criterion for witnessing. Testimony might be "insufficient for want of moral Qualifications in him that gives them." Even those who were "honest and sincere . . . might be insufficient if the matters of fact required Skill." The "better qualified a witness is, the strong Assent his Testimony deserves." For Boyle, "the two grand requisites of a Witness [were] the knowledge he has of the things he delivers, and his faithfulness in truly delivering what he knows."[117]

Hooke treated his own experiments as "history and matter of Fact," noting "How near the nature of Axioms must all those Propositions be which are examin'd before so many witnesses." Hooke, like Boyle, was sensitive to the difficulties of obtaining accurate matters of fact. Observations not "rightly and accurately made" were "pernicious and Destructive." The naturalist must be taught "what he ought to observe, how to examine it, how to preserve & register it. How to range and order it." Although this work was best done by "a society of men . . . both of Parts and Fortune, & of such as have a will as abilities," not every observer, gentleman or not, was "fitt to be a collector." The naturalist must be "knowingly versed in all the various ways of examining & trying of matter of making experiments . . . on various kinds of substances." Under these conditions, experiments might "stand like so many witnesses to give testimony of the truth or against that error, . . . a most severe examination of these witnesses must be made before a jury can . . . give their verdict or judge pronounce sentence for branding one proposition or hypothesis as erroneous . . . or for establishing another for truth or axiom."[118] Knowledge and skill were becoming more important for the scientific investigator than the witness in the courtroom.

The Royal Society sought multiple witnesses whenever possible. Hooke emphasized examination of "many witnesses," and Sprat suggested that while two or three witnesses could decide a case in law, the Royal Society might have the "concurring Testimonies of threescore or a hundred."[119] Conflicting testimony caused problems for naturalists as well as for juries making judgments about matters of fact. When respected astronomers reported conflicting observations of the comets of 1664–1665, the society was called upon to adjudicate between them. The society attempted to deal with the controversy, which "being about matter of Fact, wherein Authority, Number, and reputation must cast the Balance." The society, sought by one of the astronomers as "skilled and impartial judges," indicated that such controversies could be settled only "by weighing the numbers and the qualities of the observations." Chosen by the society to investigate, John Wallis reported that since neither astronomer would "willingly falsify" their observations, he could only suggest suspending judgment, a route not available to judges and juries.[120]

The scientific community also adopted the legal emphasis on impartial witnesses and judges. Royal Society members often proclaimed their lack of bias or interest. Mathematician John Wallis, for example, stressed the necessity for "disinterested and unbiased persons to judge" the dispute of the astronomers, as did the astronomer who appealed to the society for judgment. Boyle emphasized the need for a "disinterested mind" and the absence of "personal advantage." Statements of the need for impartial observers, impartial witnesses, and impartial judgments appeared frequently in the publications of the virtuosi and became an integral part of scientific ideology.[121]

In the scientific as well as in the legal arena, facts were not treated as believable until credible evidence had been evaluated by those capable of judgment. Like legal facts, scientific facts were to be evaluated on the basis of credible witnesses who had the opportunity to observe and possessed the requisite ability, probity, skill, fidelity, status, experience, and reputation. Social status was important and so was ability, skill, and experience. The close connection between methods of establishing both human and natural facts can also be traced in the growing number of eighteenth- and nineteenth-century philosophical and legal treatises that treated legal facts and natural facts as sharing the same epistemological basis and logic.[122]

Conclusion

To trace the development of the concept of legal "fact" in Anglo-American law, we have had not only to look at the jury trial and the English law of evidence but also the rhetorical tradition of ancient Rome and its Renaissance revival, the medieval development of and borrowings from the Romano-canon legal system, scriptural prescriptions relating to trials as well as the eighteenth- and nineteenth-century intermingling of epistemological and logical formulations of philosophers and evidence writers. We have highlighted both long-term intellectual and legal contexts and shorter term developments such as the Renaissance revival of rhetoric and the treason trials of the late seventeenth century. We have emphasized comparison with continental legal developments as well as the early modern ideological constraints that made admissions of borrowing difficult. We have also found it necessary to examine the evidentiary requirements for arrest and pretrial examination to show how these interacted with jury evaluations of witness credibility and circumstantial evidence. We have noted the early ambivalence concerning circumstantial evidence, the unexpected reversal of views about the probative values of witnesses and circumstantial evidence, and the gradual acceptance of "circumstances" as "evidence." We have shown that fact did not carry an intrinsic connotation of truth but was rather a matter whose truth was in contestation. The best evidence for alleged facts would yield a satisfied conscience or understanding or its later equivalents, moral certainty and belief "beyond reasonable doubt."

Although the concept of fact and appropriate means of attaining rational belief in facts initially developed largely in a legal context and in the language of the law, that development has been obscured as fact was appropriated by historians, by theologians, and especially by philosophers and natural scientists.[123] The role of the legal concept of fact in shaping modern empirical thought and the now ubiquitous "fact" must be recognized if we are to understand how it came to become a part of our furniture of the mind.

Notes

1. Lorraine Daston, "Baconian Facts, Academic Civility and the Prehistory of Objectivity," *Annals of Scholarship* 8 (1991): 338–339; Steven Shapin and Simon Schaffer, *Leviathan and the Air Pump: Hobbes, Boyle, and the Experimental Life* (Princeton, NJ: Princeton University Press, 1985); Steven Shapin, *A Social History of Truth: Civility and Science in Seventeenth-Century England* (Chicago: University of Chicago Press, 1994); Mary Poovey, *A History of the Modern Fact: Problems of Knowledge in the Sciences of Wealth and Society* (Chicago: University of Chicago Press, 1998). For a different view, see Barbara J. Shapiro, "The Concept 'Fact': Legal Origins and Cultural Diffusion," *Albion* 26 (1994): 1–26; Barbara J. Shapiro, *A Culture of Fact: England 1550–1720* (Ithaca, NY: Cornell University Press, 2000); Barbara J. Shapiro, "Gently Boyle," *MetaScience* 6 (1994): 113–116.

2. See Thomas A. Green, *Verdict According to Conscience: Perspectives on the English Criminal Trial Jury* (Chicago: University of Chicago Press, 1985); J. S. Cockburn and Thomas A. Green, eds., *Twelve Good Men and True: The Criminal Trial Jury in England, 1200–1800* (Princeton, NJ: Princeton University Press, 1988); Daniel Klerman, "Was the Jury Ever Self Informing," *S. Calif. Law Review* 77 (2003): 123–149; David J. Seipp, "The Reception of Canon and Civil Law in the Common Law-Courts Before 1600," *Oxford Journal of Legal Studies* 13 (1993): 388–420; J. W. Cairns and G. MacLeod, eds., *The Dearest Birthright of the People of England: The Jury in the History of the Common Law* (Oxford: Oxford University Press, 2001); Bruce P. Smith, "The Presumption of Guilt and the English Law of Theft 1750–1850," *Law and History Review* 23 (2005): 133–71; John Beattie, *Crime and the Courts in England 1660–1800* (Princeton, NJ: Princeton University Press, 1986); John Beattie, *Policing and Punishment in London, 1660–1750* (Oxford: Oxford University Press, 2000); Peter King, *Crime, Justice and Discretion in England 1740–1820* (Oxford: Oxford University Press, 2000).

3. John H. Langbein, *The Origins of Adversary Criminal Trial* (Oxford: Oxford University Press, 2003); John Langbein, "Historical Foundations of the Law of Evidence: A View from the Ryder Sources," *Columbia Law Review* 96 (1996): 1186–1190; Thomas P. Gallanis, "The Rise of Modern Evidence Law," *Iowa Law Review* 84 (1999): 499–560; Stephan Landsman, "The Rise of the Contentious Spirit: Adversary Procedure in Eighteenth England," *Cornell Law Review* 75 (1999): 497–609; Stephan Landsman, "One Hundred Years of Rectitude: Medical Witnesses at the Old Bailey," *Law and History Review* 16 (1998); Stephan Landsman, "From Gilbert to Bentham: The Reconceptualization of Evidence Theory, *Wayne Law Review* 36 (1990): 1149–1186; Bruce Smith, "The Presumption of Guilt and the English Law of Theft, *Law and History Review* 23 (2005): 133–171; Michael R. T. MacNair, *The Law of Proof in Early Modern Equity* (Berlin: Duncker & Humblot, 1999); James Oldham, "Truth-Telling in the Eighteenth Century English Courtroom," *Law and History Review* 12 (1994): 95–121; William Twining, "The Rationalist Tradition of Evidence Scholarship," in E. Campbell and L. Waller, eds., *Well and Truly Tried: Essays on Evidence* (Sydney: Law Book Co., 1982); Gerald J. Postema, "Fact, Fictions, and Law: Bentham on the Foundations of

Evidence," in W. Twining, ed., *Facts in Law* (Wiesbaden: Franz Steiner Verlag Clarendon, 1983); Allyson N. May, *The Bar and the Old Bailey, 1750–1850* (Chapel Hill: University of North Carolina Press, 2003).

4. For exceptions, see Barbara J. Shapiro, *Beyond Reasonable Doubt and Probable Cause: Historical Perspectives on the Anglo-American Law of Evidence* (Berkeley: University of California Press, 1991); Barbara J. Shapiro, "'To a Moral Certainty': Theories of Knowledge and Anglo-American Juries, 1600–1850," *Hastings Law Review* 38 (1986): 153–193; Theodore Waldman, "Origins of the Legal Doctrine of Reasonable Doubt," *Journal of the History of Ideas* 20 (1959): 299–366; Anthony A. Morano, "A Reexamination of the Reasonable Doubt Rule," *Boston University Law Review* 55 (1975): 507–528.

5. For discussion of the rhetoric and law, see Barbara J. Shapiro, "Classical Rhetoric and the English Law of Evidence," in Victoria Kahn and Lorna Hutson, eds., *Rhetoric and Law in Early Modern Europe* (New Haven, CT: Yale University Press, 2001); Alessandro Guiliani, "The Influence of Rhetoric on the Law of Evidence and Pleading," *Juridical Review* 62 (1969): 216–251; Hanns Hohmann, "The Dynamics of Stasis: Classical Rhetorical Theory and Modern Legal Argumentation," *American Journal of Jurisprudence* 34 (1989): 171–197. The Roman law of evidence was largely undeveloped. The rhetorical tradition also treated the interpretation of legal documents, the distinction between letter and intent, law and equity, conflict of laws, and reasoning by analogy. See Cicero, *De Inventione*, vol. 2: 10–11.

6. Cicero, *De Inventione*, vol. 1: 2–4, 24–25, 27, 28; vol. 2: 5–10, 1–12, 13.

7. Quintilian, *Institutes of the Orator*, J. Patsaill, trans. (London, 1777), 1, 1–5; 4.9.

8. *Rhetorica ad Herennium*, Harry Caplan, trans. (Cambridge, MA: 1964), vol. 2, 2, 3, 5–6, 8–10, 11; vol. 3, 4–5; vol. 4, 6–8.

9. I. M. Rosenberg and Y. L Rosenberg, "'Perhaps What Ye Say Is Based Only on Conjecture': Circumstantial Evidence Then and Now," *Houston Law Review* 31 (1995): 1371–1427. The Talmud barred circumstantial evidence in criminal proceedings.

10. See Richard Fraher, "'Conviction According to Conscience,' the Medieval Jurist's Debate Concerning Judicial Discretion and the Law of Proof," *Law and History Review* 7 (1989): 23–88; James Franklin, *The Science of Conjecture: Evidence and Probability Before Pascal* (Baltimore: Johns Hopkins University Press, 2001); Giorgia Alessi Palazzola, *Prova legale e pena: La crisi del sistema tra evo medio e moderno* (Naples: Jovene, 1979); John Langbein, *Torture and the Law of Proof* (Chicago: University of Chicago Press, 1977); Mirjan Damaska, "The Death of Legal Torture," *Yale Law Journal* 87 (1978): 867.

11. The most influential treatise dealing with presumptions was Jacobus Menochius's *Tractatus de praesumptionibus*. See Franklin, "The Ancient Sources of Seventeenth Century Probability," in Stephan Gaukroger, ed., *The Uses of Antiquity in the Scientific Revolution* (Dordrecht: Kluwer Academic Publishers, 1991); Palazzola, *Prova a legale et pena*, 46–48.

12. The distinction was not part of the law of the Romans. See *Le fait et le droit: Etudes de logique juridique* (Brussels, 1961), 25. The distinction is to be found in Quintilian, *Institutes of the Orator*, Loeb, ed. (Cambridge, MA: Harvard University Press, 1969), III, v, 4, 7.

13. Though frequently cited in connection with arrest, Bracton employed "suspicion" in the context of indictment. Initially in arrest, only those involved could have suspicion. Only later did the suspicions of officers empower them to make arrests. See Shapiro, *Beyond Reasonable Doubt*, 127–145. By 1608, Francis Bacon suggested that constables ought to arrest if a person was suspected by "common voice or fame," 15 *Works*, 344. See also Coke, *Second Institute*, II, 50ff. Hale felt a magistrate was "a competent judge of the probabilities offered to him of such suspicion." The language of "probable" or "reasonable cause" for suspicion became common. Hale, *History of the Pleas of the Crown*, 109–110; see also 107–108, 579, 588. See also Hawkins, *Treatise of the Pleas of the Crown* (1716). Hawkins places the causes of suspicion in the arrest rather than in the examination portion of his treatise. It then became a standard part of the arrest canon in the justicing handbook tradition.

14. John Aberdeen suggests that rather than a migration from one procedure to another, arrest was often not a distinct step from indictment. Unpublished manuscript, chap. 3, unpaginated.

15. 1 and 2 Philip and Mary (c. 1554–1555); 2 and 2 and 3 Philip and Mary (c. 1555). The language of the statute was not altered until 1826. See Shapiro, *Beyond Reasonable Doubt*, 127–145; John H. Langbein, *Prosecuting Crime in the Renaissance: England, Germany, France* (Cambridge, MA: Harvard University Press, 1974).

16. Desiderius Erasmus, *On Copia of Words and Ideas* (Milwaukee: Marquette University Press, 1963), 66–67. Richard Sherry's *Treatise of Schemes and Tropes* contains the distinction between artificial and inartificial proofs as well as signs, such as the paleness of murderers. Inferences from signs might be treated as strong or weak and reasoning from "effects" and "signs" to "cause" was frequently invoked (London, 1550), 78–79, 83.

17. Thomas Wilson, *The Arte of Rhetorique*, T. J Derrick, ed. (New York: Garland Publishers, 1982), 184–188, 190–195, 199, 234, 236.

18. William Lambarde, *Eirenarcha, or Of the Office of the Justice of the Peace* (London, 1614), 217–219. (Original work published 1581)

19. Ibid., 219.

20. Ibid.

21. Dalton, *The Country Justice*, 297.

22. See Klerman, "Was the Jury Ever Self Informing," 123–149.

23. Quoted in J. Spedding, "An Account of the Life and Times of Francis Bacon" (London, 1880), vol. 1, 513. Similar language is to be found in a royal proclamation of 1607. The Royal Proclamation for Jurors, October 5, 1607, in *Stuart Royal Proclamations*, J. F. Larkin and P. L. Hughes, eds. (Oxford: Clarendon Press, 1973), vol. 1, 168.

24. Langbein, *Prosecuting Crime in the Renaissance*, 124.

25. (London, 1681), 449.

26. The Trial of John Fisher, Bishop of Rochester, *State Trials*, vol. 1, 401. See also The Trial of Sir Thomas More for High Treason (1535), vol. 1, 392; The Trial of Sir Nicholas Throckmorton for High Treason (1554), vol. 1, 880, 881.

27. Matthew Hale, *History of the Common Law of England*, Charles M. Gray, ed. (Chicago: University of Chicago Press, 1971), vol. 1, 163, 164, 165; vol. 2, 277.

28. Hale, *History of the Common Law*, 164.

29. John Locke, *An Essay Concerning Human Understanding*, 2 vols., Alexander Frazer, ed. (New York: Dover Publications, 1959), bk. 4, chap. 4., sec. 4, 5, 6. See also Isaac Watts, *Logicke* (London, 1775), 181–182, 266–272. (Original work published 1724)

30. Before 1640, perjury was tried by the Star Chamber. The two-witness requirement continued when perjury was transferred to the common law courts. See J. H. Wigmore, "The Required Number of Witnesses," *Harvard Law Review* 15 (1901): 83, 88–90.

31. The *State Trials* indicate that the need for two witnesses was sometimes agreed on by both prosecution and defense, and other times, only the defendant insisted on it.

32. Leveller John Lilburne and the Digger Gerrard Winstanley favored a two- or three-witness rule for serious crimes. The Barebones Parliament expressed the view that the law should be more in line with "the word of God and right reason." Donald Veall, *The Popular Movement for Law Reform 1640–1660* (Oxford: Clarendon Press, 1970), 88, 159. The Massachusetts *Body of Liberties* (1641) required two or three witnesses or "that which is equivalent" in capital cases. The New Haven colony in 1644 declared that the judicial laws of Moses should be the colony's code and adopted the two-witness rule. G. L. Haskins, *Law and Authority in Early Massachusetts*, 125ff; I. M. Calder, "John Cotton and the New Haven Colony," *New England Quarterly* 3 (1930): 82–84.

33. A statute of 1623 required two witnesses to convict a woman for concealing the death of her child. Others statutes with a two-witness requirement were for breaking the Sabbath, depraving the sacrament, being at a conventicle, hunting deer, or striking with a weapon or drawing one in the churchyard. The Blasphemy Act of 1697 required two witnesses for conviction. The religious character of many may account for the two-witness requirement.

34. Hale, *The Primitive Origination of Mankind*, 130.

35. George Fisher, "The Jury's Rise as Lie Detector," *Yale Law Journal* 107 (1997): 575–708.

36. There was no settled practice as to whether the justices of the peace were to examine witnesses under oath. The Marian statutes did not direct or authorize sworn statements. Langbein, *Prosecuting Crime*, 17, 26–27.

37. *A True Relation of the Unjust Accusations of Certain French Gentlemen* (London, 1671), 19; Hale, *History of the Common Law*, 164; *The Arraignnment, and Tryal . . . of Sir John Friend* (London, 1696), 44; Gilbert, *Law of Evidence*, 147. The rule about contradiction and consistency is also found in canon and civil law. See also George Mackenzie, *The Laws and Customs of Scotland in Matters of Crime* (Edinburgh, 1678): 538–539.

38. Matthew Hale, *Primitive Origination*, 128. Character witnesses for the defense also alleviated the no-oath situation.

39. More, *Debellacyon of Salem and Bizance* (1533) in *The Complete Works of St. Thomas More* (New Haven, CT: Yale University Press, 1987), vol. 10, 157. Gilbert, *Law of Evidence*, 122, 147, 149, 155.

40. Gilbert, *Law of Evidence*, 104, 147–148, 151.

41. Michael MacNair, "'A Fragment of Proof,' by Francis North, Lord Guildford," *Seventeenth Century* 8 (1993): 143; More, *Works*, vol. 10, 157; Gilbert, *Law of Evidence*, 147.

42. Edward Bowles noted, "It is sad to see how in Courts of Justice, . . . God is prophaned with rude and irreverent swearing." *The Duty and Danger of Swearing* (London, 1655), 14–15. See also John Cheney, *A Vindication of Oaths* (London, 1677), 6, 10, 14, 23, 26; John Allen, *Of Perjury* (London, 1682), 1, 3, 15; John Tombes, *Sephersheba: Or the Oath Book* (London, 1662), 72ff, 114, 133. Many thought perjuries were "very little sins, or rather none at all." *Perjury the National Sin* (London, 1690), 4. See also Isaac Barrow, *Works*, 3 vols. (London, 1700), vol. 1, 194–195; John Tillotson, *The Lawfulness and Obligations of Oaths* (London, 1681), preface, 3–4, 6–7, 10, 34, 26, 28, 29; Thomas Bradley noted that since oaths were "often not to be trusted," it was necessary to "use all diligence, not only by examining witnesses, but observing circumstances, comparing testimonies . . . in searching out the matter." *A Sermon Preached . . . At the Assizes* (York, 1663), 34–35. William Paley referred to the "levity and frequency" of current oath taking and noted the "general inadvertency to the obligation of oaths," the effect of which was "to make them cheap in the minds of the people." *Principles of Moral and Philosophy* (Boston, 1818), 117.

43. More quoted in Hubertus Schulte Herbruggen, "The Process Against Sir Thomas More," *Law Quarterly Review* 99 (1983): 113–136.

44. Roger North, *The Lives of the Norths*, A. Jessupp, ed., 3 vols. (London, 1890), vol. 1, 303–314.

45. Witnesses swore "The Evidence that you shall give . . . shall be the truth, and the whole truth and nothing but the truth, as neere as God shall give you grace." *The Book of Oaths, and the Several Forms Thereof, Both Antient and Modern* (London, 1649), 203, 204–206, 223–224.

46. Grand jurors, who also heard prosecution witnesses, swore, "To present the Truth, the whole Truth, and nothing but the Truth." According to John Hawles, this oath was as strict as that of the petty jury. *Remarks upon the Tryals* (London, 1689), 46–48. See also *The Grand Jury-Man's Oath and Office Explained* (London, 1680); *A Guide to English Juries* (London, 1682).

47. A 1663 assize sermon indicated that precisely because oaths were not to be trusted, jurors must be particularly diligent in examining witnesses and comparing testimony if they were to find the truth. Thomas Bradley, *A Sermon Preached at the Assizes* (York, 1663), 34, 35. John Tillotson emphasized the current "evil and mischief" of breaking oaths in judicial proceedings. *The Lawfulness of Oaths* (London, 1681), preface. See also 10, 24, 26, 28, 29, 34–36. See also Shapiro, *A Culture of Fact*, 19–22, 223, n. 59, 222–224. Watts, *Logick, or the Right Use of Reason in the Inquiry After Truth* (1724/1725), 181–182, 266–271.

48. Tancred, *Treatise on Procedure*, Friedrich C. Bergamann, ed. (Gottingen, 1842, reprint Aachen, 1965), 87ff. See Charles Donahue Jr., "Proof by Witnesses in the Church Courts of Medieval England: An Imperfect Reception of the Learned Law," in *On the Laws and*

Customs of England, Morris Arnold, ed. (Chapel Hill: University of North Carolina Press, 1981), 127–158. See also Mackenzie, *Laws and Customs of Scotland*, 538–539.

49. In Scotland, defendants were not forced to testify on oath because it was considered unjust to force a man to condemn himself. Mackenzie, *Laws and Customs of Scotland*, 522.

50. Bracton, *On the Laws and Customs of England*, S. E. Thorne, trans. (Chapel Hill: University of North Carolina Press, 1981), vol. 2, 356, 386–387. See also William Staunford, *Les Plees del coron* (London, 1557), 11b.3. c.14, a text that had six editions before 1600. Franklin, nevertheless, suggests "violent presumption" was not incorporated in English law before 1600. Franklin, *Conjecture*, 28.

51. Sir Edward Coke, *The First Part of the Institutes of the Lawes of England* (1628), sec. 1, 6b. The comments are made in the context of continual and quiet possession of land.

52. Sir Edward Coke, *Third Part of the Institutes of the Lawes of England* (Philadelphia, 1953), chap. 104, 232, 373. Coke's statements were quickly added to Dalton's *Country Justice.*

53. Dalton, *Country Justice*, 1618 ed., 273. 1. cap. 107. See also Richard Bolton, *A Justice of the Peace in Ireland* (Dublin, 1683), 95. Witchcraft statutes were enacted in 1542, 1543, and 1604. Some pamphlet writers differentiated between the standards for examination and indictment where presumption, suspicion, and circumstantial evidence were permissible and the standard for conviction required "proof," proof meaning confession or the testimony of two sufficient witnesses.

54. The Trial of Sir Walter Raleigh for High Treason, *State Trials*, vol. 2, 18.

55. *The White Devil*, vol. 3, ii.

56. S. S. *The Honest Lawyer*, L, iv (1616) in *The Tudor Facsimile Texts* (1914), n.p.

57. Trial of Dover in Howell, *State Trials*, vol. 6, 559.

58. *The Trial of John Giles* (London, 1681), 54, 144.

59. *The Trial of Carr* (London, 1681), 114, 22.

60. *The True Narrative*, Old Bailey Trials, 2, 3.

61. Howell, *State Trials* (London, 1816), vol. 1, 1053–1054. He was found guilty "directly and by the most sufficient and manifest evidence." See also *Trial of Udall* (1590), *State Trials*, vol. 1, 1281. In another treason trial, the judge referred "to many apparent proofs, and evident presumptions," while the defendant, Jesuit Henry Garnett, emphasized the need for "direct proof" and the inadequacy of circumstances and presumption. *State Trials*, vol. 2, 256, 258. See also Franklin, *Conjecture*, 41–43, 85.

62. *State Trials*, vol. 2, 1053–1054, 1061, 1070, 1071. See also *State Trials*, vol. 2, 18.

63. In another 1681 treason trial, when defendant insisted there was no positive evidence, only insufficient "remote and conjectural Evidence," the judge indicated that "direct Proof of the Fact" was unnecessary and that presumptive evidence was sufficient if it was "reasonable to Conscience." *The Trial of Carr* (London, 1681), 114, 22.

64. Joseph Butler, *The Analogy of Religion* (London, 1736), 272. See also 209, 356–357, 375, 399.

65. Gilbert cites Coke on presumption but defines it "as it is defined by the Civilians." When a fact could not be proved, that "which comes nearest to the Proof, is the Proof

of Circumstances that necessarily and usually attend such Facts." Presumptions were not proof but "stand instead of the Proofs of the Fact until the contrary be proved." *Law of Evidence* (1756 ed.), 160–161. There is no attempt to place circumstances and presumptions in a philosophical context. See Gilbert, *Law of Evidence*, Capel Lofft, ed., 4 vols. (London, 1791), vol. 1, xxxvi, 137. See also Shapiro, *Beyond Reasonable Doubt*, 26–27; William Twining, *Theories of Evidence: Bentham and Wigmore* (London, 1985).

66. *State Trials*, vol. 17, 1430; see also 1429.

67. *Proceedings at Old Bailey*, Trial of John Ayliffe, October 24, 1759; Trial of William Pitts, July 12, 1716; Trial of Isaac Tyser, July 9, 1718; Trial of William Duce and James Butler, July 10, 1723. See also Trial of Thomas Bayle and Elizabeth Bale, October 15, 1740; Trial of Peter Rogers, December 7, 1743; Trial of Robert Wilson and B Whitefield, February 26, 1746.

68. Trial in Ejectment, *State Trials*, vol. 17, 1430; see also 1415, 1416.

69. *Proceedings at Old Baile*, Trial of Isaac Tyser, July 9, 1718.

70. Trial of John Woodburne, in *Collection of State Trials* (London, 1741), 378.

71. Blackstone, *Commentaries*, vol. 3, 371.

72. Trial of Mary Blandy, *State Trials*, vol. 18, 1186, 1187.

73. Trial of John Barbot, *State Trials*, vol. 18, 1292, 1293, 1296, 1297, 1299, 1300, 1301, 1314.

74. William Wills, *An Essay on the Principles of Circumstantial Evidence* (London, 1838), citing Donellan's case, 45–46.

75. Paley, *Moral and Political Philosophy*, 354–355; Wills, *Circumstantial Evidence*, 44–45, citing Burke, *Works*, vol. 2, 623. Because of the statutory rewards for conviction of offenders after 1689, there was increased public awareness of perjury and malicious prosecution. John Beattie, *Crime and the Courts*, 50–55.

76. Testimony and verdicts were "very different things." A witness swears what he has seen or heard, whereas jurors swear "to what he can infer and conclude from the testimony . . . by the act and force of his understanding." *State Trials*, vol. 6, 1005–1006, 1008, 1010. See Green, *Verdict According to Conscience*, 200–249. As early as 1650, if not earlier, jurors who wished to present evidence were to be heard on oath in court. Edward Waterhouse, *Fortescue Illustratus* (London, 1663), 259. See R. W. Baker, *The Hearsay Rule* (London, 1950), citing *Benett v. Hartford* (1650); Hale, *History of the Pleas of the Crown* (1736), vol. 2, 314.

77. Spedding, "An Account of the Life and Times of Francis Bacon," vol. 1, 513; The Royal Proclamation for Jurors, October 5, 1607 in *Stuart Royal Proclamations*, vol. 1, 168.

78. Shapiro, *Beyond Reasonable Doubt*, 13–41.

79. Baker, *Reports of Spelman*, vol. 2, 112; More, *Debellacyon*, 160.

80. *State Trials*, vol. 1, 401.

81. Hale, *History of the Pleas of the Crown*, vol. 2 (1736), 314.

82. John Hawles, *The Englishman's Right: A Dialogue Between a Barrister of Law and a Juryman* (London, 1680), 11, 35, 38, 47. See also Henry Care, *English Liberties* (London, n.d.), 214; Thomas Williams, *The Excellency and Praeheminence of the Laws of England* (London, 1680).

83. The "law of conscience" for Locke was "that fundamental judgment of the practical intellect concerning any possible truth of a moral proposition about things to be done in

life. Moral actions belong therefore to the jurisdiction of the outward and the inward court, and are subjects to both dominations of the civil as well as the domestic governor; I mean both of the magistrates and of conscience." John Locke, *Essays on the Law of Nature*, W. von Leyden, ed. (Oxford, 1954), 225. For Samuel Pufendorf, the rightly informed conscience required either persuasion built on certain principles or persuasion that is "true and certain; and sees no reason to doubt it." This formulation is explicitly related to law in *Of the Law of Nature and Nations* (London, 1703), 17, 21. Locke and Pufendorf suggest how the language of casuistry helped to shape moral and legal philosophy.

84. McAdoo, *Caroline Moral Theology*, 77, quoting Robert South, *Works*.

85. *State Trials*, vol. 26, 286, 350, 351, 457.

86. "Beyond reasonable doubt," however, appears in *State Trials* only in 1795 and is not found in Hale or Blackstone.

87. *State Trials*, vol. 26, 811. *Whole Proceedings of Old Bailey* (London, 1777), 110–111. In 1696, jurors in the Trial of Andrew Glennan were told "I will leave the case to you; and if you have a reasonable doubt, not such as idle or fanciful men may take up on remote probabilities, but such as cannot satisfy your judgments upon your oaths, then you will acquit." *State Trials*, vol. 2, 256–257. See Shapiro, *Beyond Reasonable Doubt*, 21–24. Anthony Morano suggests that the beyond reasonable doubt test was introduced by the prosecution to give defendants less protection than the "any doubt" test. "A Reexamination of the Reasonable Doubt Rule," *Boston University Law Review* 55 (1975), 507–528.

88. *Commonwealth v. Webster*, 59 Mass. (5 Cush.), 320 (1850).

89. Isaac Watts, *Logick, or the Right Use of Reason in the Inquiry After Truth* (1724), 175, 177, 247, 266–271.

90. David Hartley, *Observations on Man* (London, 1749), 204–230, 362; George Campbell, *The Philosophy of Rhetoric*, L. Bitzer, ed. (Carbondale: Southern Illinois University Press, 1963), 44, 55.

91. Gilbert, *Law of Evidence*, 1–3. Gilbert cites Coke on presumption but defines it "as it is defined by the Civilians." When a fact could not be proved that "which comes nearest to the Proof, is the Proof of Circumstances that necessarily and usually attend such Facts." Presumptions were not proof but "stand instead of the Proofs of the Fact until the contrary be proved. "*Law of Evidence* (1756 ed.), 160–161. Gilbert does not attempt to place circumstances and presumptions in a philosophical context. See Gilbert, *Law of Evidence*, Capel Lofft, ed., 4 vols. (London, 1791), vol. 1, xxxvi, 137. See also Shapiro, *Beyond Reasonable Doubt*, 26–27; William Twining, *Theories of Evidence: Bentham and Wigmore* (London, 1985).

92. John Morgan, *Essays upon the Laws of Evidence*, 2 vols. (London, 1789), vol. 1, 1–5. Morgan discusses witness testimony, circumstantial evidence, and presumptions, vol. 1, 39, 48–49.

93. James Wilson, *Works*, 2 vols., R. McCloskey, ed. (Cambridge, MA: 1987), vol. 1, 503–504, 518, 519; vol. 2, 232, 235. See also Thomas Reid, *Essays on the Intellectual Powers of Man*

(Cambridge, 1850), 313–317, 328–329, 413–415; John Abercrombie, *Inquiries Concerning the Intellectual Powers and the Investigation of Truth* (1820); James Glassford, *Essay on the Principles of Evidence and Their Application to the Subject of Judicial Inquiry* (Edinburgh, 1820).

94. Richard Kirwan, *Logick, or An Essay on the Elements, Principles and Different Modes of Reasoning*, 2 vols. (London, 1807), vol. 1, x, 146, 151, 224. Kirwan's treatment of presumption is identical to that of the legal texts vol. 1, 238.

95. Daniel McKinnon, *The Philosophy of Evidence* (London, 1812).

96. James Gambier, *Guide* (Boston, 1834), 17, 49–50, 55–57, 59, 66.

97. Thomas Starkie, *Practical Treatise on the Law of Evidence*, 2 vols. (London, 1824/1833), 15, 478, 514. Both testimony and circumstantial evidence were capable of reaching moral certainty. Starkie cites Roman law writers on presumption and circumstantial avoidance.

98. There were also specialized treatises dealing with circumstantial and presumptive evidence. See William Wills, *An Essay on the Principles of Circumstantial Evidence* (London, 1838); William Best, *The Principles of the Law of Evidence* (6th ed.) (London, 1875); William Best, *A Treatise of Presumptions of Law and Fact with the Theory and Rules of Presumptive or Circumstantial Proof in Criminal Cases* (London, 1844). Best, like Starkie, rejected the notion that circumstantial evidence was superior to other kinds of proof.

99. These developments are treated only briefly here. For a fuller treatment, see Shapiro, *A Culture of Fact*. See also Andrea Frisch, *The Invention of the Eyewitness: Witnessing & Testimony in Early Modern France* (Chapel Hill: University of North Carolina Press, 2004).

100. Thomas Blundeville, *The True Order and Method of Writing and Reading Hystories*, H. G. Dick, ed., *Huntington Library Quarterly* 3 (1939–1940): 157.

101. John Rushworth, *Historical Collections*, 8 vols. (London, 1682), preface; William Howell, *The Elements of History* (London, 1670/1700), preface; *Ravillac Redivivus* (London, 1678), 4; D. Jones, *The Secret History of White-Hall* (London, 1692), preface. Some historians, however, felt that it was also necessary to discuss the causes of events.

102. Thomas Hobbes, *Leviathan*, M. Oakeshott, ed. (New York: Macmillan, 1962), 69.

103. Bolton, *Hypercritica*, vol. 1, 91; see also 91–95; Thomas Fuller, *The Appeal of Injured Innocence* (London, 1650), 16; Peter Heylyn, *The History of the Sabbath* (London, 1636), preface.

104. Thomas Gumble, *The Life of General Monck* (London, 1671), preface.

105. Thomas Sprat, *A True Account of the Horrid Conspiracy* (London, 1885), preface; Robert Brady, *A Complete History of England* (London, 1685), dedicatory letter.

106. Gilbert Burnet, *Memoirs of . . . Dukes of Hamilton* (London, 1677), preface; Lord Bolingbroke, *Historical Writings*, I. Kramnick, ed. (Chicago, 1972), 76.

107. Roger North, *Examen* (London, 1740), dedicatory preface, 16, 17, 110, 119. If the historian or historical relation was determined to be "within the bounds of evidence and certainty," it was necessary to examine whether the historian "had sufficient means of knowledge," whether he was "an eye or ear witness," and whether the things he reported were "publickly acted and known." Bolingbroke, *Historical Writings*, xxxviii.

108. Historians distinguished fact and matter of fact from causal explanation as well as from "conjecture," "inference," and "reflection."

109. See "Religion and the Law: Evidence, Proof and Matter of Fact, 1660–1700." in *Law, Crime and English Society, 1660–1830*, Norma Landau, ed. (Cambridge: Cambridge University Press, 2002), 185–207; Shapiro, *A Culture of Fact*, 168–188. See also Joseph M. Levine, "Matter of Fact in the English Revolution," *Journal of the History of Ideas* 64 (2003): 317–335.

110. Edward Stillingfleet, *Origines Sacrae* (London, 1662), 28, 286–288, 297. For similar views, see Edward Stillingfleet, *A Rational Account of the Grounds of Protestant Religion* (London, 1662); John Tillotson, *The Rule of Faith* (London, 1666); Robert Boyle, *Some Considerations About the Reconcileablness of Reason and Religion* (London, 1675); Gilbert Burnet, *A Rational Method for Proving the Truth of the Christian Religion* (London, 1675).

111. Sir Matthew Hale, *Primitive Origination of Mankind* (London, 1677), to the reader, 29.

112. John Ray, *The Wisdom of God Manifested in the Works of Creation* (London, 1692), preface, 24.

113. Francis Bacon, *The Works of Francis Bacon*, 14 vols., James Spedding, Robert Lodge Ellis, and Douglas Denon Heath, eds. (London 1857–1874), vol. 4, 123, 260; see also vol. 1, 203, 210, 218; vol. 4, 12, 19, 32, 102, 110, 123, 161, 252, 254, 299. See Perez Ramos, *Francis Bacon's Idea of Science and the Maker's Knowledge Tradition* (Oxford: Clarendon Press, 1988); Paolo Rossi, *Francis Bacon: From Magic to Science* (Chicago, 1979); Shapiro, *A Culture of Fact*, 107–110. For the relationship between science and law in Bacon, see Paul Kocher, "Francis Bacon on the Science of Jurisprudence," *Journal of the History of Ideas* 18 (1957): 3–26; Harvey Wheeler, "The Invention of Modern Empiricism: Juridical Foundations of Francis Bacon's Philosophy of Science," *Law Library Journal* 76 (1983): 76–120; Harvey Wheeler, "Science out of Law: Francis Bacon's Invention of Scientific Empiricism," in *Toward a Humanistic Science of Politics: Essays in Honor of F. D. Wormuth*, F. D. Nelson and R. L. Sklar, eds. (London, 1983), 101–143; Rose-Mary Sargent, "Scientific Experiment and Legal Expertise: The Way of Experience in the Seventeenth Century," *Studies in the History and Philosophy of Science* 20 (1989): 19–45; Julian Martin, *Francis Bacon, The State and the Reform of Natural Philosophy* (Cambridge: Cambridge University Press, 1992).

114. Hobbes, *Leviathan*, 69. For Hobbes, "scientific" knowledge was based on reason, not the "facts" of natural history.

115. Thomas Sprat, *The History of the Royal Society*, Jackson Cope and H. W. Jones, eds. (St. Louis: Washington University Press, 1958), 70, 83, 99, 100. See also Peter Dear, "Totius in Verba: Rhetoric and Authority in the Early Royal Society," *Isis* 76 (1985): 145–161; Shapiro, *A Culture of Fact*, 147–160; Barbara Shapiro, "Testimony in Seventeenth-Century English Natural Philosophy: Legal Origins and Early Development," *Studies in History and Philosophy of Science* 33 (2002): 243–263.

116. Robert Boyle, *New Experiments Touching the Spring of Air* (London, 1662), preface; Robert Boyle, *The Christian Virtuoso* (London, 1690), 52; Robert Boyle, *The Works of the*

Honourable Robert Boyle, 6 vols., Thomas Birch, ed. (London, 1772), vol. 1, 34, 313–314; vol. 2, 569, 741, 742. See also R. W. Serjeantson, "Testimony and Proof in Early-Modern England," *Studies in History and Philosophy of Science* 30 (1999): 195–236.

117. "Unpublished Boyle Papers Relating to Scientific Method," R. S. Westfall, ed., *Annals of Science* 12 (1956): 71, 73, 115, 116; Boyle, *Christian Virtuoso*, 72. See also Robert Boyle, *Some Considerations About the Reconcileableness of Reason and Religion* (London, 1675), 61.

118. D. R. Oldroyd, "Some Writings of Robert Hooke on Procedures for the Prosecution of Scientific Inquiry," *Notes and Records of the Royal Society* 41 (1987): 146–147, 155, 157; Henry Oldenburg, *Correspondence*, 13 vols., A. R. Hall and M. B. Hall, eds. and trans. (Madison: University of Wisconsin Press, 1965–1986), vol. 2, 383; Robert Hooke, *Micrographia* (London, 1665), preface.

119. Sprat, *History of the Royal Society of London*, 100; Hooke, *Micrographia*, preface. Sprat greatly exaggerated the number of members who observed experiments and observations.

120. See Shapiro, *A Culture of Fact*, 125–127. Oldenburg, *Correspondence*, vol. 2, 653; vol. 3, 6, 24, 30, 170–171, 219. See also Albert Van Helden, "Telescopes and Authority from Galileo to Cassini," *Osiris* 9 (1994): 19. For a different view, see Shapin, *The Social History of Truth: Civility and Science in Seventeenth-Century England* (Chicago: University of Chicago Press, 1994), 286–287.

121. Royal Society, *Boyle Letters*, vol. 1, 108r, 131 4; Boyle, *Works*, vol. 2, 626; Oldenburg, *Letters*, vol. 3, 342; Hooke, *Micrographia*, preface.

122. It must be noted, however, that "fact" was distinguished from "hypothesis," "causal explanation," and "theory." For a discussion of the relationship of fact, hypothesis, causal explanation, conjecture, and theory see Shapiro, *A Culture of Fact*, 144–160.

123. The process by which fact, as something that had to be established by evidence, was transformed into a truthful or believable statement has still not adequately been examined. For an initial foray, see Shapiro, *A Culture of Fact*, 157–160.

Theoretical and Methodological Issues in the Study of Legal Knowledge Practices

MARIANA VALVERDE

What Do We Study When We Study *How Law Knows*? Questions of Scope and Method

Most questions about law have legal answers—but not all. Questions about law that do not have legal answers are sometimes very specific. Examples of specific nonlegal questions about law are: What effects did statute X have on group Y? Will court decision A improve or harm ongoing sociolegal struggles regarding B? Theoretically inclined sociolegal scholars, however, often ask nonlegal questions about law that cannot be definitively answered by means of empirical research. "How does law know?" is a good example of the sort of question that is not posed to get a definitive, specific empirical answer but rather to stimulate reflection upon the general processes of knowledge and power that ordinary everyday sociolegal research leaves in the background.

When confronted with a question of such generality, most of us have been trained to look for equally general answers. Theses about the general state of things legal are readily available for those who follow the beaten path and evaluate competing answers to nonspecific questions about law and knowledge. There are those, for example, who examine the growing influence of science and technology in certain legal arenas and go on to predict the scientization of law and the replacement of both legal and common-sense knowledges by expertise. Others then enter the fray and either confirm the thesis or deny it. And then, whether the thesis is thought to be correct or incorrect, arguments can be made about whether the scientization of law is a good thing or a bad thing, normatively.

At a more philosophical level, arguments can be made about whether law (in general) is a closed system, cognitively, or whether it is a partially open system.

Debates about the "autopoeisis" thesis put forward by Niklas Luhmann and Gunter Teubner revolve around this issue.[1]

These debates certainly have their uses, both at the level of philosophical reflection and at the level of shedding light on legal processes. But in this chapter, I would like to begin by challenging the debates' unspoken premise that the purpose of theoretical work in legal studies is to devise, test, and refine general propositions about law as such. Thus, in regard to the question of knowledge processes, I would like to propose that we resist the temptation to ask "whether law knows in this way or in that," reflecting instead on what we have learned about the actual epistemological workings of various legal complexes. Such a reflection, I suggest, may encourage us to think of philosophical approaches and methodological traditions as resources that can be used as needed and as appropriate—rather than as general theories that must be either accepted or rejected or modified.

Thinking about theory and method in a craftlike manner, in the context of the common law and of English-language philosophies, calls to mind the pragmatic tradition. The chapter thus begins with a brief consideration of pragmatism, conceived as a set of concerns and approaches that I suggest should be (pragmatically) regarded as a flexible resource rather than as a philosophy. After this introductory reflection on what I call law's pragmatist habitus, I turn to one selected recent methodological tradition that I think holds much promise for sociolegal studies: the tradition that began in science studies but has now been adapted for use in many other settings under the banner of actor network theory (ANT). Studies using this approach are very germane to the challenge of going beyond the by-now rather trite opposition of "law in the books" (the study of texts) versus "law in action" (the study of social relations). In addition, such studies can help those of us who are interested in developing analytic tools that are themselves as dynamic as the processes we study, instead of continuing to generate static models that supposedly reflect struggles and contestations.

Legal events lend themselves extremely well to an ANT-inspired analysis, as I hope to show. But ANT, I will suggest, is not a theory and hence not a self-contained model. Scholars who are interested in critiquing established power relations, for example, can explore ways of combining existing critical tools for analyzing power with ANT approaches. In the end, this chapter will have served this purpose if it helps readers to think somewhat more reflexively about just what we mean by doing theory: The exploration of ANT is not meant as an advertisement for "the next big thing" but rather as an exercise in theoretical reflection regarded as one of many equally valid such exercises.

The Pragmatist Habitus in Law

Looking at both conventional and avant-garde discussions of law's knowledge, one claim that seems to reverberate across approaches and disciplines (in English-language publications) is that law and pragmatism have a strong affinity. Pragmatism has here a broad and nonspecialized meaning, although the association with philosophical pragmatism is by no means irrelevant.[2] The affinity between law and pragmatic reasoning is not always praised. Duncan Kennedy, for example, has recently written that the proliferation of "balancing" tests within rights adjudication demonstrates that constitutional law has become a mere political/policy game, something that he laments, identifying it with a general "loss of faith in legal reasoning."[3]

But whether pragmatism is denounced (often by being identified with law and economics, quite unfairly) or praised, there is general agreement that it is inescapable. Stanley Fish famously remarked that law "is not philosophical (except when it borrows philosophy's argument for its own purposes) but pragmatic; and, from the pragmatic standpoint, the inconsistency of doctrine is what enables law to work."[4] Fish presents this as a radical attack on formalism and hence on black-letter law, but in the U.S. context, it is not at all radical. It is, on the contrary, fully in keeping with the most famous statement about law's knowledge ever made in the Western hemisphere—namely, Oliver Wendell Holmes's "the life of law has not been logic, but experience."

Appealing to experience—the most renowned pragmatist knowledge move—is not necessarily a legal realist move. It does not amount to letting law be driven by social science evidence. In respect to Holmes, Kunal Parker has recently shown that Holmes's experience has little to do either with the sense perceptions favored by American psychology of his day or with personal experience in the contemporary sense. Neither does it gesture toward social science evidence. Parker's careful examination of Holmes's thought reveals that most of what he mentions by way of experience consists of the well-known, trite facts of famous *cases* taught in law schools. When Holmes appeals to "experience" to grant the common law greater legitimacy, he is not actually appealing to either social science evidence or individual personal experience but rather to a particular lifeworld—the world of the middle-class, late nineteenth-century gentleman who might be riding on a horse down a city street and might be accidentally hit by a barrel falling out of a factory window. This lifeworld was to a large extent itself shaped not only by the common law's sensibilities but even by its specific precedents.[5]

Despite its covert reliance on law itself to provide dead law with the life of experience, Holmes's rejection of "pure" theories of law, both historicist and formalist, is an important step in the theorization of law. In general, valuing responsiveness over coherence or formal elegance and seeing law as always subject to reform and improvement are by no means outmoded elements in the constitution of what one could call law's pragmatist temperament or habitus (or perhaps more accurately, the common law's pragmatist habitus). Whether common-law responsiveness to "experience" is seen in Holmes's humanistic manner, as embodied in the habitus of wise judges, or whether it is regarded more objectivistically as listening to social science evidence, as in the work of Roscoe Pound, there is a common emphasis on change and on responsiveness to the social. Pound's own overview of the history of the common law emphasizes this continuity; for example, instead of chastising earlier generations for failing to pay attention to social science, as many contemporary law-and-society scholars do, he constructs a quasi-Hegelian narrative in which nineteenth-century equity jurisprudence is regarded not as a quaint survival but rather as law's attempt to be responsive to social facts not envisioned by the codifiers.[6]

Pound's overview of the common law teleologically constructs the United States of his day as common law's natural home, and yet, contrary to the usual national narrative, the American Revolution plays a very minor role. The United States is simply more modern and hence more exemplary; the more "social" aspects of U.S. law are not American contingencies. In Pound's narrative, the common law itself appears as the main subject of history, and this macrosubject is endowed with all of the virtues generally ascribed to English people. It is the English legal system that, in contrast to French rationalism, is practical, sensible, and so forth. (In English Canada, A. V. Dicey's influential treatise on constitutional law was a key vehicle for the dissemination of a very similar and equally circular narrative about the common law's innate practical wisdom.) Experience, then, in Pound's account as well as in Holmes's, turns out also to merge imperceptibly into law. In other words, the pragmatic habitus cannot be once and for all ascribed either to law/common law or to "society"/English culture. It jumps from one side to the other whenever one tries to find an origin or a firm causal relation.

To complicate matters further, philosophical pragmatism itself is highly variable and contested. At the level of systematic philosophy, Holmes's humanism is seriously at odds both with sociological jurisprudence and with the mechanical models of rational-choice economics, and all of these in turn are at odds with Stanley Fish's left-wing postmodern pragmatism. As many recent studies have emphasized, there is no one thing called pragmatism, even if one looks only within legal circles.[7]

While recognizing the large differences in philosophy and in politics that separate the various approaches are in part inspired by pragmatism, for present purposes it is possible to sweep those differences under the rug and speak of a pragmatist temperament or habitus that runs throughout English-language legal theorizing and that is compatible with a number of philosophical models and with a variety of political stances.

The existence of a multifarious pragmatist stance or habitus should not mislead us into concluding that English/American law is "essentially" pragmatic, however. Perhaps more than other approaches and philosophical stances, pragmatism is, by definition, not a total theory or self-sufficient model. It would not be very pragmatic to absolutely ban antipragmatic knowledge moves. If we look at recent judicial pronouncements (at least the nonrepresentative sample I have encountered in my work and teaching), we see what one could call a silent dialectic of pragmatism and antipragmatism. Perhaps in an unconscious guilty reaction against the canonization of capitalism that American law has facilitated, English-speaking judges and legislators are very fond of occasional crypto-Christian diatribes not only against greed but even against utilitarian rationalities. Martha Stewart can be sent to jail for what was basically an administrative offense so that citizens can rest assured that capitalism is subjected to some kind of legal/ethical limits. In another sphere, Justice Scalia's homilies on unnatural sexual acts get much mileage out of old-fashioned deontological reasoning. Elsewhere in law, continuing restrictions on the physical location and the advertising opportunities applying to "vice" capitalism—for example, restrictions on casinos, on offtrack betting, on cigarette advertising, and of course, on the sale of anything sexual, and in some jurisdictions, the sale of alcohol—suggest that deontological rationalities are still very much part of contemporary law. Deontological reasoning is also used almost to the exclusion of other logics in certain domestic and international human rights contexts.

But more or less occasional lapses into the deontology of moral outrage, whether by Puritans who stand for absolute moral codes or by liberals who fetishize absolute rights, seem to be easily accommodated within the everyday pragmatism of most everyday law, as I have noted elsewhere.[8] Moralistic crusades have usually coexisted with everyday capitalist greed, as Kierkegaard pointed out long ago in regard to the "Sunday supplement" approach to combining Christianity with worldliness. Legal discourse reflects this, in that judicial homilies about "evil" rarely seek to actually drive the moneylenders out of the temple.

Thus, the pragmatist temperament or habitus that can be seen both in legal theorizing and in the everyday work of law (in common-law countries, at any rate) cannot be rigorously defined. It can, however, be described. It is a stance that is concerned more with effects than with formal elegance and coherence. It is also one that takes law as an ever-changing formation that is deeply embedded in a complex world that can never be adequately captured in static theoretical models.

Needless to say, this description of a general stance does not take us very far at all. What Holmes means by "experience" is not what Roscoe Pound meant by "sociological evidence" and is very far from what rational-choice law professors mean by utility. How are we then to document the very striking differences that quickly arise when legal actors or legal scholars, agreeing that law's effects are important, go on to examine and count the relevant effects?

One key difference—which acts to separate law school lawyers from the law-and-society movement, roughly—lies in the scope of the inquiry. Someone like Holmes assumes that if anyone other than legislators makes law, it is judges. The wisdom of the common law and the wisdom of particular gentlemanly judges thus merge easily into one another. Similarly, many left-wing legal scholars who decry the rise of law and economics speak as if legal reasoning is at its best when the only extralegal knowledge that is allowed in the door is that of classical philosophy (Kant, for example)—but they too think of law as fully contained in legislation, the principles of legislation, and judgments. The effects of law that count here are those that are visible either within formal law itself, such as effects on later courts, or at the level of philosophical constructs. This or that judgment by court X is said to be "bad for individual freedom," for example, or "a blow to the Fourteenth Amendment," rather than being bad for people.

Mainstream and left law-centered writers thus share an a priori knowledge move, a move that excludes anyone other than legislators and judges from the lawmaking function and that therefore confines pragmatic inquiries into effects to investigations of the formal legal system of discourse and some related conceptual constructs (e.g., "individual freedom"). Law-and-society scholars, by contrast, have for a long time now stressed that lawmaking has deep roots in social struggles and in economic conflicts. In tracing the effects of law, then, law-and-society studies draw much larger and more diffuse boundaries around their research projects.

And yet, law-and-society scholarship has been guilty, as a genre, of reacting rather too negatively to blackletter intellectual habits and priorities. In many studies, the effects of sociolegal events on law itself are almost ignored to the point that relevant court decisions and statutes sometimes remain unread. Political and social causes, interests, and effects are sometimes assumed to be the only objects worth studying. This bias is understandable given the minority status of law-and-society scholarship vis-à-vis the tremendous volume of strictly legal scholarship daily generated by blackletter lawyers; but it nevertheless distorts the field in that the "society" part of "law and society" ends up much better researched than the "law" part. Of course, nobody can study everything, and choices need to be made. It is not selectivity that is the problem but rather the unreflective and unreflexive selectivity that makes assumptions about what is worth studying at all.

Whether privileging law narrowly defined or society, the act of taking up the standpoint of law or the standpoint of society without much discussion has the effect of reconstituting and reaffirming the very boundary that law-and-society scholarship claims to be deconstructing. It seems to me that what we need now, after forty years of law-and-society scholarship, is not more studies that demonstrate yet again that law is not self-sufficient or autonomous. Rather, we need new studies that resist the temptation of waving the flag of society as against law. After all, plenty of law professors now beat us at our own game, albeit by transforming society into an abstract rational-choice model. It is thus time to call a truce in the old battle between formal law and sociological jurisprudence or, more accurately, to recognize that in practice a truce has long been in effect.

More specifically, a key methodological challenge for us today, in my view, involves putting into question old assumptions about what constitutes legal versus social *effects* of law—as well as old assumptions about what types of objects to include in this study if one is more interested in sociopolitical power struggles than in law's own questions. We do not necessarily have to study ordinary people or social movements to study law's social effects, and conversely, studying legal texts does not have to be done legalistically. If even that Holy Grail of American pragmatism, "life," turns out to be inside rather than outside of law (as Parker's analysis of Holmes elegantly shows), then studying law itself—including carrying out such apparently old-fashioned projects as Parker's intellectual history of American law—is not without its importance for our understanding of the dynamics of extralegal relations.

Legal Texts or People: Bracketing the Binary

Sociolegal studies, especially in North America—where much more empirical work is carried out than in British or continental sites of sociolegal research—routinely include within their scope a whole range of institutions, actors, and research sites. But although North American sociolegal scholarship has for a long time now dispensed with the law–nonlaw binary that still marks both doctrinal work and European sociology of law, North American sociolegal scholars have only recently begun to question a different set of binary oppositions. In keeping with the deep-rooted humanism that characterizes qualitative (and even much quantitative) work in the social sciences, North American scholars asking about law and society have only just started asking questions about the line separating persons from things and, more generally, humans from nonhumans.

In France and in Britain, actor network theory (ANT) and other posthumanist approaches to the social study of knowledges (mainly arising from science and technology studies, or STSs) have recently started to be used for the study of legal processes. The noted anthropologist Marilyn Strathern has been key in stimulating this kind of work among younger scholars, such as Alain Pottage and Annelise Riles.[9] And in France, Bruno Latour, a professor in France's elite mining engineering school, recently decided to turn his attention away from scientific laboratories and study the workings of a "legal factory" (*La fabrique du droit*). His particular object[10] is the Conseil d'État, a hybrid political-legal body.[11] In North America, this work has had little influence on sociolegal scholarship thus far, despite the efforts of a few valiant anthropologists (Bill Maurer, Annelise Riles, and Susan Silbey) and a few other sociolegal scholars.

A key insight shared by all of these scholars is that there is much to gain by treating one's research site as if the distinction between human and nonhuman could be bracketed. Note that this is primarily a methodological decision, not a substantive claim about whether humans exist or are important. Some scholars do claim that "the legal boundary between persons and things, rather like that between nature and culture, is no longer self-evident"[12]—a statement that assumes we are now more complex and fluid than our ancestors, in keeping with the postmodern narrative.[13] But while some scholars using ANT accept postmodern theorists' substantive claims about the world having become more unstable, or in Zygmunt Baumann's word more "liquid," most of the work along these lines does not make ontological claims about society or the world. The claim is rather that it is very fruitful to proceed, analytically, without making any initial assumptions about the role and the weight of things, people, artifacts, human thought, paperclips, the papers they organize, and so on. Persons, devices, rules, laboratory animals, chemical reagents, and knowledge bits are all regarded as "actors"—with the word *actor* having little or no link with the sociological concept of "agency."

From the ANT perspective, what is and is not an actor is a matter for investigation. Thus, the designation "actor" is always specific and always relational. The scallops studied by Michel Callon[14] only become actors when scientists make claims about their impending disappearance or when fishermen try to sell them; that is, they only become actors if some other actor tries to enlist them in a network. In the same way, what is or is not a network is a site-specific question. Networks are made and remade every day through a process known as *translation*, a term evoking the archaic meaning of "translation" as physical travel.

Here is an example from my ongoing research on urban law in action. A residents' group opposing a public housing development will constitute itself more successfully as an actor in the legal network whose most authoritative actor is the zoning appeals board if it puts its objections in the form of complaints about land uses rather than attacks on people. This translation process is of course totally familiar to sociolegal and urban studies scholars; but an ANT perspective would emphasize that the strategic rewording of one's affidavit is not a merely politico-discursive maneuver because it also involves a physical movement of persons and things (photos, petitions, PowerPoint presentations) from the residents' homes to the downtown offices where the hearings are held. Including the physical movements of objects, persons, and other entities in one's analysis is not often done outside anthropological writing. ANT helps us to reflect upon the specific effects of translation choices. For instance, in one hearing I attended, the adjudicator objected to the PowerPoint slides, asking repeatedly to be given printed copies and forcing the residents' group to admit that the information delivered through professional-looking slides was not academic research but was taken from a newspaper article. The residents looked dejected because they had assumed that translating their "facts" into objective-looking PowerPoint slides would strengthen their own legal network. But PowerPoint, a technical actor engaged in translation, has different degrees of authority in different contexts (networks). Sociologists would generally classify PowerPoint as a technical medium, but an ANT perspective encourages the analyst to consider the possibility that in some instances PowerPoint may be an actor alongside human and other nonhuman actors.

As Latour and others were experimenting with the language of actors and networks, a literature developed within sociology that also spoke a great deal about networks; the work of Manuel Castells is among the best known.[15] Two differences between the two ways of using networks can be usefully mentioned here. First, contrary to the general logic of network sociology, which emphasizes the success and the ubiquitousness of networks and claims that we now live in a networked world whereas our ancestors did not, ANT-inspired work makes no claims about what the world is really like. Second, while most sociological accounts of the networked global world focus on successful changes, ANT-inspired work often draws our attention to failures, to situations in which networks grind to a halt for lack of a translation, as Latour often puts it.[16] Documenting in some detail unexpected failures in the work of constituting networks puts claims about "the knowledge society" and "networked society" in doubt.

Along the same lines, Michel Callon's recent reflection on a man who point-blank refused to speak about his genetic condition—a man who not only refused the self-help discourse being visited upon him by his wife and brother as well as by medical experts but, more remarkably, also refused to voice anything that could be construed as "resistance," confining himself to remaining silent and watching football on television—demonstrates that even global-scale networks drawing on considerable material and symbolic resources are always fragile. Their fragility lies in the fact that they depend for their existence on day-to-day moves and translations that do not always occur, even if they occur habitually.[17]

Documenting failures of translation without recourse to the resistance–accommodation binary, as Callon and Rabeharisoa do and as Marilyn Strathern does in a study titled "Refusing Information"[18] is important for sociolegal scholars who want to go beyond the political binaries of the 1970s and 1980s. Precisely because they bracket the question of structural power relations, ANT approaches are able to document microknowledge moves without immediately proceeding to classify them as either collaborationist co-optations or as acts of crypto-resistance.

Another key binary of sociolegal studies—that which divides the study of people and their "agency" from the study of legal texts—can also be usefully undermined and bracketed with the help of ANT tools. I have argued elsewhere that it is well worth experimenting with methodologies for the study of legal processes that do not separate people from things (or texts), the social from the textual, law in action from law in the books.[19] One does not need ANT to see the problems caused by the law in the books versus law in action binary. But the ANT insistence on treating all elements in a network as actors, without dividing the human from the nonhuman in an a priori fashion, helps to move sociolegal scholarship beyond the polemical attacks on studying the books of law that were necessary in the 1960s but which have become increasingly unnecessary and even inaccurate, given the prestige of law and economics within law schools.

It should be clear by now why ANT studies are always particular studies; theoretical models and typologies are of little if any help if one's aim is to combinations of human and nonhuman actors in a dynamic and site-specific manner. But then how is one to write theoretically informed analyses? A hypothetical example can help to address this question. Lorraine Daston, one of the most influential historians of scientific knowledges writing today, has stimulated a wide range of studies under the banner of "biographies of scientific objects."[20] It would be possible (and interesting, in my view) to generate a similar series of biographies of legal objects, with *objects* defined as broadly as possible. An anthology of biographies of legal objects could include a property lawyer writing the biography of "the easement," a scholar of family law writing about "the disappearing wife" of family law, an anthropologist studying the invention and use of the judge's gavel, a cultural historian investigating the history of the English judge's wig, and a constitutional scholar pondering the development of the key American legal technology of the constitutional amendment. Such an anthology would not demand methodological consistency, but it would have a certain unity in that the articles taken together would emphasize the fruitfulness of setting aside the separation of things and people, the textual and the social.

A final word about ANT within legal studies. There are those that see ANT as a self-sufficient method. Bruno Latour's study of the Conseil d'État,[21] for example, refuses to address any of the obvious political questions about state power and class hegemony that arise as one reads about the "conseillers," their individual biographies, and their decisions. The term *class* is studiously avoided.

But if we take ANT and related analytic tools with a pragmatist pinch of salt rather than as the solution to our methodological crisis, we could proceed to combine an ANT-inspired analysis of the internal workings of a legal institution with a consideration of the social and political context that is not directly visible to the ethnographer. If we see ANT studies as resources rather than as examples of a theory that one has to either accept or reject because it is in a competitive relation with other theories, we will be able to experiment with ways of combining methods, insights, and agendas in whatever way seems appropriate for each particular research project. The pragmatist legacy is best understood not as a philosophical position to be defended against others, in my view, but rather as a way of examining the possible uses and effects of existing methodological and theoretical resources.

Legal Claims About the Social: Some Examples of Law's Knowledge Moves

I have just argued that social effects and legal effects cannot be assumed to lie in different research sites and that a "law-and-society" location (such as mine) should not automatically prejudge what one studies—or how. In addition, I earlier argued that the actor–network habit of putting all actors on the same plane, initially at least, without automatically dividing persons from things or the human from the nonhuman, is a very useful way to stimulate new research. And yet, I parted company with most of the actor–network scholars insofar as they tend to present their method as an exclusive and self-sufficient one, whereas in my view certain insights from ANT can be usefully supplemented by more conventional social science investigations, including those in the "everyday life of law" stream.

It is high time to show rather than tell and to give some sense of what aspects of legal knowledge processes one might be able to see by following my suggestions that are not so visible otherwise. Given the focus on knowledge rather than power/authority, law here is considered not as system of power endowed with a unique authority but as a system of knowledge among many such systems, as a machine to process knowledge claims that coexists with scientific knowledge machines, bureaucratic knowledge machines, and so forth. And since most previous studies have focused either on the content of law's knowledges or on the formal reasoning structures typically used by officially certified legal actors, it will be helpful to turn our attention away from philosophical habits and preferences and concentrate on the "minor" technologies of knowledge, what I call the "knowledge moves" that one commonly sees in legal contexts. Furthermore, given the discussion of pragmatist mentalities and habits, it makes sense to select knowledge moves that enable legal actors to acknowledge, receive, reject, transform, and otherwise "translate" knowledge claims about aggregate social effects. Some of these claims are externally generated (e.g., by expert social science evidence), some are internally generated (e.g., out of the reasonable person standard and its wealth of knowledges of risks), and many are neither or both. An example of the latter is judicial notice, a way of translating knowledge claims that, as Susan Drummond has shown, simultaneously names and invisibilizes factual claims.[22]

While autopoeisis writers and many other scholars would proceed by differentiating external from internal knowledge claims—a move that does allow hybrids, but with these being seen as mixtures of two established entities rather than as sui generis assemblages—here we attempt to do without that basic binary. Thus, whether knowledge claims being transmuted and translated in the examples that follow are "originally" extralegal or legal, or whether they are properly made by legal rather than some other actors, is not our question.

Given the creativity and unpredictability of knowledge networks, even those that, as is the case for law, suffer from an abundance of rules designed specifically to curtail creativity in both interpreting previous texts and formulating new texts, an exhaustive inventory of knowledge moves—even if confined to moves that make claims about "the social"—is impossible. And given that my own reading of legal and paralegal texts is confined to a few areas, the moves mentioned here are unlikely to be representative. I thus offer them in the spirit of experimentation and dialogue in the hope that someone will take issue with my descriptions or proceed to add a whole other series.

Anonymous Allusion

That legal documents—such as affidavits, statutes, and decisions—have citational practices that are totally at odds with those of the nonlaw academy is hardly a new insight. But the intertextual practice of "anonymous allusion" has not received analytical attention, as far as I know. Anonymous allusion works as follows. Anyone writing a text that seeks to become part of a legal network (note that the seeking is here attributed to the text in the manner of ANT) has to be aware of the fact that legal sources have to be carefully and extensively referenced. Once in a while, a phrase such as "the whole of the common law" is found, but this refusal to reference is rarely found in the lower reaches of the system. Citing cases and statutes is absolutely essential, and law schools devote much more time to teaching students how to find and correctly cite relevant texts than social science departments spend teaching students how to write bibliographies.

In relation to nonlegal sources, however, a great deal of discretion obtains. Countless court decisions use phrases such as "studies show . . ." or "expert evidence supports . . ." without any citations. Expert evidence is sometimes specified, but interestingly, the name of the expert witness is more likely to make it into a legal text than the reference to a specific study. That the credibility of the witness as a moral person is crucial is one of those facts about law's knowledge that social scientists simply deplore, rarely seeking to understand it.[23] But the key point here is that even when expert evidence is deemed relevant and credible, one often sees allusions rather than references. Legal texts I have examined in the course of my research on urban law often mention "the experience of cities" or "the concerns of homeowners" without specifying which cities, much less referencing the exact source.

Anonymous allusion may seem at first sight as a typical legal-imperialist "dissing" move because it literally erases scientific networks of referencing, refereeing, and authorization. But given its noted success and ubiquitousness, there may be more than a professional investment in dissing other disciplines at work here. Anonymization does work to eliminate all possible debate about the details and the authority of particular claims, but the allusion simultaneously recognizes (in a generic manner) the very expertise/experience that seems to be downgraded. A judge mentioning "the concerns of the neighborhood" when declaring that a zoning variance was indeed properly granted by the zoning appeals board is making the neighbors visible and invisible at the same time. Neighbors are visible but only generically, en masse as it were. In this manner, conflicts among them are erased; furthermore, no individual is named or profiled in such a way as to enable that individual to contest the judge's translation. The experiences of others—and the expert evidence generated by other disciplines—are thus acknowledged and deprived of independent power at the same time, surely the mark of a successful translation.

The particular political and social effects of various ways of deploying the anonymous allusion would close study. Who and what end up deauthorized or validated are not questions that can be answered in a general manner. But one thing that is clear from a purely formal analysis of this knowledge move is that it manages to perform that key function of law in a modern liberal state: to speak authoritatively while at the same time claiming either to represent "the people" and/or to heed, on behalf of the people, the realities of "experience." Sovereigns of all kinds, including legal ones, rarely speak in their own name now; they are expected to speak either as representatives of the popular will, as funnels for the wisdom of the experts, or as both. Anonymous allusion enables both of these acts of ventriloquism, acts that are in themselves political, quite apart from the specific political consequences that may ensue and that would require separate investigation.

Exemplary Excerpting

Instead of merely alluding to a generalized knowledge of a generalized experience, sometimes a legal text will actually quote a passage from a nonlegal or paralegal document. Public hearings held on a proposed new law are a favorite gold mine for lawyers and articling students working as judicial clerks. What one resident of a neighborhood said—about street prostitution, about gangs, etc.—is literally cut out of a 1,000-page record of the hearings and pasted into a very short document with a much larger and more authoritative circulation.

Since almost nobody involved in the legal network (or for that matter, in the actual hearing) reads the physically intimidating volumes of evidence that are generated from these events, the bit that is cut and pasted automatically becomes exemplary. The physicality of the volume is transformed but not wholly eliminated as the articling student puts the volume away after having excerpted one or two bits because the citation to volume and page number will make it clear to the reader/consumer of the higher level text that the giant volume did exist and was read by someone.

Exemplary excerpting is by no means uniquely legal: Journalism lives by this technique. Journalistic texts assume—and encourage readers in turn to assume—that the individuals quoted are somehow representative, that they were somehow chosen out of many others whose words were also potentially available, and that they speak for a group, not just for themselves. This impression of having been chosen out of a large sample creates a sense of "weight" in the sense given to the word *weight* in the law of evidence. But within law, the technique has particular effects. Apart from the social and economic effects that arise from the particular demographics of the chosen speakers, there is a more formal effect that is very similar to what film critics call the "reality effect." The lawyer drafting the brief or the articling student who clerks for a judge are like journalists in that they are institutionally prevented from putting in their own opinions. But views that exactly match their own but which are taken from someone else's mouth are not only permitted but valued. Exemplary excerpting takes a few sentences out of context and out of the control of their original speakers and uses them merely to lend weight to the opinion that the legal actor had already formed before setting out to elaborate the text. In this way, exemplary excerpting, like anonymous allusion, contributes to the overall objectivist reality effect of legal writing.

Epistemological Sidelining

Courts today, especially appellate courts, are bombarded with expert evidence, amicus curiae briefs, and other knowledge claims that cannot be leached out of the network as easily as the eyewitness evidence presented at trial. It is well known that in some situations expert evidence is quickly transmuted into law, as when the existence and legality of a certain environmental standard or a certain highway traffic rule are validated by an appeal court by reference to expert studies, but in other situations, expert evidence is rejected either as irrelevant or as lacking in credibility.

What is perhaps less well known, or rather less theorized, is the fact that a great deal of evidence introduced "from the outside," as it were, is neither accepted nor rejected. A scientific article cannot ignore past relevant studies but must either confirm or deny the preliminary findings of other scientists. In legal networks, however, and specifically in appeal courts, available relevant studies are often sidelined rather than accepted or rejected or distinguished. The studies and/or the experts who literally bring studies into the court's network (either in person or in writing affidavits) are often put literally on the legal sidelines, such that they are still available if required in a later part of the legal match but without being allowed to play for the time being.

One current example of epistemological sidelining concerns biomedical evidence regarding the nature of sexual orientation. While in some U.S. cases with nationwide importance, a parade of experts testified at trial regarding the ontological status of homosexuality and/or sexual orientation,[24] appeal courts have consistently refused to either certify or decertify any of these competing knowledge claims. That the "nature–nurture" debate, as the courts simplistically put it, is not one for courts to settle has become a cliché in this kind of litigation. In Canada, the sidelining took place at an earlier point in the network—earlier both chronologically and legally. Since 1995 or thereabouts, no high-level Canadian legal pronouncement on homosexuality and/or sexual orientation has even mentioned the gay gene, the gay brain thesis, or anything else that is part of the nature–nurture "causes of homosexuality" debate. The sidelining was thus earlier and more complete in the Canadian judicial network of decisions about homosexuality and sexual orientation.

Epistemological sidelining is a move with which anyone who reads court decisions is familiar. But its importance has not been analyzed. Those who see law as an imperialist institution that is always capturing and absorbing extralegal knowledges (and these include autopoeisis scholars but also some Foucaultians and many CLS-style critics) generate models of law's knowledges based on the assumption that law is always, amoeba-like, swallowing up other knowledges/powers. They thus fail to see what amounts to a refusal to pronounce on the role, within the legal game, of certain knowledge players. The would-be players waving their sheaves of studies are neither included nor explicitly excluded; they are merely sidelined. In general, the ubiquitousness of this knowledge move emphasizes the need to generate concrete analyses of law's knowledge processes that are as attentive to refusals and abdications as they are to imperialist moves.

Transmuting Jurisdiction into Knowledge

As part of a project on urban/municipal law, I have read many U.S. and Canadian court decisions regarding the legality of particular ordinances and bylaws, decisions which often turn on the issue of jurisdiction. Although jurisdiction is sometimes regarded, in blackletter fashion, as a question that can be definitively settled through statutory interpretation and stare decisis, in many cases courts stray far beyond the letter of the law and engage in their own evaluation of the reasonableness or otherwise of a municipal council's lawmaking activities. A common trope in this type of inquiry is that of "the streets": a familiar semimythical, semiphysical, semilegal space that is generally taken to be automatically known by the city councilors who passed the impugned bylaw or ordinance. If asked to rule on the legality of an ordinance regulating, say, the distance that must obtain between "adult entertainment" establishments, courts are likely to say that city councilors are the ones who know the streets of their city, not courts, and that their legal rules are thereby reasonable and hence constitutional.[25]

This knowledge move, which justifies a lawmaking process by reference to an extralegal knowledge process (namely, the city councilors acquiring knowledge of "their" streets), is very similar to that performed by Oliver Wendell Holmes when attributing to law the ability (and the duty) to change itself so as to match what is going on in life, in experience. In both cases, the reasoning appears to ground law in extralegal social and material relations instead of merely referring to a statute or a precedent. But in both cases, the supposedly extralegal relations that are invoked so they can lend their solidity, their weight, to law turn out to have a curiously legal essence. In none of the cases that I have read did courts ever clearly state, as part of the summary of facts, that city councilors did actually set out on nocturnal walks to know the city's vice districts. Neither are city councils said to be learned in urban studies and other relevant disciplines. City councilors are simply declared to be in possession of knowledge of the streets. Such a declaration manages to get by unnoticed, it seems to me, because city councilors have legal *jurisdiction* over streets, as every resident phoning city hall about a pothole knows.

When one considers the arbitrary manner in which councils are declared to have true knowledge of the streets, even when they have not themselves made any such claims, it becomes clear that courts are, first, treating jurisdiction as if it were based on extralegal knowledge, and then, circularly, transmuting this legal capital (jurisdiction) into the social and political authority to govern urban space—the authority to pass ordinances that breach First Amendment rights, for example. That hybrid political-social-legal authority is then used, again circularly, to affirm their jurisdiction: The ordinance in question is not ultra vires, we are told, or not really subject to judicial review, because city councils know their streets and know them better than courts do. One curious aspect of this move is that council's knowledge seems to fall between two stools, being neither the personal knowledge of the eyewitness nor the learned knowledge of the expert. But even more curious is the fact that councils don't generally make claims to know the streets as such. They merely claim—in the submissions of city lawyers—that they have the (legal) authority to regulate them. But in this day and age, courts don't like to simply affirm a strictly legal power found in statute and in common law; they like to write as if jurisdiction were not purely legal but were in turn based on extralegal knowledge and authority.

The sociopolitical effect of this curious (and legally unnecessary) reading of municipal jurisdiction is that city councils end up being granted an authority that the councils themselves don't necessarily seek from courts. Councils want courts to affirm that they do have a right to regulate public space as they see fit. But courts give more than they are asked when they stray beyond blackletter law to make claims about who does or does not *know* "the streets."

Responsibilization Through Imputed Knowledge

In earlier work on liquor inspections and on drinking and driving cases, I have shown that courts (and some recent statutes) are often keen to impute knowledge of the psychobiological effects of alcohol on human bodies, even to people who do not themselves drink and thus have neither personal nor expert evidence of alcohol's effects.[26] This move relies on the well-worn common law ontology of reasonableness, in which the hypothetical prudent person is more real than the actual person in court. Not surprisingly, then, the imputing knowledge move is not unique to drinking law. Tort law is full of judicial declarations of what Mr. X should have known or what the reasonable person is expected to know, declarations that can proceed in the absence of any empirical evidence about what Mr. X had the opportunity to actually learn. Ordinary people are not always responsibilized, of course. The infamous case of the lady who sued McDonald's after she burnt herself with coffee is always trotted out to argue that people these days aren't being sufficiently responsibilized and that juries in this kind of lawsuit are turning adults into infants. But for our purposes, it is not necessary to find out how typical (or more likely, atypical) the famous McDonald's case is; it is simply sufficient to note that a number of legal machineries, from tort law to drinking and driving law, work by means of a particular epistemological trick involving imputing knowledge.

What can we say about the effects of this move? It is clear that imputing knowledge works to eliminate experts and their advice from a specific network and to thereby responsibilize ordinary people for monitoring and managing the risks of everyday life. The continuing liveliness of tort cases in which this sort of knowledge move is performed demonstrates that even though there are many risks that have been taken out of the purview of the reasonable person and put within the sole epistemological jurisdiction of experts, nevertheless, experts have not taken over the work of assessing and managing risks to the extent that is claimed by many risk-society theorists. Thus, looking at the uses of this particular knowledge move can shed some light on the persistence of that old Protestant category of prudence in contemporary law in the age of hot-coffee lawsuits. And it can also shed some light on the sociological question of the locus of risk management.

Conclusions: Studying the Dynamics of Legal Knowledge

Sociolegal scholars have been concerned to document the ways in which substantive claims made within and around law perpetuate social inequality, as part of the "critique of ideology" project also carried out since the 1960s in a large number of other scholarly fields. The study of knowledge forms is of more recent vintage. It has been greatly facilitated by borrowing approaches and insights from anthropology, a discipline that, unlike sociology, has long been interested in the formats and the codes of knowledge claims. Even more recently, actor network theory (ANT) has also been put to good use by sociolegal scholars in such a way as to highlight the dynamics of knowledge formation and knowledge circulation.

ANT and certain approaches cultivated within the history and sociology of scientific knowledges have provided us with highly sophisticated analyses of the *form* and the dynamics of knowledges in contrast to the emphasis on content and on interests that marked the law-and-society scholarship of the 1960s and 1970s. In our own day, technological and social innovation has alerted us to the importance of formats and of translation codes, but an interest in documenting these should not blind us to the fact that in many cases the process through which knowledges are disassembled and reassembled has the effect of allowing "the haves" to still come out ahead. Thus, despite the risks of eclecticism that one runs when combining heterogeneous methods, there is a very good reason for attempting to combine ANT-style analyses of particular knowledge networks with the insights and the methods of more established law-and-society studies. The reason is simply that old questions of justice and injustice have by no means become irrelevant. Because relations of injustice are notoriously prone to becoming invisible through various techniques of naturalization (including what Pierre Bourdieu called "misrecognition"), we may well need more than one method if we are going to continue engaging in the always necessary, never finished task of revealing injustice in all its forms, especially its more everyday, taken for granted forms.

Notes

1. Niklas Luhmann, *A Sociological Theory of Law* (London: Routledge and Kegan Paul, 1985); Niklas Luhmann, *Law as a Social System* (Oxford: Oxford University Press, 2004); Gunter Teubner, *Autopoeitic Law: A New Approach to Law and Society* (The Hague: Walter de Gruyter, 1988); Gunter Teubner, "How the Law Thinks: Toward a Constructivist Epistemology of Law," *Law and Society Review* 23, no. 5 (1989), 727–758; and Gunter Teubner, *Law as an Autopoeitic System* (Oxford: Blackwell, 1993).

2. For example, see Alfonso Morales, ed., *Renascent Pragmatism: Studies in Law and Social Science* (Dartmouth: Ashgate, 2003); and Annelise Riles, "Introduction," special issue of *Political and Legal Anthropology Review* on "Ethnography in the Realm of the Pragmatic" 26, no. 3 (2003).

3. Duncan Kennedy, "The Critique of Rights in CLS," in Wendy Brown and Janet Halley, eds., *Left Legalism/Left Critique* (Durham, NC: Duke University Press, 2002).

4. Stanley Fish, "The Law Wishes to Have a Formal Existence," in A. Norrie, ed., *Closure and Critique: New Directions in Legal Theory* (Edinburgh: Edinburgh University Press, 1993), 169.

5. Kunal Parker, "The History of Experience: On the Historical Imagination of Oliver Wendell Holmes Jr.," *Political and Legal Anthropology Review* 26, no. 2 (2003), 60–85.

6. Roscoe Pound, *The Spirit of the Common Law* (Francestown, NH: Marshall Jones, 1921), 186.

7. See M. Dickstein, ed., *The Revival of Pragmatism: New Essays in Social Thought, Law, and Culture* (Chapel Hill, NC: Duke University Press, 1998); Alfonso Morales, ed., *Renascent Pragmatism: Studies in Law and Social Science* (Dartmouth: Ashgate, 2003); and Annelise

Riles, "Introduction," special issue of *Political and Legal Anthropology Review* on "Ethnography in the Realm of the Pragmatic" 26, no. 3 (2003).

8. Mariana Valverde, "Pragmatist and Non-pragmatist Knowledge Practices in American Law," *Political and Legal Anthropology Review* 26, no. 2 (2003), 86–108.

9. Alain Pottage and Martha Mundy, eds., *Law, Anthropology, and the Constitution of the Social* (Cambridge: Cambridge University Press, 2004); and Annelise Riles, *The Network Inside Out* (Ann Arbor: University of Michigan Press, 2000).

10. Bruno Latour, *La fabrique du droit: une ethnographie du Conseil d'État* (Paris: La Decouverte, 2002).

11. Pottage and Mondy, *Law, Anthropology, and the Constitution of the Social,* has a chapter in English translation.

12. Ibid., 2–3.

13. Donna Haraway, *Simians, Cyborgs, and Women* (New York: Routledge, 1991).

14. Michel Callon, "Some Elements of a Sociology of Translation: Domestication of the Scallops and of the Fishermen of St. Brieux Bay," in J. Law, ed., *Power, Action, and Belief: A New Sociology of Knowledge* (London: Routledge and Kegan Paul, 1986).

15. Manuel Castells, *The Rise of Network Society,* 2nd ed. (Oxford: Blackwell, 2000).

16. Bruno Latour, *ARAMIS, or the Love of Technology* (Cambridge, MA: Harvard University Press, 1996).

17. Michel Callon and V. Rabeharisoa, "Gino's Lesson on Humanity: Genetics, Mutual Entanglements and the Sociologist's Role," *Economy and Society,* 33, no. 1 (2004), 1–27.

18. Marilyn Strathern, *Property, Substance, and Effect: Anthropological Essays on Persons and Things* (London: Athlone, 1999), chapter 4.

19. Mariana Valverde, Ron Levi, and Dawn Moore, "Legal Knowledges of Risk," in *Law and Risk,* Law Commission of Canada, ed. (Vancouver: University of British Columbia Press, 2005); and Mariana Valverde, "Authorizing the Production of Urban Moral Order: Appellate Courts and Their Knowledge Games," *Law and Society Review* (2005).

20. Lorraine Daston, ed., *Biographies of Scientific Objects* (Chicago: University of Chicago Press, 2000).

21. Bruno Latour, *La fabrique du droit.*

22. Susan Drummond, "Judicial Notice: The Very Texture of Legal Reasoning," *Canadian Journal of Law and Society* 15, no. 1 (2000), 1–37.

23. But see Sheila Jasanoff, *Science at the Bar: Law, Science and Technology in America* (Cambridge, MA: Harvard University Press, 1995), 54; and Simon Cole, *Suspect Identities: A History of Fingerprinting and Criminal Identification* (Cambridge, MA: Harvard University Press, 2001).

24. Mariana Valverde, *Law's Dream of a Common Knowledge* (Princeton, NJ: Princeton University Press, 2003), 120–122.

25. See Mariana Valverde, Ron Levi, and Dawn Moore, "Legal Knowledges of Risk," for the details of several such cases.

26. Mariana Valverde, *Law's Dream of a Common Knowledge,* chapters 6 and 7.

Legal Realism as Psychological and Cultural (Not Political) Realism

DONALD BRAMAN AND DAN M. KAHAN

How does law know? Do judges faithfully follow doctrinal precedent and heed legislative language even when contrary to their own intuitions about justice?[1] Or are they, like the politicians who appoint them, *de facto* policymakers who reshape the law of the land to privilege the values they prize most dearly?[2] Do jurors scrupulously apply the law to the facts of the case? Or are they ideological saboteurs who willfully ignore facts or nullify the law to suit their own sense of justice?[3]

Journalistic accounts generally feature what can be called the "crude politics" thesis.[4] Each round of judicial appointments and every high-profile case in which a jury is suspected of nullification prompt a host of stories about the movement of politics into the chambers of the judge and the jury. A substantial number of academics agree and have produced a bounty of empirical analyses purporting to reveal the partisan nature of legal decision making.[5] On this account, the law is the site of fierce battles over electoral, racial, gender, and religious politics conducted under only a thin screen of gestures toward objectivity and neutrality. For these observers, the strategic nature of legal decision making has become so blatant and has been exposed so often that the law is best described as just another site in the culture wars.[6]

This assessment provokes resistance from most judges and jurors (not to mention legislators, police, and prosecutors), who disavow partisan motivations and profess unqualified commitment to doing their jobs impartially and objectively.[7] Academics have come to their aid as well, furnishing evidence that judges and jurors are strongly influenced by the law and the facts of the case and that the impact of political partisanship, where it exists, is relatively muted by the constraints one would expect a reasonable judge or juror to honor.[8]

So are legal actors obedient formalist agents or politically motivated lawmaking principals? The answer, we think, is neither. The problem with these depictions stems from the fact that neither has a realistic empirical account of how legal actors do what they do.[9] Casual and statistical observers have some knowledge of the outcomes of cases, and legal actors themselves have some access to their own subjective motivations,[10] but neither side can settle the debate about whether "politics" or "principle" controls because neither accurately apprehends the social and cognitive mechanisms by which legal actors come to understand the law and facts in any given case. In this chapter, we present a theory that does account for these mechanisms and argue that it not only helps to explain the seemingly contradictory nature of the evidence in debates over legal partisanship but provides a more secure foundation on which to structure legal and policy reforms.

The answer to the question of how law knows, we argue, is that law knows in the same way that ordinary democratic citizens know. When deliberating about what dangers are real and which are specious, and about which policies are efficacious and which are futile or even self-defeating, ordinary folk will rarely have direct access to the answers themselves. Instead, they must make decisions about what information and which sources warrant their trust. They must judge whether the stories in which the information is embedded are plausible and consistent with one another. They must consider which norms are relevant, given the facts as they know them. And all the empirical evidence we have suggests they will do all of this through interlocking social and cognitive mechanisms that cause them to rely on a culturally contingent situation sense, an implicit knowledge of how the material and social world works and who can be trusted to report it accurately.

We call this form of active knowledge *cultural cognition*[11] because it is sensitive to values that vary along culturally distinguishable lines and because the information that shapes and interacts with these values is conveyed through the same social networks that are the lifeblood of socialization and cultural transmission.[12] What one knows to be true, it turns out, depends a great deal on what one values and whom one trusts.

Contrary to formalist accounts, values do matter—and they matter a lot—for both jurors and judges. But the way in which they matter is grossly misrepresented by the popular accounts of judicial ideology and jury nullification. It's not that political values *motivate* legal actors to reach particular outcomes but rather that cultural values *orient* them in determining what outcome is dictated by the law and evidence at hand. Legal actors with differing values will decide culturally sensitive cases differently not because they want to impose their values on others but because the mechanisms of cultural cognition move them to view the facts and the law differently.

At first blush, this may appear to imply a radical critique of not only legal knowledge but of knowledge itself. Nothing could be further from the case. We don't presume that, at bottom, there is no truth to the many matters over which there is fierce disagreement within the law or without, nor do we insist that people can't overcome the various cultural heuristics and biases that are necessarily present in their lives. Rather, we argue that there *is* a truth to the matter about human cognition, and this truth can help explain why legal knowledge, like knowledge outside the courtroom, can become embroiled in contest and conflict. Understanding why this is so, we believe, can ultimately lead us closer to a world in which conflict over the law is less intense, where both reason and reasonableness prevail.

We are certainly not the first to plow the field of law with theories of human cognition. For the last century, legal realism has contributed a great deal to our understanding of how those who administer and practice law think.[13] But if legal realism provided a more accurate account of the law than did formalism, it was also unsatisfactory in a number of ways. Legal realist accounts either portrayed legal reasoning as too idiosyncratic to be predictable[14] or as guided by a professional "situation sense"[15] that seems too general to explain readily apparent patterns of variation. Indeed, the only variations described or implied were usually dismissed (or perhaps worse, embraced) as partisan manipulations of fact and precedent to fit political agendas[16]—precisely the assumption that fuels the current debate over ideology and the law.

Understanding the conflict over law as a form of cultural cognition lends itself to a more elegant development of legal realist claims. People, even when they are not motivated by partisanship—indeed, even when they understand themselves to be completely impartial—will be subject to the same orienting force of their cultural values as they make sense of the facts and the law. Moreover, because cultural values differ in systematic ways, legal actors will regularly disagree on the nature of the reality that lies plainly in front of them; indeed, their differences will be structured along relatively predictable lines that reflect familiar cleavages in the particular norms that inform competing systems of "situation sense." Judges and jurors (not to mention legislators, police, and prosecutors) will thus often appear to behave in a strategic and partisan manner even when they are intent on not doing so—a phenomenon that is currently breeding a great deal of distrust not only in the legislative process but in the judicial process, including (most saliently at the moment) the selection of judges.

Moreover, because cultural cognition suggests that the most important cultural norms are structured along predictable dimensions, we can look for empirical evidence of their influence. Cultural cognition thus rescues legal realism from accusations that it is, at bottom, either a theory about the influence of self-interest and partisanship or a theory about the influence of breakfast on jurisprudence.[17] This, we believe, is a suitably empirical account that begins to deliver on the deeper promise of legal realism.

We develop our claims in four parts. In the first section, we offer a schematic overview of cultural cognition, identifying its foundations in anthropology and social psychology. We also summarize evidence of the relationship between orienting values and factual beliefs that our model implies. In the second section, we summarize existing empirical evidence of the impact of cultural cognition in the courtroom, focusing first on juries and then on judges. The third section relates our theory of cultural cognition to other theories of legal knowledge and culture. We conclude in the fourth section by suggesting ways that cultural cognition may bear on practical questions of the law.

How People Know: Cultural Cognition

Values, attitudes, and factual beliefs come in clusters. Extensive public opinion data tell us that the person who opposes gay marriage and believes that the death penalty deters is also likely to think that nuclear power is underutilized and that claims of environmental fragility are overstated. Similarly, the person who dismisses claims that gun ownership and abortion pose much of a risk is also likely to think that market regulation is quite risky but that pornography is not.

What explains this shared variation? In this section, we describe the theory of cultural cognition, according to which factual beliefs are shaped by a series of interlocking cognitive and social mechanisms that move lay citizens and scientific experts alike to coordinate their factual beliefs with the cultural norms they prize. On this account, an individual's conception of how the material world works is tied to his or her conception of how the social world should be ordered.

The social and cognitive mechanisms we describe explain not only this shared variation but also the durability of cultural disputes over law and policy. Because people are resistant to factual information that threatens their cultural identity, increasing reliance on empirical data and other ostensibly objective forms of knowledge is unlikely to succeed in resolving disputes over culturally charged issues.

The Cultural Theory of Risk

The sensitivity of both moral and factual beliefs to cultural norms is most famously described by anthropologist Mary Douglas and political scientist Aaron Wildavsky in their book *Risk and Culture.*[18] Douglas and Wildavsky attribute variance in risk perception to competing clusters of values—individualism, egalitarianism, and hierarchy—that construct opposing visions of how society should be organized. Individuals conform their view of what sorts of activities are dangerous and what policies for abating danger are efficacious to these visions. For example, those who prize individualist values tend to see commerce and industry as relatively safe for the environment and the regulation of those activities as potentially disastrous for society. Highly egalitarian individuals, in contrast, view industrial commerce—a font of social inequality—as posing environmental risks, the regulation of which poses little danger to economic prosperity. And finally, individuals of a hierarchical orientation view social deviance as increasing the risk of all manner of social ills, including disease, crime, and subversion—concerns dismissed by individualists and egalitarians alike.

These competing cultural norms shape perceptions of the world in an overt manner by overlaying moral considerations onto "what dangers should be feared most" and "what risks are worth taking."[19] Thus, individuals may openly disagree about the relative importance of the risks associated with various activities—whether skydiving, hunting, motorcycle riding without a helmet, having an abortion, or using illegal drugs—relative to the benefits of engaging in them.

But more subtly, cultural norms also shape risk perception by entering into the social and cognitive processes by which individuals identify the existence and magnitude of risks. It is easier to believe that what is evil is harmful and what is good is useful than vice versa. If one is uncertain about a risk, one can ask for guidance, but because individuals are likely to trust the advice of those who share their values, they are likely to obtain answers that are guided by similar cultural norms. Your values and your community will tell you a great deal not only about the social meaning of hunting, riding a motorcycle, and abortion but also about the magnitude of the risks that attaches to each of these acts. In this way, the values that inhere in a preferred way of life are woven into the fabric of everyday existence through supportive factual beliefs and social networks.

The Mechanisms of Cultural Cognition

In the years since Douglas and Wildavsky introduced their theory, researchers have developed a broad body of social scientific research describing cognitive and social mechanisms that help to explain the phenomenon of cultural cognition. Together, these mechanisms provide an increasingly detailed empirical account of how culture and information interact in the formation and transmission of belief, an account of what we call *cultural cognition*. The mechanisms of cultural cognition work both to shape beliefs as they emerge and to defend them against culturally hostile challenges. We briefly describe both sets here.

Belief Formation. There are three interlocking cognitive and social mechanisms of cultural belief formation. *Cognitive-dissonance avoidance*, as numerous studies have demonstrated, moves individuals to seek psychic comfort by viewing those things believed to be noble as also benign and those things believed to be base as also dangerous.[20] Rather than accepting beliefs that threaten the beliefs, commitments, and affiliations central to their identity, "people may dismiss, deny, or distort"[21] the information they receive in a defensive fashion.

Affect, also coded in cultural terms, shapes the visceral reactions individuals have to many objects and acts, from guns and hunting to condoms and same-sex intercourse to environmental pollution and the production of nuclear power. In particular, perceptions of the harmfulness of such objects and activities are powerfully influenced by affect, and the positive or negative valence of that affect is determined largely by cultural values.[22]

Finally, *interpersonal trust* dramatically shapes how individuals receive and evaluate information.[23] Few people, for example, can investigate the full effects of gun regulation on crime, the health risks related to the presence of nuclear power plants, or the behavioral effects of including sex education in a public school curriculum. Instead, they must rely on trusted sources for information to help them evaluate competing claims and conflicting evidence. And they tend to trust, naturally enough, others who share their worldviews—and who, for that reason, are likely biased toward one conclusion or another by virtue of forces such as cognitive-dissonance avoidance and affect.[24]

This is not to say that culture's influence is limited to those who must rely on others for advice and guidance. Indeed, research with expert toxicologists indicates that cultural values also orient the beliefs of individuals who are in a position to investigate facts for themselves.[25] The very experts we turn to for assistance in evaluating sophisticated scientific data, these studies tell us, are constrained by the same cognitive mechanisms that guide those of us in society at large.

The Impotence of Culturally Threatening Evidence. The same mechanisms that help explain how individuals form beliefs that cohere with their cultural commitments also explain why individuals are often resistant to contrary evidence, particularly when the new information appears culturally incongruous or threatening. One phenomenon that works against the acceptance of culturally incongruous information is *biased assimilation.*[26] Individuals don't mechanically accept new information; rather, they evaluate each new piece of evidence based on its conformity with prior beliefs, dismissing evidence that is contradictory and integrating evidence that is compatible with those prior beliefs. Biased assimilation is likely to be especially significant when new information challenges a belief that is related to one's cultural identity and values because this is where cognitive-dissonance avoidance and affect, the mechanisms that generate biased assimilation, are particularly pronounced.

Coherence-based reasoning is another mechanism that works against individuals changing their beliefs in light of culturally incongruous information.[27] After accepting one of two competing claims, individuals tend to revise their evaluations of the supporting evidence, inflating the persuasiveness of the evidence in favor of their choice and devaluing the persuasiveness of the opposing evidence. This in turn reinforces the individual's confidence in her belief, which then causes her to inflate and devalue still further the opposing evidence. Coherence-based reasoning helps individuals avoid the lingering suspicion that they may be wrong and thus avoid cognitive dissonance.

Two other phenomena, related to affect and trust, further diminish the persuasive power of information that threatens culturally sensitive beliefs, particularly when proffered (as most likely it will be) by a cultural outsider. *Naïve realism* describes the ability of individuals to perceive bias in others while failing to perceive the bias in themselves. Thus, to the extent that people come bearing threatening information—particularly if they are already identified as not sharing one's cultural values—they will be perceived as unobjective and unreliable. *Reactive devaluation* describes the related phenomenon whereby individuals assign a lower value to proposals and evidence when they perceive the offering party to be a cultural adversary.[28]

Again, these findings are not limited to laypeople. Other research reveals that scientists reviewing reports of experiments—presumably under the influence of cognitive-dissonance avoidance—are far more likely to find the methodology of the experiment defective if the findings conflict with their prior beliefs, even though they would have found the methods to be perfectly acceptable had the results supported their prior beliefs. In one ingenious study, for example, scientists were asked to judge the experimental and statistical methods of what was represented to be a real study of the phenomenon of ESP. Those who received the version of the fictitious study that found evidence of ESP rated the methods to be low in quality, whereas those who received the version that found no evidence of ESP rated the methods to be high in quality, even though the methods were in fact identical.[29]

Cultural Cognition and Conflict. How does this relate to concerns about cultural conflict in the society at large and in the law in particular?

Two positions dominate the academic debate over cultural conflict in American politics. One account, call it the "culture war thesis," asserts that such conflict is of decisive importance and that the prominence of symbolic issues like gay marriage, abortion, capital punishment, and gun control reflects the struggle of opposing cultural groups to impose a moral orthodoxy through law.[30] On this view, "[c]ulture outweighs economics as a matter of public concern."[31] Politicians and the public aren't motivated by questions of general welfare but rather by the pitched battle of cultural warfare.

The "end of ideology thesis," in contrast, treats the appearance of cultural conflict in American politics as largely an illusion: "The simple truth is that there is no culture war in the United States—no battle for the soul of America rages, at least none that most Americans are aware of."[32] The vast majority of voters aren't focused on cultural issues but rather on the performance of the economy and other matters that affect their material welfare.[33] Only political elites are moved by cultural concerns, concerns that these more disproportionately vocal constituencies thrust upon what would otherwise be a fairly tame and evenly divided debate.[34]

The phenomenon of cultural cognition suggests that both of these accounts misplace the epistemic origins and thus the nature of political conflict. The end of ideology thesis grossly understates the role that culture plays in organizing mass, and not just fringe, political opinion in the United States. But the culture war thesis just as decisively misunderstands the *way* in which cultural values figure in mass politics.

Rather than supplying people with conflicting ends, cultural values will divide citizens by supplying them with different beliefs about how best to achieve outcomes, the desirability of which is not in question. Conflicting worldviews will create conflicting understandings of whose fears are more pressing and whose policy proposals are more feasible. On this account, cultural conflict is not the object of politics; it is a byproduct of the social and psychological processes through which culturally diverse citizens *apprehend* their common interests.[35]

The theory of cultural cognition helps explain the persistence of factual disputes that run alongside value disputes and why the production of empirical evidence that bears on culturally sensitive disputes has so little impact. Indeed, it suggests that the turn to empirics in the face of cultural conflict can actually harden positions and heighten distrust. Because individuals' perceptions of the facts are largely derivative of their cultural worldviews, a debate focused on the facts fosters the perception that one's opponents are willfully ignorant or, worse, knowingly subverting the truth to further their own cultural claims. To insist that the debate is about truth rather than about competing visions of the good society persuades both sides only that their opponents are biased and unprincipled, creating a deep distrust and undermining effective deliberation.[36]

How Legal Actors Know: Cultural Cognition and the Law

Debates over how law knows parallel these political debates. The explosion in reporting on jury nullification and partisan judicial rulings represents what we call the "crude politics" theory of law—the legal equivalent of the "culture wars" thesis in politics at large.[37] The dramatic increase in interest in nullification began more than a decade ago, and popular interest shows no signs of ending.[38] Many point with alarm to the supposed increasing incidence of jury lawlessness (thinly veiled as "reasonable doubt" in cases in which guilt seems obvious), whereas others alternatively applaud nullification or dismiss evidence of it as overblown.

If anything, judges are even more embattled. Commentators decry the demise of the apolitical judiciary, lamenting that "the traditional conception of the judicial role,"[39] battered by partisan politics, is all but dead. Yet there are also those who deny that the influence of partisanship has anything like the pronounced effect that crude politics commentators suggest.[40] Although they may concede that the Supreme Court has become politicized, the vast majority of judges, and certainly most jurors, generally do a fair and honest job. Certainly, most judges and jurors themselves deny that they are motivated by anything but respect for the law and an impartial review of the facts.

But just as it does about the debate over cultural conflict in politics, the theory of cultural cognition suggests that debate about political conflict in law is misconceived. Judges apprehend law and jurors apprehend fact through the same social and psychological mechanisms that guide citizens' apprehension of facts in policy debates. Jurors and judges, like ordinary people, inevitably evaluate the trustworthiness and credibility of people, arguments, and evidence through the prism of cultural norms. In most respects, these norms will overlap, and individuals, guided by cultural cognition, will agree. But in cases where there is conflict over which norms the law should privilege in society at large, there will be serious disagreement in the courtroom as well. Moreover, while this disagreement will occasionally appear in consciously motivated terms and thus register as a debate over the form of the just society, given the constraints on legal discourse, it will appear far more frequently in the subtly differing orientations of individuals to the law and the facts. And when it takes the latter form, legal actors who are motivated to be objective and nonpartisan will nonetheless disagree over reasonable interpretations of law and standards of proof for evidence.

This proposition, as we'll discuss later, is supported by ample evidence on the behavior of both jurors and judges. That evidence on jurors includes studies of jury deliberations that suggest that cultural norms inform the scripts or prototypes jurors use to piece together the evidence they are presented with. These culturally derived scripts help them evaluate the credibility of actors, arguments, and evidence as the legal drama unfolds. Not only do jurors downplay the relevance of evidence that fails to conform to these scripts, but they are less likely to even recall such data. This variation predictably leads to heightened levels of distrust, as individuals who intently focus on what they consider the objective nature of the law and the facts find themselves arguing not over visions of the good society—something reasonable people can disagree about—but over truth itself. This phenomenon explains why the incidence of hung juries rises dramatically with the diversity of jury composition.

Cultural cognition is also at play, the evidence suggests, in judicial decision making. Judges themselves believe that the individual judge's sense of justice plays a significant part in the outcome of most cases, and empirical evidence supports this intuition. Judges may reason in relatively similar fashion in cases where there is little cultural conflict. But in cases that are the focus of competition between cultural groups in society at large—cases that deal with environmental regulation, the death penalty, states rights, and the like—the evidence suggests that cultural cognition leads them in different directions. Here, the differing cultural orientations of judges predictably shape legal outcomes. And although we have less data on the cognitive mechanisms of judicial decision making than we do on juries, the most plausible explanation is that their evaluations of the law and facts are shaped by cultural cognition.

We turn, now, to the evidence.

Juries

Of all the traditional legal actors, the juror has been the most thoroughly studied. Because jurors are often debriefed by the press following a verdict, and because researchers have constructed thousands of mock juries to understand how selection, individual juror attributes, and jury group composition shape deliberation, we know a great deal about how jurors and juries behave. And all the evidence we have suggests that juror cognition is guided by the same psychological biases and social processes that are present in the public at large.[41]

The most comprehensive account of how jurors reach verdicts is the "story model" of juror decision making,[42] a model first developed by psychologists Reid Hastie and Nancy Pennington[43] and subsequently refined and expanded by others.[44] Using a series of experimental studies, story-model researchers have shown that jurors decide cases by fitting the evidence presented by the parties into one or more "verdict stories" and then selecting the story that appears most plausible and coherent to them. Jurors, these researchers find, have "preconceptions and attitudes that lead them to entertain particular stories about what may have happened, . . . stories [that] are used to process the facts presented in the case . . . [and] to arrive at a legal decision or verdict."[45]

The verdict stories that jurors rely on come from shared experiences and socially constructed understandings of the natural and social world—in other words, from culture.[46] These culturally contingent associations profoundly shape considerations of evidence. In fact, jurors are less likely to even *recall* evidence that is inconsistent with their preferred verdict story, removing culturally unacceptable evidence from consideration.[47] And of course, to the extent that jurors in a culturally diverse society are likely to enter the jury room with diverse and even antagonistic cultural prototypes, they will sometimes disagree over verdicts because they won't agree on what the evidence means—or even what the evidence is.[48]

Also highlighting the primacy of culture are the "total justice" and "common-sense justice" theories of jury decision making. Studies supporting the "total justice" theory suggest that jurors "strive to work their emotions and their judgments into a satisfying totality"[49] even when this directly contradicts jury instructions about how to evaluate evidence.[50] Similarly, studies of common-sense justice suggest that in their legal role jurors often rely on "adages, images, and rules of thumb"[51] that they would use in everyday reasoning.[52] Under both theories, jurors will conform their understanding of the evidence to their cultural values, which determine *how* jurors morally and emotionally conceive of what total justice is and what common sense dictates.[53]

Finally, culture influences juror cognition through the mechanism of "culpable causation."[54] Culpable causation can be described as the tendency to attribute causal import to acts, and responsibility to those who perform them, in proportion to the moral blameworthiness of those acts or actors. Thus, a driver involved in an accident will be perceived as more causally responsible for the accident if he was speeding on his way home to hide some illegal drugs than if he was speeding on his way home to hide an anniversary present.[55] Now imagine the moral valence if his motivation was a matter of cultural dispute—say, he was rushing his girlfriend to an appointment for an abortion, was late to meet friends for a hunting trip, or was on his way to a strip club. Each of these activities would orient reasonable people of diverse values to different evaluations of the driver's culpability. As extensive empirical research and everyday experience reveal, the same variation in moral sensibilities leads to dramatic variation in assessments of culpability in mass tort cases against manufacturers of guns, breast implants, and toxic waste.

As a result of this variation, juries will sometimes deadlock over matters of fact and law, with different jurors crediting different evidence. Indeed, just as the theory of cultural cognition would predict, "hung juries" who deadlock on one or more counts typically *don't* disagree about what the law requires, nor do they fail to reach consensus because cases are particularly complex. Instead, they disagree about the credibility of witnesses and what the evidence presented to them proves. Also, where this occurs, jurors tend to perceive one another to be "unreasonable."[56] In light of cultural cognition, this makes perfect sense: From the perspective of those jurors who are in agreement on one side of the case, the other jurors are evaluating the evidence in light of cultural norms alien to the first group, in other words, unreasonably.

That differing cultural values lead to juror disagreements, hung juries, and differences across juries of diverse composition is not only intuitive and consistent with what we know about human cognition, but it is also supported by sophisticated statistical analysis. Researchers who use demographic variations as proxies for value differences have estimated that increasing jury diversity can dramatically increase the likelihood of a hung jury from 3% to 33%.[57] Ethnographic and anecdotal evidence suggests that these differences are value driven and that the effects on legal verdicts, particularly in cases involving highly disputed norms, are significant.[58]

Verdicts in suits against gun manufacturers supply a real-world case study of how conflicting cultural values generate disagreements of *fact* among jurors. In *Hamilton v. Accu-Tek*,[59] for example, both sides relied heavily on expert witnesses to present voluminous, and radically conflicting, statistical analyses of the contribution that the defendant gun manufacturer's marketing practices were making to violent crime. "The jurors ignored almost all of it."[60] Almost immediately after deliberations commenced in the case, two jurors (one a statistician employed by Publishers Clearing House Sweepstakes and the other an accountant) "dismissed [the expert] testimony, telling their fellow jurors that numbers can be twisted to make almost any point."[61] Thereafter, according to one of the jurors, "[we] didn't really discuss the statistics for either side."[62] Instead, for six days, the jurors traded competing stories and impassioned speeches about crime and who is responsible for it; and because these were matters on which the jurors themselves were apparently bitterly divided, the deliberations produced, unsurprisingly, a process of recriminatory give-and-take that was just as excruciating and conflictual as the American gun debate itself.[63]

This is not to say that jurors and juries will always disagree. Just as citizens agree on most matters of fact and policy, in most cases the norms on which jurors draw will overlap considerably, and there will be little, if any, dispute. But in areas where cultural norms and the facts are contested, we can expect the same kind of divergence that we witness in society at large. And this will occur not because jurors privilege cultural politics over respect for the law and the facts but rather because in their determination to read the facts and apply the law objectively, they will necessarily rely on the mechanisms of cultural cognition to tell them what is true and what is just.

Judges

Disputes over judicial appointments are battles, in large part, waged on the assumption that judges are now partisan political operatives. We reject the assumption. As with jurors, lay citizens, and scientific experts, judges will be steered in culturally biased and conflicting directions by cultural cognition *notwithstanding* judges' genuine efforts to be impartial. Thus, even the judge who is most determined to render the law objectively and to review the facts with neutrality may behave like a cultural partisan.

Empirical studies of judges generally support this view. Because the evidence is thinner and more distant from the kinds of experiments that have been conducted with ordinary citizens and jurors, our argument here is admittedly more conjectural. Still, the data link our account of human cognition with broader patterns of judicial conduct in ways that are supportive, if not dispositive, of our claim.

The idea that judges are subject to the same biases and heuristics that shape the cognition of lay citizens has been tested in various areas. Judges, researchers have found, are influenced by "anchoring (making estimates based on irrelevant starting points); framing (treating economically equivalent gains and losses differently); hindsight bias (perceiving past events to have been more predictable than they actually were); the representativeness heuristic (ignoring important background statistical information in favor of individuating information); and egocentric biases (overestimating one's own abilities)."[64] Indeed, we know of no bias or heuristic that exists in the general population that has been shown not to exist among judges. Judges are human, and like the rest of us, "their judgment is affected by cognitive illusions that can produce systematic errors in judgment."[65]

Still, it might be argued that judges are special in some way so that, although they are subject to all of the other biases and heuristics that shape laypeople's cognition, they are somehow exceptionally adept in disabling the mechanisms of cultural cognition. And admittedly, we have no carefully controlled studies specifically assessing the influence of cognitive-dissonance avoidance, affect, and trust on judges. But if it were true that judges were immune to cultural cognition, we would expect that their decisions wouldn't vary along the lines that cultural theory suggests. Instead, the variation in judicial decision making on issues over which cultural battles in the world at large are waged—racial and sex discrimination, exclusion of evidence under the Fourth Amendment, states rights, environmental protection, for example—would be random or motivated by some directly relevant characteristic (the race or sex of the judge, whether they were ever wrongly searched, or whether they lived close to an environmental site).

The portrait of the judge as a cultural partisan or as merely a selfish rational actor is simply not supported by the data on judicial behavior. Instead, the evidence suggests that while personal motivations and characteristics may weakly influence the decisions of some judges in some areas,[66] values are far more influential in shaping judicial behavior. Indeed, in nearly every detailed empirical analysis,[67] proxies for judicial value preferences (e.g., the identity of the appointing president, the political party of the judge, and the region in which the judge grew up) are significant predictors of judicial behavior. In the recent explosion of empirical research into the link between these proxies and judicial behavior, evidence of the patterns that the theory of cultural cognition predicts would occur are pervasive and uncontested by any serious empirical analysis. In reviewing this data, we'll start with evidence describing judges voting on their own and then turn to analyses of judges sitting on panels.

The best data to date bearing on the influence of judicial worldview on individual judicial decision making are those assembled by Nancy Scherer.[68] It contains information about every district court judge in the federal judiciary, including the identity of the appointing president, the majority party in the Senate at the time of the judge's appointment, the regional background of the judge, and the voting behavior of those judges on several classes of cases. Just as cultural cognition would predict, judicial behavior was significantly predicted by several value proxies. Carter appointees and judges from the East, West, and Midwest were significantly more likely than other judges to cast pro-"criminal rights" votes in search and seizure cases,[69] whereas Reagan and Bush appointees and judges from the South were significantly more likely to cast "anti-minority" votes in race discrimination cases and "anti-federal government" votes in state's rights cases.[70]

The theory of cultural cognition suggests that these patterns are the effect of cognitive-dissonance avoidance and affect rather than crude politics. Just as toxicologists were oriented toward toxicity by cultural cognition, judges are oriented to procedural and evidentiary claims. This is not to say that judges aren't principally motivated to be objective and neutral in their adherence to the law. Rather, it is to acknowledge that, as a majority of judges readily concede, a "judge's personal views of justice" are "very important" determinants of case outcomes.[71] The variation in judicial decisions is shaped not by bald politics but rather, as the theory of cultural cognition describes, by the subtle orientation of the mind to facts and arguments that cohere with the "background and philosophy"[72] of the judge.

Data on district court judges support the notion that cognitive-dissonance avoidance and affect are likely at play in judicial decision making. But what about the orienting influence of one's social networks? Although we would expect circuit court judges, like district court judges, to be oriented to the facts and the law, because federal circuit judges know one another quite well and sit with one another quite often, we would also expect that they would develop relatively high levels of *trust*, even across cultural divides. Thus, they may disagree on issues vehemently, but they would also be likely to give closer consideration to one another's arguments than, say, members of juries who gather together for a single case and are unlikely to meet or interact with one another again. As a result, we would expect that both the values of individual judges and the values of their copanelists would exert a significant influence on the outcomes of cases in a number of culturally sensitive areas. Moreover, where cultural values are centrally implicated in the case, we would expect less cross-cultural influence and more panels split along cultural lines. All of these hypotheses are supported by the data.

The research that bears most closely on this question involves analyses of the voting patterns of federal circuit court judges sitting in panels. Richard Revesz developed the seminal analyses in this area, focusing on judicial backgrounds and decisions in environmental law.[73] Several other scholars have since expanded on his analysis and findings to abortion, affirmative action, campaign finance, capital punishment, the Contracts Clause, disability discrimination, piercing the corporate veil, race discrimination, and sex discrimination.[74]

The judge panel data suggest that judicial decision making conforms to the same social and cognitive mechanisms that govern ordinary citizens, mediated by the structure of their social interactions with one another. First, as with district court judges, proxies for judicial values have a significant influence on voting patterns.[75] Second, judges are significantly influenced by their copanelists. Like-minded judges, when sitting together, are far more likely to vote in a "liberal" or "conservative" manner than judges sitting on panels with judges of diverse values.[76] Thus, we see both the influence of cognitive and social aspects of cultural orientation at play. And third, we see that the cognitive aspects are particularly pronounced, trumping social aspects, in cases that are particularly freighted with cultural meaning: abortion and capital punishment.[77] Indeed, in those instances when culturally sensitive issues are at stake, judges may be particularly alert to the competing and contrary cultural values of their copanelists, making them less trustful and less receptive to the arguments and evidence offered by them.

These admittedly are extrapolations of existing research. But again, the evidence is borne out in the details of individual cases. Decisions in criminal sentencing cases are often quite sensitive to cultural norms, and there are many issues in criminal law and procedure over which judges predictably split along the lines the theory of cultural cognition would suggest. In *U.S. v. Labonte*,[78] for example, the Supreme Court had to undertake a simple case of statutory interpretation over which lower courts had split. The issue hinged on whether federal judges were to be required under the sentencing guidelines to sentence drug offenders to the maximum of the standard sentence for an offense or the maximum of that sentence plus an enhancement for prior offenses. Writing for the Court, Justice Thomas found that the authorizing statute "is unambiguous and requires a court to sentence a career offender 'at or near' the 'maximum' prison term available once all relevant statutory sentencing enhancements are taken into account."[79] The dissent, however, viewed the meaning as entirely ambiguous and thus preferred to defer, as the lower court (or rather, some of the lower courts) did, to the Sentencing Commission's interpretation.[80]

What drives this (or any other) disagreement over the ambiguity of a statute?[81] Here again, the evidence points toward cultural cognition. Judges, as the statistical analyses described earlier suggest, are more likely to defer to the agencies of an ideologically congenial administration than they are to an ideologically hostile one.[82] This, of course, makes perfect sense within the theory of cultural cognition; judges, like the scientists reviewing evidence disproving ESP, will subtly and unknowingly lower their deferential bar when they are encountering a culturally coherent claim.[83] That the party making the claim is culturally congenial will, cognitively speaking, only further lower the bar to deference.

Both the district court data and the circuit court panel data support the hypothesis that cultural cognition is at work. But the data are admittedly an imperfect test of our claim and somewhat ambiguous. An alternative reading (indeed, the more common reading) of the data would be that judges are quite consciously ideological, but strategically (and thus, stealthily) so. On this account, they are less likely to go to ideological extremes when sitting on a diverse panel simply because they know that the other panel member may dissent, revealing their arguments to be more political than legal in motivation.[84]

Perhaps this is so. But accepting this alternative claim would require us to discard all of the data supporting the claim that judges do their best to interpret the law objectively—and the "objective attempt" claim is supported by a substantial amount of data. Just about every account from every federal judge and their clerks suggests that ideology is not a conscious motivating factor in judicial decision making.[85] While the "crude politics" theory has to ignore these data, the cultural cognition thesis is entirely consistent with the claim that "most judges in most cases are simply trying to give an accurate construal to what the Supreme Court said in the most relevant precedent or to what Congress wrote in the controlling statute."[86] Ours, we think, is a more realistic account, one that comports with the self-image of judges who give serious weight to role morality, respect for the fact, and the rule of law.

Interpretive Method

One possible objection to our claim as presented thus far is that it fails to account for the variation in interpretive method. On this view, most of judging will depend on whether one prefers, as Stanley Fish wryly puts it, "strict constructionism versus judicial activism, originalism versus present-oriented interpretation, interpretivism versus non-interpretivism, deontology versus consequentialism, individual rights versus utilitarianism, indeterminacy versus plain meaning, or pragmatism versus almost anything."[87]

The first answer to this is that choice of interpretive method, like the interpretation itself, will be influenced by one's extralegal normative commitments.[88] Thus, those who prize traditional forms of social ordering will be more likely to employ methods that focus on the traditional meanings of the language in the law, whereas those who embrace more egalitarian norms will focus on the modern antihierarchical meanings of terms. Hence, when judges actually commit themselves to "presentist" or "originalist" modes of interpretation, those modes may be in some sense prior to their decisions, but their cultural norms are prior to their selection of a mode of interpretation.

But even if one were to assume that those judges who proclaim a particular interpretive method do so independently of their commitment to competing cultural norms, this would leave a great deal of apparently contradictory evidence unexplained. For if interpretive method drove the variation in judicial decision making, then we would expect that judges who employed the same interpretive method would reach the same results: Textualists would agree with textualists, proceduralists with proceduralists, pragmatists with pragmatists, democratic reinforcers with democratic reinforcers, deontologists with deontologists, and so on. And this is simply not so. This would have Justice Antonin Scalia agreeing with Akhil Amar because they both look to the historical meaning of the language of the Constitution, and Judge Richard Posner agreeing with Justice Thomas Ruffin simply because they are both pragmatists (one self-declared[89] and the other so described by historians[90]).

The accusations of disingenuous interpretation stem from precisely this point. When legal actors swear to the same neutral principle of investigation, they expect (like all who rely on neutral and objective standards) to reach the same conclusions. The constraints they place on themselves, they imagine, will lead inexorably to a single conclusion. But as legal realists were at pains to point out, nearly every rule and every constraint will point in several directions. This doesn't mean that it can point in *any* direction or *all* directions[91] but that there will be ambiguity and conflict. The mechanisms of cultural cognition tell us that this conflict will be structured along predictable lines. And further, they tell us that the variations in reasoning stem, most likely, not from a secret agenda dressed up in a professed but ultimately deceptive interest in the law and facts of the case but precisely from the honest interest of the judge in the law and the facts.

Legal Philosophy

If one expands the claim from interpretive methodology to judicial philosophy, the case for the influence of cultural orientation only becomes more obvious. It's a truism, for example, to say that opposing theories of morality will move judges to differing interpretations of the law. A judge who prizes egalitarian over hierarchical ideals will look on sex and race discrimination as decidedly (and intrinsically) wrong. A judge who prizes individual autonomy over ideals of equality or tradition will look on claims of government restrictions of speech and action with great suspicion.

But the influence of culture isn't limited to judges who explicitly blend cultural values into their jurisprudence. Predictably, consequentialist judges will also have differing conceptions of the consequences of various legal policy choices that will vary along the lines cultural cognition predicts. We say "predictably" not only because this is the central tenet of cultural theory but also because this is what the empirical data show—that cultural norms are strong predictors of consequentialist beliefs. A series of national surveys conducted by a variety of researchers (including the authors) have consistently found, for example, that cultural orientations are strong predictors of perception of the health risks associated with nuclear power, abortion, gun ownership, environmental pollution, illegal drug use, and a host of other culturally sensitive issues.[92] Cultural norms also strongly predict the societal and economic risks perceived to accompany business regulation[93] and gun control measures.[94] Indeed, cultural worldviews more powerfully predicted individual beliefs about the seriousness of these risks than any other factor, including gender, race, income, education, and political ideology.[95] Judges may interpret laws with an eye to consequences, but the consequences they are attentive to are structured by cultural cognition.

In sum, cultural cognition tells us that the conflict we see in the law isn't the crude politics that animates popular accounts. But neither is it the "high"[96] politics of interpretive method or judicial philosophy that are necessarily incomplete, requiring a prior set of norms and values to give them a substantive hue, or orientation. This orientation is precisely what cultural cognition generates, even among those whose focus is on neither politics nor ideology but on the law and the facts. Put another way, we might say that while a philosophical stance won't tell a judge what method to use, a methodological commitment won't tell her what philosophical stance to take, and neither will determine what outcome a case should have, cultural cognition will help the judge answer all three questions with minimal effort.

Modern Empirical Legal Realism

We offer our account as a cognitively and culturally realistic form of legal realism. It differs from the classical accounts of legal realism in important ways. A rough approximation of legal realism would suggest that judges and jurors find in the law the justice that fits the specific facts in any given case, and because the law is drawn from the same well of collective sensibilities, the common-sense justice that courts hand down will generally be in line with, but not determined by, legal rules and standards.[97] This account, to our mind, is unsatisfactory in two ways.

First, where legal realists and their inheritors suggest that legal knowledge is "drawn from the culture's general understanding of how we 'know' things to be true,"[98] we argue that this understanding varies along discernible lines. Relying on the mechanisms of cultural cognition in a heuristic fashion, most Americans, including most jurors and judges, attain a roughly similar situation sense about most issues. But this situation sense is not as singular within a society (or the legal profession) as Karl Llewellyn implied,[99] nor is it as variable and unpredictable as Jerome Frank suggested.[100] Rather, on issues where competing groups are embattled—in the domain of the culture wars—the mechanisms of cultural cognition move individuals to view both facts and the law in strikingly different terms. That is to say, legal knowledge is in large part *cultural*, varying along lines that most Americans understand intuitively as such. And this variation makes for conflict within and over the law.

Second, legal realists like Llewellyn argued that legal decision makers use "situation sense"—a shared intuitive capacity based on immersion in professional and societal norms—to derive consistent and generally accepted results from otherwise hopelessly indeterminate formal doctrines.[101] We, in contrast, believe that cultural cognition orients individuals toward different and often conflicting understandings of both the law *and* the facts. This, the theory of cultural cognition suggests, helps to explain the origins of hung juries and the variation in decisions on similar fact patterns across juries and courts.

A culturally and psychologically realistic theory of jurisprudence also has normative implications. Perhaps the most obvious is this: Courts are unlikely to be the best forum for resolving cultural contests such as those over guns, crime, abortion, illicit drugs, pornography, and sexual orientation. Not only are the decisions of courts likely to vary in predictable ways along with the values of the legal actors involved (creating a diversity of outcomes), but the answers they provide are unlikely to resolve the controversy over norms that brought the case to court in the first place. For evidence, simply ask yourself whether litigation over abortion, same-sex marriage, or gun control has calmed cultural conflict and helped resolve those issues in the minds of ordinary citizens. Expecting to make progress toward resolving normative questions through litigation alone is thus, as we have argued elsewhere, "culturally obtuse."[102]

There is, on this account, no singular "constitutional [or legal] culture"[103] that can be achieved or referenced, only the possibility of legal responses to cultural conflict in the polity at large that are more or less attentive and respectful of the diverse cultural values of the public. A second normative implication that follows from this concerns the qualities that should be sought in judges who are likely to be confronted with cases implicated in broader cultural conflicts. These jurists should not only be able to satisfy the traditional constraints of judicial reasoning and interpretation; they should also be capable of navigating the law through such conflicts with a situation sense that is attuned to the public's varied cultural commitments. Often described by jurists and commentators in terms of "judicial statesmanship,"[104] this quality addresses the importance of a culturally sensitive jurisprudence that, while never fully articulated in the realist tradition, is entirely in keeping with it.

Conclusion

Mainstream accounts cast jurors and judges either as strategic political actors or as faithful and politically inert servants of legal authority wielded by others. We think both accounts get it wrong. We've argued instead for a realistic account of legal knowledge grounded in the social and cognitive mechanisms that we know guide human belief formation and decision making more generally, mechanisms that can be described as *cultural cognition*.

On this account, jurors and judges, like ordinary people, must evaluate the trustworthiness and credibility of people, arguments, and evidence through the prism of their cultural norms. In most respects, their values and the norms they are embedded in will be widely shared by others, and guided by cultural cognition, most will find no difficulty reaching agreement. But in cases where there is competition between cultural groups over which values should be privileged in the law, there will be serious disagreement. Moreover, this disagreement will only sometimes be an overtly normative and consciously motivated disagreement over the form of the just society. Far more often, it will appear in the subtly differing orientations of individuals to the law and the facts. And as a result, legal actors who are motivated to be objective and nonpartisan will nonetheless disagree over the truth of the matter—and will come to distrust those whose cultural commitments lead them to a different interpretation.

The effects of cultural cognition are evident in data on jury deliberations where cultural norms shape the story scripts that jurors use as prototypes of reasonable behavior when piecing together the evidence they are presented with. These culturally derived scripts help them evaluate the credibility of actors, arguments, and evidence as the legal drama unfolds. Not only do jurors downplay the relevance of evidence that fails to conform to these scripts, but they are also less likely to even recall such data. This variation predictably leads to heightened levels of distrust, as individuals who intently focus on what they consider to be the objective nature of the law and the facts find themselves arguing not over visions of the good society—something reasonable people can disagree about—but over truth itself. This helps explain why the incidence of hung juries rises dramatically with the diversity of jury composition.

Cultural cognition is also at play, we've argued, in judicial decision making. Judges themselves believe that the individual judge's sense of justice plays a significant part in the outcome of most cases, and empirical evidence supports this intuition. Judges may reason in relatively similar fashion in cases where there is little cultural conflict. But in cases that are the focus of competition between cultural groups—cases that deal with environmental regulation, the death penalty, states rights, and the like—the evidence suggests that cultural cognition leads them in different directions. Here the differing cultural backgrounds predictably shape legal outcomes. And although we have very little experimental data on why this is so, the most plausible explanation is that their evaluations of the law and facts are shaped by cultural cognition.

The account we've offered here, we think, begins to deliver on the deeper promise of legal realism by providing a more accurate and empirically grounded description of the process through which legal actors come to know the law and the facts necessary to deciding any case. Some might find this accuracy a little disheartening; after all, what does it matter what judges think they are doing if, in the end, they are acting like cultural partisans?

The answer is that this more accurate account lays the groundwork for a mode of political and legal analysis that is cognizant of the influence of cultural cognition. Indeed, the most effective forms of law and politics will take full advantage of the mechanisms of cultural cognition to develop legislation, policies, holdings, and opinions that are respectful and affirming of diverse norms. Although this style of law and politics isn't new—some of the most effective jurists and legislators employ it quite intuitively—it is only now being grounded in cognitive and social scientific research. It's an endeavor, we believe, that only an empirically realist account of the law can credibly and reliably support.

Notes

1. See, e.g., Alex Kozinski, "What I Ate for Breakfast and Other Mysteries of Judicial Decision Making," *Loyola of Los Angeles Law Review* 26 (1993), 993, describing Senator Strom Thurmond's notion that judges "feel that you have got to do what is right, whether you want to or not" as "corny, perhaps, but true"; Stuart Buck, "Legal Realism," *The Buck Stops Here*, at http://stuartbuck.blogspot.com/2003/11/legal-realism.html: "I am positive that in the overwhelming majority of cases, ideology or morality or what-have-you just [doesn't] have that much to do with the decision."

2. Sandy Levinson, for example, has argued: "Though judges are 'political,' the politics are 'high' rather than 'low'; that is, decisions are based on ideology rather than a simple desire to help out one's political friends in the short run." Sanford Levinson, "The Return of Legal Realism," *The Nation* (Jan. 8, 2001).

3. See generally Irwin A. Horowitz and Thomas E. Willgins, "Changing Views of Jury Power," *Law and Human Behavior* 15 (1991), 180, describing the evolution of competing beliefs that juries either (a) "lack . . . predictability and rationality" and are moved by emotions rather than reason; or (b) are competent at "applying common sense notions of equity and rationality to conflicted and ambiguous cases." Compare, e.g., Judge Lawrence W. Crispo, Jill M. Slansky, and Geanene M. Yriarte, "Jury Nullification: Law Versus Anarchy," *Loyola Los Angeles Law Review* 31 (1997), 3, describing the nullifying jury as "serv[ing] as a mini-legislature"; and "The Perfect Juror?" *National Law Journal* (May 2, 1994), A18: "As shown in last year's *National Law Journal* poll of nearly 1,000 jurors, most of them take their jobs seriously and try to follow the law as best they can."

4. See, e.g., "Live with It," *Business Week* (Mar. 17, 2005), describing a "trend of judges being more ideologically than legally involved in their work"; Joshua Spivak, "Judicial Nomination Battles Are Not New," *N.J. L. Journal* (Mar. 14, 2005), describing the court system as engulfed in "partisan ideology"; "Editorial: Victory May Be Small," Copley News Service (Jan. 20, 2004), voicing concern about "the ideological war over the federal judiciary"; Ann Woolner, "The Big Issue That Dems Ignored: Judicial Nominations," *Fulton County Daily Report* (Aug. 3, 2004), decrying judges who "rule as ideological lackeys"; "Independent Women's Forum," *PR Newswire* (Nov. 17, 2003), noting public concern about politicians bent on "achieving ideological domination of the federal judiciary."

5. See, e.g., Linda R. Cohen and Matthew L. Spitzer, "Solving the Chevron Puzzle," *Law & Contemporary Problems* 57 (Spring 1994): 65 (special issue); Frank B. Cross, "Decisionmaking in the U.S. Circuit Courts of Appeals," *91 California Law Review* 1457 (2003); Frank B. Cross and Emerson H. Tiller, "Judicial Partisanship and Obedience to Legal Doctrine: Whistleblowing on the Federal Courts of Appeals," *Yale Law Journal* 107 (1998), 2155; Theodore Eisenberg and Sheri Lynn Johnson, "The Effects of Intent: Do We Know How Legal Standards Work?" *Cornell Law Review* 76 (1991), 1151; Tracey E. George, "Developing a Positive Theory of Decisionmaking on U.S. Courts of Appeals," *Ohio State Law Journal* 58 (1998), 1635; Deborah Jones Merritt and James J. Brudney, "Stalking Secret Law: What Predicts Publication in the United States Courts of Appeals," *Vanderbilt Law Review* 54 (2001), 71, 110; Richard L. Revesz, "Environmental Regulation, Ideology, and the D.C. Circuit," *Virginia Law Review* 83 (1997), 1717; Cass R. Sunstein, David Schkade, and Lisa Michelle Ellman, "Ideological Voting on Federal Courts of Appeals: A Preliminary Investigation," *Virginia Law Review* 90 (2004), 301.

6. See, e.g., Wayne Slater, "Christian Conservatives Fight Filibusters," *Dallas Morning News* (May 17, 2005), describing the judiciary as the "new front in the culture war"; Carl M. Cannon, "The Uncompromising Mr. Bush," *Washington Post* (May 29, 2005), describing the judicial nominating process as a way for politicians to leave a political "legacy" for their

supporters; Gail Russell Chaddock, "Where Congress Agrees," *Christian Science Monitor* (May 17, 2005): "Sen. Bill Frist (R) of Tennessee described the fight over judges as 'much more important than most of the legislation that goes through here.' And for much of both partys' activist base, highly engaged in the culture wars, it is."

7. See, e.g., *Republican Party of Minn. v. White*, 536 U.S. 765, 799 (2002) (Stevens, J., dissenting): "The elected judge, like the lifetime appointee, does not serve a constituency while holding that office. He has a duty to uphold the law and to follow the dictates of the Constitution."; Ibid., 805 (Ginsburg, J., dissenting): "Judges . . . are not political actors. They do not sit as representatives of particular persons, communities, or parties; they serve no faction or constituency. . . . They must strive to do what is legally right, all the more so when the result is not the one 'the home crowd' wants." See also Harry T. Edwards and Linda Elliott, "Beware of Numbers (and Unsupported Claims of Judicial Bias)," *Washington University Law Quarterly* 80 (2002), 723; Harry T. Edwards, "Collegiality and Decision Making on the D.C. Circuit," *Virginia Law Review* 84 (1998), 1335, disputing the claim that judges are guided by political considerations.

8. See, e.g., Cross, supra note 5, 1515: "The greatest constraint [on judicial decision making] appears to be that of the law: the 'neutral principles' of the traditional legal model fare quite well as a descriptive model for judicial decisionmaking."

9. As one researcher remarks: "There is no coherent framework yet developed that can make sense of the seemingly contradictory findings to date." Wendy L. Martinck, "The Effect of Confirmation Politics on United States Courts of Appeals Decision Making," paper presented at the 2003 annual meeting of the American Political Science Association, Philadelphia, Aug. 28–31, 2003.

10. Although individuals may have some sense of their conscious motivations, they often have little insight into the social and cognitive factors that influence their decisions. See Richard E. Nisbett and Lee Ross, *Human Inference: Strategies and Shortcomings of Human Judgment* (Englewood Cliffs, NJ: Prentice Hall, 1980).

11. See Dan M. Kahan and Donald Braman, "Cultural Cognition and Public Policy," *Yale Law School, Public Law Working Paper 87* (Jun. 2005), http://research.yale.edu/cultural-cognition/content/view/43/77/.

12. Wildavsky described cultural theory as "attempt[ing] to unify heuristics by suggesting that these chains have but one link: the internalization of social relations." Aaron Wildavsky, "Choosing Preferences by Constructing Institutions: A Cultural Theory of Preference Formation," *American Political Science Review* 81 (1987), 10. Preferences, on this account, are endogenous to culture because the heuristic mechanisms by which preferences are formed are also endogenous to culture.

13. For discussions of legal realists' empiricism, see John H. Schlegel, *American Legal Realism and Empirical Social Science* (1995); Morton J. Horwitz, *The Transformation of American Law, 1870–1960: The Crisis of Legal Orthodoxy* (1992), 10–30; William W. Fisher III, Morton J. Horwitz and Thomas A. Reed, eds., *American Legal Realism* (1993); Horwitz, supra note 1; Wilfred E. Rumble Jr., *American Legal Realism: Skepticism, Reform, and the*

Judicial Process (1968). For a specific account of the development of legal realism at Yale Law School, see Laura Kalman, *Legal Realism at Yale, 1927–1960* (Chapel Hill: University of North Carolina Press, 1986).

14. See Robert Jerome Glennon, *The Iconoclast as Reformer: Jerome Frank's Impact on American Law* (Ithaca, NY: Cornell University Press, 1985), 44–45: "Most important, according to Frank, are the 'uniquely individual factors' that are the product of the judge's 'entire life-history,'" quoting Jerome Frank, *Law and the Modern Mind 106* (New York: Brentano's, 1930). See also Brian Leiter, "Rethinking Legal Realism: Toward a Naturalized Jurisprudence," *Texas Law Review* 76 (1997), 280, describing this characterization of legal realism as implying that "the foundation of judicial decision is the various idiosyncrasies of the individual judge, which not only govern his sense of justice on a given set of facts, but 'the very processes by which he becomes convinced what those facts are.'"

15. Karl Llewellyn, *The Common Law Tradition* (Boston: Little, Brown, 1960), 194.

16. See, e.g., Ronald Dworkin, *Taking Rights Seriously* (Boston: Cambridge University Press, 1977), 3, characterizing realism as the belief that "judges actually decide cases according to their own political or moral tastes, and then choose an appropriate legal rule as a rationalization."

17. The attribution of the claim that what judges eat will bear on their decision to legal realists is both apocryphal and misleading. See Brian Leiter, "American Legal Realism," *Public Law and Legal Theory Research Paper No. 042* (2002), 9, available at http://papers.ssrn.com/sol3/ papers.cfm?abstract_ibid=339562. But the claim is influential nonetheless. See, e.g., Kozinski, supra note 1. See also Leiter, supra note 14, 267–268, describing a number of surprising misreadings of legal realism.

18. Mary Douglas and Aaron Wildavsky, *Risk and Culture* (Berkeley: University of California Press, 1987).

19. Ibid., 6.

20. See Leon Festinger, *A Theory of Cognitive Dissonance* (Stanford, CA: Stanford University Press, 1957).

21. David K. Sherman and Geoffrey L. Cohen, "Accepting Threatening Information: Self-Affirmation and the Reduction of Defensive Biases," *Current Directions in Psychology Science* 4 (2002), 119–120.

22. See, e.g., Paul Slovic, "Trust, Emotion, Sex, Politics and Science: Surveying the Risk-Assessment Battlefield," in *The Perception of Risk* (London: Earthscan Publications, 2000), 404–405, noting that perceptions of risk and benefit for risky technologies are always inversely correlated, a finding suggesting that risk perceptions are influenced by cognitive dissonance. See also George A. Akerlof and William T. Dickens, "The Economic Consequences of Cognitive Dissonance," *American Economic Review* 72 (1982), suggesting that cognitive dissonance deflates demand of workers to be compensated for accepting occupational risks.

23. See Geoffrey Cohen, "Party over Policy: The Dominating Impact of Group Influence on Political Beliefs," *Journal of Personality & Social Psychology* (2003), 85; Robert J. Robinson, Dachter Keltner, Andrew Ward, and Lee Ross, "Actual Versus Assumed Differences in Construal: 'Naive Realism' in Intergroup Perception and Conflict," *Journal of Personality & Social Psychology* 68 (1995), 404, 405, 415.

24. See Donald Braman, Dan M. Kahan, and James Grimmelmann, "Modeling Facts, Culture, and Cognition in the Gun Debate," *Journal of Social Justice Research* 18: 3 (2005).

25. Slovic, supra note 23, 406–409.

26. See Charles G. Lord, Lee Ross, and Mark R. Leper, "Biased Assimilation and Attitude Polarization: The Effects of Prior Theories on Subsequently Considered Evidence," *Journal of Personality & Social Psychology* 11 (1979), 2098–2109.

27. See Keith J. Holyoak and Dan Simon, "Bidirectional Reasoning in Decision Making by Constraint Satisfaction," *Journal of Experimental Psychology* 128 (1999), 3; Dan Simon, Lien B. Pham, A. E. Quang, and Keith J. Holyoak, "The Emergence of Coherence over the Course of Decisionmaking," *Journal of Experimental Psychology* 27 (2001), 1250.

28. See Lee Ross, "Reactive Devaluation in Negotiation and Conflict Resolution," in *Barriers to Conflict Resolution*, Kenneth J. Arrow, Robert H Mnookin, Robert Wilson, and Amos Tversky, eds. (New York: W. W. Norton, 1995), 27.

29. See Jonathan J. Kohler, "The Influence of Prior Beliefs on Scientific Judgments," *Organizational Behavior & Human Decision Processes* 56 (1993), 28.

30. See, e.g., James Davison Hunter, *Culture Wars: The Struggle to Define America* (New York: Basic Books, 1991).

31. E.g., Thomas Frank, *What's the Matter with Kansas?* (New York: Henry Holt, 2004), 6.

32. Morris P. Fiorina, Samuel J. Abrams, and Jeremy C. Pope, *Culture War? The Myth of a Polarized America* (New York: Longman, 2005), 1.

33. Many news media outlets identified "moral values" as the primary concern of voters in the 2004 election. However, a Pew Research Center poll of 2004 voters found that the disposition of voters to identify moral values as the most important factor in their decision was extremely sensitive to question wording and that in fact 57% of voters identified either "Iraq" (22%), "Economy/Jobs" (21%), or "Terrorism" (14%) as the most important when those choices were offered as alternatives to "moral values" (27%). See http://people-press.org/reports/display.php3?ReportID=233.

34. Fiorina et al., supra note 33, 7–8.

35. See John Gastil, Dan M. Kahan, Donald Braman, and Paul Slovic, "The Wildavsky Heuristic," unpublished manuscript on file with authors.

36. See Dan M. Kahan and Donald Braman, "More Statistics, Less Persuasion," *Pennsylvania Law Review* 151 (2003), 1291: "Instead of challenging one another's worldviews, those who continue the debate simply challenge one another's honesty and integrity."

37. The Federalist Society, in fact, held a panel entitled "Judge Wars" to describe the heated politics of judicial nominations. See "Judge Wars" at http://www.fed-soc.org/Publications/Transcripts/judgeswars.pdf.

38. About ten major articles have been published every year for the last ten years. See Teresa L. Conaway, Carol L. Mutz, and Joann M. Ross, "Jury Nullification: A Selective, Annotated Bibliography," *Valparaiso University Law Review* 39 (2004), 393. It also remains a live doctrinal question, with the Ninth Circuit recently splitting on whether grand jurors should be instructed as to their nullifying powers. See *U.S. v. Navarro–Vargas*, 367 F.3d 896 (9th Cir. 2004).

39. Stephen B. Presser, "Is The Judicial Confirmation Process Broken? What Would Hamilton, Tocqueville, and Montesquieu Do?" *Jurist* (Apr. 15, 2004), available at http://jurist.law.pitt.edu/forum/symposium-jc/presser.php.

40. See, e.g., "Remarks of Ronald Rotunda," in *Judge Wars*, supra note 38.

41. We describe some of the evidence on juries elsewhere. See Dan M. Kahan, Donald Braman, and John Gastil, "A Cultural Critique of Gun Litigation," in *Suing the Gun Industry*, Timothy Lytton, ed. (2005).

42. See Neil Vidmar and Shari Seidman Diamond, "Juries & Expert Evidence," *Brooklyn Law Review* 61: 38 (2001), 1121: "The Story Model is widely accepted as a general description of how jurors process information and reach their decisions."

43. Nancy Pennington and Reid Hastie, "A Cognitive Theory of Juror Decision Making: The Story Model," *Cardozo Law Review* 13 (1991), 520.

44. See, e.g., Jill E. Huntley and Mark Costanzo, "Sexual Harassment Stories: Testing a Story-Mediated Model of Juror Decision-Making in Civil Litigation," *Law & Human Behavior* 27 (2003), 29; Yvette Tinsley, "Juror Decision-Making: A Look Inside the Jury Room," *Selected Papers from the British Criminology Conference*, Roger Tarling, ed. (2001), 4.

45. Lynda Olsen-Fulero and Solomon M. Fulero, "Commonsense Rape Judgments: An Empathy-Complexity Theory of Rape Juror Story Making," *Psychology, Public Policy & Law* 3 (1997), 273.

46. See Vicki L. Smith, "Prototypes in the Courtroom: Lay Representations of Legal Concepts," *Journal of Personality & Social Psychology* 61 (1991), showing that jurors follow socially constructed prototypes, not legal definitions, in assessing evidence; Norman J. Finkel and Jennifer L. Groscup, "Crime, Prototypes, Objective Versus Subjective Culpability, and a Commonsense Balance," *Journal of Law & Human Behavior* 21 (1997), cultural prototypes, not abstract moral theories, determine judgments of blame.

47. *See* Nancy Pennington and Reid Hastie, "Explanation-Based Decision Making: The Effects of Memory Structure on Judgment," *Journal of Experimental Psychology: Learning, Memory, and Cognition* (1988), 14: "[I]n a memory test, jurors' recognition of elements consistent with their verdict stories was significantly higher than their recognition of elements not consistent with their verdict stories."

48. See Reid Hastie, "The Role of 'Stories' in Civil Jury Judgments," *University of Michigan Journal of Legal Reform* 32 (1999); see also Sherry S. Diamond and J. D. Casper,

"Blindfolding the Jury to Verdict Consequences: Damages, Experts, and the Civil Jury," *Law & Social Review* 26 (1992), 513: It is the "expectations and preconceptions" that jurors bring with them to the jury box, the divergent ways that they "consciously or unconsciously process information" and "interpret[] ambiguities" that ultimately accounts for their divergent decisions; Sherry Diamond, "Scientific Jury Selection: What Social Scientists Know & Do Not Know," *Judicature* 73 (1990), 178: "The evidence presented at trial cannot account for initial disagreements among jurors: all jurors are exposed to the same evidence. The difference in juror reaction must stem from preexisting differences among the jurors."

49. Neil Feigenson, *Legal Blame* (Washington, DC: American Psychological Association, 2000), 14.

50. See ibid., 14: "Jurors want to decide the accident case in a way that reduces or eliminates the bad feelings that perceived injustice arouses." See also Gerold Mikula, Klaus R. Scherer, and Ursula Athenstaedt, "The Role of Injustice in the Elicitation of Differential Emotional Reactions," *Personality & Social Psychology Bulletin* 24 (1998).

51. Norman Finkel, *Commonsense Justice: Jurors' Notions of the Law* (Cambridge, MA: Harvard University Press, 1995).

52. See generally Finkel, supra note 52. See also Jason Schklar and Shari Diamond, "Juror Reactions to DNA Evidence: Errors and Expectancies," *Law & Human Behavior* 23 (1999), 180, indicating that jurors are often unimpressed by statistical evidence, however rigorous or definitive.

53. Feigenson, supra note 50, 103.

54. Mark D. Alicke, "Culpable Causation," *Journal of Personal & Social Psychology* 63: 3 (1992), 368.

55. Ibid., 369–370.

56. Paula L. Hannaford-Agor, Valerie P. Hans, Nicole L. Mott, and G. Thomas Munsterman, "Are Hung Juries a Problem?" *The National Center for State Courts* (Sept. 30, 2002), available at http://www.ncsconline.org/WC/Publications/Res_Juries_HungJuriesExecSumPub.pdf&e=7388.

57. Kenneth S. Klein and Theodore D. Klastorin, "Do Diverse Juries Aid or Impede Justice?" *Wisconsin Law Review* 1999 (1999), 565: "The general ethnic diversity of a jury clearly was related to the likelihood of reaching a verdict. Based on OLS regression analysis, we predict that only eight cases would have been undecided if the 188 juries had been composed of a single ethnic group, while sixty-two juries of the 188 would have hung had the juries been composed of equal numbers from all ethnic groups."

58. The best (and best-known) studies in this area have been done by Pheobe Ellsworth. See, e.g., W. C. Thompson, C. L. Cowan, Pheobe C. Ellsworth, and J. C. Harrington, "Death Penalty Attitudes and Conviction Proneness: The Translation of Attitudes into Verdicts," *Law & Human Behavior* 8 (1984), 95, finding that those who are willing to impose the death penalty are also more likely to consider prosecution witnesses more credible, events favorable to the prosecution more likely to have occurred, and the defendant more responsible for her

actions; see also Pheobe Ellsworth, "Some Steps Between Attitudes and Verdicts," in *Inside the Juror*, Reed Hastie, ed. (New York: Cambridge University Press, 1993).

59. 62 F. Supp.2d 802 (E.D.N.Y. 1999), vacated, 264 F.3d 21 (2d Cir. 2001).

60. Vanessa O'Connell and Paul M. Barrett, "Open Season: How a Jury Placed the Firearms Industry on the Legal Defensive," *Wall Street Journal* (Feb. 16, 1999), A1.

61. Ibid.

62. Ibid.

63. See ibid., detailing emotional strife and deliberative deadlock within the jury.

64. Chris Guthrie, Jeffrey J. Rachlinski, and Andrew J. Wistrich, "Inside the Judicial Mind," *Cornell Law Review* 86 (2001), 778. See also Chris Guthrie, Jeffrey J. Rachlinski, and Andrew J. Wistrich, "Judging by Heuristic: Cognitive Illusions in Judicial Decision Making," *Judicature* 86 (Jul.–Aug. 2002), 44, summarizing these findings.

65. Ibid.

66. Judges who tend to be in the religious minority, some researchers have found, also tend to be particularly concerned about separation of church and state. See Gregory C. Sisk, Michael Heisc, and Andrew P. Morris, "Searching for the Soul of Judicial Decisionmaking: An Empirical Study of Religious Freedom Decisions," *Ohio State Law Journal* 65 (2004), 491, suggesting that religious beliefs play a part.

67. One possible exception is judicial decision making in Establishment Clause cases. See ibid.

68. See Nancy Scherer, "Who Drives the Ideological Makeup of the Lower Federal Courts in a Divided Government?" *Law & Society Review* 35 (2001), 191; Nancy Scherer, *Scoring Points: Politicians, Activists, and the Lower Federal Court Appointment Process* (Stanford, CA: Stanford University Press, 2005). See also George, supra note 5, 1635; Tracey E. George, "Judicial Independence and the Ambiguity of Article III Protections," *Ohio State Law Journal* 64 (2003), 221.

69. Scherer, supra note 69, 207.

70. Ibid., 208–209.

71. J. Woodford Howard, *Courts of Appeals in the Federal Judicial System* (Princeton, NJ: Princeton University Press, 1981), 164, tbl.6.2, reporting that 80% of judges polled felt this way.

72. Cross, supra note 5, 78.

73. Revesz, supra note 5; Richard L. Revesz, "Congressional Influence on Judicial Behavior? An Empirical Examination of Challenges to Agency Action in the D.C. Circuit," *N.Y.U. Law Review* 76 (2001), 1100, providing evidence that the political affiliation and ideological preferences of judges affect judicial outcomes. Other valuable analyses preceded those of Revesz. See, e.g., Cohen and Spitzer, supra note 5, finding that justices are far more likely to defer to an agency's statutory construction when the agency is controlled by a president of the same political party as the justice.

74. See generally Cross, supra note 5; Sunstein et al., supra note 5.

75. The proxies, in this case, are the identity of the appointing president or the president's party and the region in which the judge practices or the judge's circuit.

76. See generally Revesz supra note 5; Sunstein et al., supra note 5.

77. See Sunstein et al., supra note 5, 305: "In . . . these areas, judges apparently vote their convictions and are not affected by panel composition."

78. 520 U.S. 751 (1997).

79. Ibid., 762.

80. Ibid., 763: "the words 'maximum term authorized' are ambiguous."

81. For a similar disagreement over supposedly unambiguous statutory language, see *Deal v. U.S.*, 508 U.S. 129 (1993).

82. See Cross and Tiller, supra note 5, 2171, providing evidence that a three-judge panel was 31% more likely to defer to an agency "when the agency's policy outcome is consistent with the policy preferences of the panel's majority"; Revesz, supra note 74, describing data indicating that the political affiliation and ideological preferences of judges affect judicial outcomes; Cohen and Spitzer, supra note 5, finding that justices are more likely to defer to an agency's statutory construction when the agency is controlled by a president of the same political party as the justice.

83. See supra note 30 and accompanying text, describing the ESP study.

84. See, e.g., Cross and Tiller, supra note 5; George, supra note 5, finding ideological decision making on en banc panels to be similarly strategic; Cross, supra note 5, detailing the "strategic" model and finding that, while judges are influenced by ideology, they are primarily driven by legal considerations.

85. See, e.g., Edwards, supra note 7, disputing the claim that judges are guided by political considerations.

86. Stuart Buck, http://stuartbuck.blogspot.com/2003/11/legal-realism.html.

87. Stanley Fish, "Theory Minimalism," *San Diego Law Review* 37 (2000), 761.

88. The phrase "strict constructionist," for example, was popularized by Richard Nixon, who used it to describe the qualities he sought in his judicial appointees. He was introduced to the phrase by none other than former Chief Justice Rehnquist, who provided the following definition: "A judge who is a 'strict constructionist' in constitutional matters will generally not be favorably inclined toward claims of either criminal defendants or civil rights plaintiffs—the latter two groups having been the principal beneficiaries of the Supreme Court's 'broad constructionist' reading of the Constitution." Memorandum by William H. Rehnquist, *Re: Judicial Selection* (May 29, 1969) (National Archives & Records Administration, Washington, DC, White House Special Files).

89. See, e.g., Richard Posner, *Law, Pragmatism, and Democracy* (Cambridge, MA: Harvard University Press, 2003), arguing that pragmatic discretion should guide legal decision making.

90. In *State v. Mann*, for example, a case in which a slave owner shot a slave who was running away after he beat her, a jury convicted the owner of battery, but Ruffin overturned

the conviction, arguing that "the power of the master must be absolute, to render the submission of the slave perfect." 13 N.C. 263, 266 (1829). In this decision, Timothy Heubner describes, *Mann* combined considerations of expediency, experience ("in the actual conditions of things, it must be so"), and reasoning based on legal precedent as a judicial pragmatist would. See Timothy S. Huebner, *The Southern Judicial Tradition: State Judges and Sectional Distinctiveness, 1790–1890* (Athens: University of Georgia Press, 1999).

91. This is the claim that Judge Kozinski, with unintentional irony, attributes to legal realism. See Kozinski, supra note 1, describing legal realism as a theory that holds that "a grouchy mood, the theory went, is likely to cause the judge to take it out on the litigant he least identifies with, usually the guy who got run over by the railroad or is being foreclosed on by the bank." The claim is ironic because while Kozinski claims that language places "an objective constraint" on the interpretations judges can make, his interpretation of legal realist theory appears to be entirely *unconstrained* by the writings of the major legal realists. In fact, none of the constraints that Judge Kozinski regards as influential (clerks, reputation for honesty, self-respect) appear to have constrained his reading of legal realist texts. And yet, as cultural cognition suggests, he is very likely to believe that he has evaluated legal realism objectively.

92. See, e.g., Ellen Peters and Paul Slovic, "The Role of Affect and Worldviews as Orienting Dispositions in the Perception and Acceptance of Nuclear Power," *Journal of Applied Social Psychology* 26 (1996), 1427; Michael Siegrist, George Cvetkovich, and Claudia Roth, "Salient Value Similarity, Social Trust, and Risk/Benefit Perception," *Risk Analysis* 20 (2000), 3; Dan M. Kahan, Donald Braman, John Gastil, Paul Slovic, and C. K. Mertz, "Gender, Race, and Risk Perception: The Influence of Cultural Status Anxiety," available at http://papers.ssrn.com/sol3/papers.cfm?abstract_id=723762.

93. Unsurprisingly, egalitarians and solidarists perceived business regulation to be conducive to economic prosperity; hierarchists and individualists perceived it to be destructive of it. See Gastil, Braman, and Kahan, supra note 36.

94. Firearm ownership and regulation are areas particularly freighted with cultural concerns. Gun-control proponents argue that greater restrictions will promote public safety by reducing gun violence and accidents; see, e.g., Philip J. Cook and Jens Ludwig, *Gun Violence: The Real Costs* (New York: Oxford University Press, 2000). On the other hand, control opponents argue that such restrictions will diminish public safety on net by rendering innocent persons unable to defend themselves from violent criminals; see, e.g., John R. Lott Jr., *More Guns, Less Crime: Understanding Crime and Gun Control Laws*, 2nd ed. (Chicago: University of Chicago Press, 2000). Individuals' cultural worldviews predictably determine which of these empirical claims they accept. Persons of hierarchical and individualistic orientations conclude that gun control has perverse consequences, a belief congenial to the association of guns with hierarchical social roles (hunter, protector, father) and with hierarchical and individualistic virtues (courage, honor, chivalry, self-reliance, prowess). Relatively egalitarians and solidaristic individuals, on the other hand, believe that

gun control enhances safety because of their association of guns with patriarchy and racism and with distrust and indifference to the well-being of strangers. See generally Kahan and Braman, supra note 37. Our results again strongly bore out these conclusions. Not only did cultural worldviews have the predicted influence on beliefs. Cultural orientations explained such beliefs more powerfully than any other individual characteristic, including whether a person is male or female, white or black, urban or country dwelling, liberal or conservative. See Kahan, Braman, Gastil, Slovic, and Mertz, supra note 93.

95. See ibid.

96. Levinson, supra note 2.

97. Realists' main point was not that law was somewhat indeterminate; that was a corollary to their deeper point that the legal decision makers were constrained by extralegal facts and moral concerns that were not always aligned with a single reading of doctrine. See, e.g., Llewellyn, "Some Realism About Realism," 1237: "[T]raditional . . . rule formulations are not the heavily operative factor in producing court decisions."

98. Cf. Barbara J. Shapiro, "'To a Moral Certainty': Theories of Knowledge and Anglo-American Juries 1600–1850," *Hastings Law Journal* 38 (1986), 153, making this point about modern rules of evidence more generally.

99. Rather than talking of conflicting norms as the product of social contest, Llewellyn talks instead of imperfect solutions to practical problems that may be improved upon. See, e.g., Karl Llwellyn, "One 'Realist's' View of Natural Law for Judges," *Notre Dame Law Review* 15 (1939), 3.

100. See generally Jerome Frank, "Are Judges Human? Parts I & II," *University of Pennsylvania Law Review* 80 (1931), 17–53, 233–276. It bears noting that Frank, though often taken as representative of legal realism by its critics, was not representative of the movement. See Brian Leiter, "Is There an 'American' Jurisprudence?" *Oxford Journal of Legal Studies* 17 (1997), 376: "Over time, our image of Legal Realism has suffered 'Frankification,' resulting in what Duxbury rightly calls 'the popular burlesque' of Realism according to which judicial decisions are determined by 'the moods and whims of the particular judge.'"

101. See generally Llewellyn, supra note 15 (1960).

102. Dan M. Kahan, Donald Braman, and John Gastil, "A Cultural Critique of Gun Litigation," in *Suing the Gun Industry: A Battle at the Crossroads of Gun Control and Mass Torts*, Timothy D. Lytton, ed. (Ann Arbor: University of Michigan Press, 2005).

103. See Robert C. Post, "Fashioning the Legal Constitution: Culture, Courts, and Law," *Harvard Law Review* 117 (2003), 4, arguing that "constitutional law and culture are locked in a dialectical relationship."

104. See, e.g., Post supra note 104, note 181, citing Brandeis and Taft as vigorous advocates of judicial statesmanship. The practical qualities of respectful attentiveness to cultural diversity in legal decision making have been most carefully developed by Mary Anne Glendon in her work on abortion and divorce in Europe. See Mary Anne Glendon, *Abortion and Divorce in Western Society* (Cambridge, MA: Harvard University Press, 1984).

How Law Knows in the American Trial Court

ROBERT P. BURNS

On Knowing How Law Knows in the Trial Court: The Problem of Knowing How the Trial Knows Through Situated Practical Ideals

In this chapter, I describe the pattern of linguistic practices in which we actually engage at trial and then how the trial occasions a distinctive form of awareness, a distinctive understanding of the events and persons being tried. It is possible to stop there. When one asks "How does law know?" one may be accepting or bracketing normative questions about whether the law *succeeds* in *knowing*. The question may be equivalent to a "purely descriptive" inquiry into the methods, practices, or cognitive operations by which law claims, however wrongly, to "know." It is true that major developments in the philosophy of science, understood as a partly normative discipline, have emerged from studying what scientists actually do, rather than relying exclusively on philosophically driven notions of what they must be doing if they are really doing science. But it is also possible that certain forms of awareness occasioned by the trial may have their own forms of validity, but these other forms of validity may not count as "knowledge." We may grant their validity but say they don't give us ("amount to") knowledge. I will briefly recount how powerful strands in modern philosophy make such a position eligible and the kinds of intellectual moves that would be necessary to overcome a division between, let us say, practical understanding and "knowledge."

It is true that in English the word *know* has an inevitably normative denotation. One can believe a proposition that is false, but one cannot know it. (I can believe that the moon is made of green cheese, but I cannot know it.) The account of our practices in the trial court that I sketch out stresses that the trial is a practical enterprise and embodies situated ideals about how we should act in certain concrete public contexts. The ultimate question the jury asks is, "What is to be done?" It turns out that if the law knows at trial, it is because its "consciously structured hybrid of languages" allows us to achieve practical knowledge of how best to proceed in the face of competing alternatives that reflect incommensurable values. "Trial judgments will be true [and so the awareness occasioned at trial will really be knowledge] if (1) there exist no institutions—and more robustly, no possible inquiry will identify institutions—that are better designed to achieve the practical purposes of the trial, and (2) those purposes are rooted in the most important human interests" (Burns, 1999, 235). If there is a distinctively legal form of truth (and so knowledge), then only through a better trial, judged by the trial's own internal norms, could we know that.

We tend to think that this is not true because, after all, *something* happened that has led to the trial and we tend to think that this "something" must be something whose factual, moral, and political meaning is definite before we determine what it is—"already-out-there-now-real," as Bernard Lonergan puts it. We tend to think that there is some *other* means to know what the trial is addressing other than the trial itself, some means by which the truth of the trial's results may be reliably determined. I will suggest that this is quite wrong. It has some *limited* sense at the level of "brutally elementary data" (Did certain physical movements in space and time take place?). But it seems that methods somewhat similar to the adversary trial have a kind of ultimacy even when scientific evidence is concerned. Even what appears to be strong evidence of what was already-out-there-now-real, such as provided by the Rodney King video, can be subject to differing interpretations. Yes, there are brutally elementary data. But when those facts are about a single event, often involving one or two people, our access to those facts is inevitably through the testimony of interested witnesses, even when those witnesses are scientists. Recent revelations about systematic lab error in the process of "infallible" DNA evidence make this point. Determinations of witness credibility have been traditionally viewed as distinctively "within the province of the jury," and something like the methods of the adversary trial seem appropriate for those judgments. As we move along the normative spectrum away from "Did he do it?" kinds of questions (brutally elementary data) to questions involving the interpretation of the meaning of circumstantial evidence and then to the provisional acceptance of morally and politically charged narratives, the dramatic and critical qualities of the trial seem even more appropriate. This is true most obviously for the acts of moral and political self-constitution by which jurors or judges decide how much uncertainty is acceptable before authorizing the state to act coercively in the particular case, a matter about which "standards of proof" offer little guidance. The question of *whether*, as opposed to *how*, the trial knows can only be resolved by specifying a version of the trial whose situated ideals are superior to those of the contemporary trial, whose practices better achieve the same practical purposes of the trial or which achieve more important human purposes. To do *that*, one first must fully specify what the situated ideals of American trials are. Otherwise, "reforms" are likely to diminish what the trial routinely achieves.

I will argue that the trial embodies a form of practical intelligence and has been shaped, through a series of often jagged historical steps, to allow us to achieve, again imperfectly, certain practical goals. I use "practical" in its traditional sense to connote instrumental, moral, or political ends beyond the theoretical grasp of a state of affairs. (In this sense, philosophical contemplation is theoretical, and "pure science" is usually thought to be theoretical.[1]) Achieving the best concrete integration of those ends in a given case is what we call "justice." It could then be fairly said that the trial's practices embody a set of situated ideals. They are situated because they embody only a limited set of the norms that we value in practical situations. (For example, they may not be fully expressive of ideals of reconciliation that are better embodied in mediation.) They are *ideals* because they actually are forms of practical *intelligence*, and those practices cannot easily be replaced by other practices that better achieve the trial's human purposes.

This understanding of the trial may be analogized to a traditional understanding of drama. Tragedy allows us to see something that could not be seen any other way. It is not one of those "reproductions of a reality that can be identified independently of the work . . . and used to judge the adequacy of its representation." Like a work of art, the trial is a unique and transforming lens through which a problematic situation is interpreted and so seen:

> [T]he features of the objects works of art represent . . . are illuminated only by means of the representation itself; certain events or features are exaggerated, the importance of others minimized and the like. Hence the representation does not provide a mirror of reality that exactly reflects it; rather, on Gadamer's view, artistic presentation shows the "truth" of reality, as he puts it. "Reality" is defined as what is untransformed and art as the raising up of this reality into its truth. (Warnke, 1987, 57)

To the extent that the trial realized its situated ideals, there would be no better form of awareness of the events being tried by which to deal practically with the situation at hand than those provided through the trial's internal practices. Because this awareness is practical, it does not involve a mental screenplay of past events but something much more difficult to describe: a simultaneous grasp of facts, norms, and possibilities for action that may not be pictured or represented. That the trial is primarily addressing a single past event and the practically intelligent response to that event affects the foregoing only somewhat.

I have been talking about the trial and how the law knows at trial, but we cannot help talking at the same time about how *we*—those of us inquiring into the nature of the trial—can know how it knows. (Hannah Arendt, who always thought the less said about methodological questions the better, quite consciously avoided the question by calling her own attempts to understanding public practices "*thinking* what we do.") In an earlier exchange, Martha Umphrey distinguished her own inclination to "dwell in the concrete materializations of cultural and legal rhetoric and representation both inside and outside the courtroom" from my inclination to be a "synthesizer deeply interested in proposing and perfecting an ideal model of trial processes." Likewise, she contrasted the "messy specificity" that she tends to find in her studies of particular trials to the "beautiful ideality" that my accounts seem to aspire to. She argued as well that my "idealist" arguments are easier to maintain to the extent that I abstract from the relationship between what goes on in the courtroom and the "ballyhoo" of popular culture and outside institutions with which it is enmeshed. This is true, and a fuller account would place the trial in its complete institutional and practical context. The trial regularly goes wrong because its practices are encased within and so dependent on bureaucratic and market institutions that distort what it has come to be. Because the trial's situated ideals are limited, for us to *know* when the trial really knows and when it doesn't, we need to see it in a broader context of practices.

But this raises two fundamental problems. The first is to identify those aspects of the trial that are indeed intrinsic to what it is when understood "in its best light," as Dworkin likes to say. It is my burden to show that certain aspects of what the trial has come to be represent considered judgments of justice, in Rawlsian language, or "situated ideals," the Hegelian term I have been using. The practices can be revealed in thick description and must resist arguments that they are inconsistent with what the trial *should* be, as revealed by jurisprudential perspectives that would limit the trial to a role that is not fully consistent with current practices. Critics would say that any aspect of the trial—and there are many—that is inconsistent with the trial as a machine for stamping the law of rules onto a value-free already-out-there-now-real narrative of events should be eliminated. Which aspects of the trial express situated ideals? Which express decadent misunderstandings of its true role? These are interrelated questions and their resolution can only be made hermeneutically, "by the mutual support of many considerations, everything fitting together into one coherent view."

There is a second, even more difficult, problem awaiting any attempt to place the trial in the full context of all the institutions and practices with which it is connected. The challenge is to do that in a language that is as rich as the language of the trial so that, to use the unfashionable Straussian language, the higher is not understood in light of the lower, the lower being a journalistic *or* functionalist *or* formalistic account of the place of this relatively "minor" institution. In these latter forms of metalevel accounts, it is *impossible* that the trial be seen as expressing powerful practical ideals—the sun around which all the planets in the procedural solar system travel, as James Boyd White has put it. Further, the small and declining numbers of cases going to trial and the ascendancy of bureaucracy, formalism, and bargaining (much of which involves offers the parties cannot refuse) as the dominant forms of dispute resolution in the "legal system" tend to credit the normatively impoverished functionalist or formalist account that *does*, in fact, fairly describe them. And so the war about the appropriate means of social ordering at the institutional level is replicated in the theoretical battle about the best way (or best hybrid of ways) in which to understand legal practices and institutions. As usual, there is no simple way out of the circle. At the metalevel, the practitioner of social inquiry seeking to *know* how the trial *knows* is in a position closely analogous to that of the judge attempting to know the events before him. Both enterprises have an inevitably normative element because the "objects" of knowledge in both cases can best be understood in light of the situated ideals within them. (The trial and the event being tried are both human actions.) When I wrote *A Theory of the Trial*, I attempted to multiply a set of accounts at the metalevel that in many ways paralleled the methods used at trial, not as a kind of *tour de force*, but because they seemed to be exactly appropriate to understand what the trial was. This is because the way the trial itself knows can only be shown, not fully stated in propositional form. I was trying to engage in a form of intelligent practice (interpretive social inquiry) designed to understand a form of intelligent practice (the trial). I wanted an account that could understand how the trial could realize its own (our) purposes. How could one begin to do the same thing for *all* the practices—legal, political, and social—that surround the trial without almost immediately oversimplifying and objectivizing those practices as forms of social behaviors to be "explained" using scientific modes of thought that emptied their objects of internal significance? But that is exactly what the comprehensive interpretive social science that Umphrey calls for would require, both at the level of interpreting a single institution like the trial and at the level of comprehensive social theory. In either project, it seems to me important that some investigators try to be foxes and hedgehogs at the same time. Both at trial and in the fuller understanding of the trial, understanding comes from dwelling in the tensions between the concrete particulars and often theoretical accounts. As Clifford Geertz has reminded us, it is by cycling between the most detailed description of institutionalized practices and the broadest generalizations that we are likely to achieve insight into both those details and our theoretical self-understandings. Although Hannah Arendt celebrated the importance of concrete and detailed storytelling, she clearly became a political *theorist.*

How We Have Gotten Here: A Very Short Intellectual History

This question of whether there are valid forms of comprehension that should not be called "knowledge," itself intertwined with the question of how we can know social practices constituted by situated practical ideals, played an important role in modern philosophy. There is a tension in Kantian thinking on this point that has radiated through the past two centuries. He calls the categorical imperative the only "fact of reason," implying that moral truth can thus be "known." The major thrust of his philosophy was, however, to limit the range of what it is that we can know to common sense and scientific knowledge of the sensible world. The issue is implicit in the famous Kantian saying, "I found it necessary to deny knowledge [of the supersensible world] to make way for [moral] faith." Subsequent German idealism tried to move beyond Kant by building on a related tension between Kant's presenting the critical philosophy itself as "true" when it surely did not conform to his own critical canons for knowledge. Both moral and philosophical consciousness seem to require an understanding, let us call it, that cannot easily within the confines of the critical philosophy be termed knowledge. (Similarly, in Anglo-American philosophy, a strict positivism foundered on the recognition that positivism itself was quite meaningless given the positivist principle of meaning.) Hegel argued that a "critical" philosophy was necessarily a performative contradiction and that philosophy had to embrace a notion of knowledge that was fully achieved only in the single absolute grasp of the whole that his dialectical philosophy provided.

After the waning of absolute idealism, neo-Kantians and philosophers in the phenomenological tradition struggled with the task of saying something meaningful about usually practical dimensions of the human world of which we could no longer have knowledge. Neo-Kantians tended to offer transcendental or reflexive arguments to show that certain moral concepts were necessary for us but had solely practical, not theoretical, employment. That is, though they could not yield knowledge, we could not do without them without undermining the human world. But put this way, practical notions such as justice seemed to be pure "as ifs." Even if one accepted a Kantian account of such notions as deeply embedded in the human mind,[2] dominant naturalistic understandings of human capacities carried by Darwinian perspectives tended to rob those contingent capacities of any real normative significance. Kant himself had probably thought of our awareness (call it knowledge or not) of our moral obligations to be a form of participant-observer status in a real (*noumenal*) intelligible order. This was Kant's Platonism. Although some twentieth-century philosophers, usually explicit Platonists, such as Whitehead, or those writing in a religious idiom, such as John Macmurry, were willing to paint more or less self-consciously mythical pictures of the world to give ontological support to practical concepts, they were generally out of step with the naturalism of our age. The "likely stories" that Plato thought necessary to tell in the *Timaeus* (and Whitehead in *Process and Reality*) to be adequate to all aspects of our experience lacked the rigor necessary for the successful prediction and control of natural processes that the "acting into nature" of modern science made the touchstone of knowledge, just as Kant understood.

Legal thought was, of course, affected by these major philosophical developments and by the dominance of modern science. The sociological wing of realism (Leiter, 1999, 1148) sought to know the law as concrete legal practices in a way that traditional doctrinal methods could not provide because those doctrines could not, realism taught, yield knowledge of the real bases for judges' determinations. These were to be found, at least in aspiration, in a scientific account of the court's situation sense, known as a "psycho-social fact" and connected with specific decisions, ideally through scientific covering laws (Burns, 2001, 223–226). But a scientific account could not, of course, provide anything that looked like a normative "appreciation," let us call it, of the trial. Because the trial itself could not claim to know scientifically, sociological realism, which could know both the trial and the event being tried in its own way, almost inevitably, even in its descriptions, judged the trial through situated ideals of prediction and control that were foreign to the situated ideals that animate the trial and provide what illumination the trial offers.

The task, then, is to give an account of a practical enterprise that illuminates how it can succeed and the forms of understanding germane to that success. Much of twentieth-century pragmatism has attempted precisely such accounts, though in the very different keys associated with the names Heidegger, Wittgenstein, and Dewey. In the phenomenological tradition, for example, Heidegger's embrace of truth as disclosedness or unhiddenness provides for a human comprehension of the truth of a situation ultimately irreducible to a propositional, and certainly a scientific, knowledge of objects. Truth is revealed through an ultimate correlation, itself only partially explicable, between human practices and the world. "[E]ntities are self-disclosive (*alethes*) only insofar as they are in *correlation* with the various modes of the human co-performance of disclosure (*aletheuein*), primarily the practical ones." The understanding of the truth of practical enterprises, then, depends on "the always already operative empowering of the essential togetherness of disclosive human comportment and of entities qua accessible" (Sheehan, 1993, 81–82). Within this view, our *practices* are disclosive but do not yield propositional knowledge. They are disclosive of a background, a world within which we always already are and to which we need make no Cartesian leap. Indeed, providing an account of the intelligibility of this world, discernible from our practices, was philosophy's central task. And this is the hardest part of all: a philosophy that was to provide that account could not itself be a "theory," least of all a scientific theory. For example, in Heidegger's later writings, it becomes clear that "philosophy is more a form of life on the edge of expression rather than a science," and phenomenology "more a preconceptual, provisory comportment than a conceptual science" whose "formally indicating 'concepts' are first intended to serve life rather than science" (Kisiel, 1993, 57).

Philosophy could then seek to disclose how our ordinary practices disclose the world. These ideas, and similar notions in Wittgenstein's analytic and Dewey's biological idioms, have been enormously influential and have been as controversial as they have been influential. In the hands of the scholars who embrace them, they provide some hope of giving an account of our practices, including the practices of self-government such as those deployed in the trial, that is not reductionist and that can amount to both a comprehension of and appreciation of those practices and the situated ideals within them. They must do so, however, in a post-Hegelian environment where an absolute point of view from which to assess institutions and practices is not available. Thus, in their actual practices, they must be multivoiced and multiperspectival even as they construct their accounts. Thick description, doctrinal elaboration, moral philosophy, and quantitative inquiry are four of those voices. The hope is that something is shown that cannot wholly be said once the propositions that are uttered are kicked away like a ladder. At trial, multiple voices spoken by and to many people with different perspectives can produce a single verdict. Something like that may, it seems to me, emerge in an *appreciation* of the trial adequate to its voices.

One Standard View of How the Law Knows Facts and Law in the Trial Court

How the Jury Knows "the Facts"

I have called perhaps the dominant understanding of how the trial knows the "received view" of the trial. This perspective, including the important "rationalist tradition" in evidence law, assumes that the jury learns the factual truth as a value-free narrative of events constructed from circumstantial evidence and purely empirical generalizations connecting bits of evidence to factual conclusions. The creation of that narrative is the jury's prime responsibility as the "trier of fact." After the narrative is constructed, the jury is then to decide the case by determining whether the factual narrative previously constructed without essential reference to the law falls within or outside the categories established by the substantive law. Once that act of inspection has occurred, the case is decided without the intrusion of any norms other than those found in the instructions. In this picture, the facts are representations, value-free atoms that are connected by empirical generalizations to construct an accurate account. Empirical generalizations are embedded within the web of belief that constitutes our common sense. The latter is understood as containing generalizations of the form "generally and for the most part. . . ." (For example, "generally and for the most part, mothers have affection for their children.") The cognitive operations the jury is to engage in to constitute this value-free narrative are mainly inferential. Notice that the rationalist tradition understands the trial as a theoretical enterprise in the sense described earlier. The jury's immediate interest in creating its value-free narrative of what occurred is theoretical: It is simply to know the past as accurately as possible. Likewise, its interest at the level of judgment is simply to categorize the narrative previously inferred as accurately as the legal rules will allow.

Notice too that this account invokes what one theorist has called the tripartite model of judgment. This model provides:

> Any judgment—as the bringing together somehow of a universal and a particular—would seem to require at least three things: (1) the universal qua concept must be identi-

> fied, and this means being able to specify at least some of the conceptual features that make it what it is; (2) the particular must be identified, and this means being able to specify at least some of the characteristics that individuate it; and (3) there must be a mental faculty that allows us to establish some kind of demonstrable and explicable connection between the universal's features and the particular's characteristics such that we can say with some justification that "X is (or is not) Y." (Steinberger, 1993, 91)

We will see shortly that even at the first stage of the received view, the jury must depend on a determination of the *meaning* of the events tried. As analytical philosophers sometimes put it, these events can only be known "under a description." The jury cannot make even a determination of relative "purely" factual probabilities unless it understands *what* has occurred

The received view understands the linguistic practices of the trial to be consistent with this understanding of the jury's cognitive operations. The opening statements of the lawyers serve to provide a preview of the evidence to come. The law of professional responsibility prohibits the lawyer from mentioning any fact for which there will not be admissible evidence. The law of evidence requires that physical and documentary evidence be "authenticated," be shown by a person with firsthand knowledge that it is indeed "what it purports to be." The hearsay rule requires that verbal declarations offered to prove the truth of the matter asserted be made in court, under oath, and subject to cross-examination, "the greatest legal engine ever invented for the discovery of truth," as Wigmore put it. At least as important, the direct examination of witnesses must proceed in the form of a rhythm between physical description and an artificially stripped-down chronological narrative, all based on the witness's "personal" (that is, perceptual) knowledge and in the language of perception (that is, without the witness's own interpretations, opinions, evaluations, or recommendations for action). Cross-examination provides an additional guarantee of factual accuracy by testing the witnesses' credibility. Closing argument argues the empirical strength of the generalizations on which the party relies to establish the accuracy of the ultimate value-free narrative of events (and then argues that this narrative falls exactly within the meaning of the legal categories in the jury instructions).

There is power to this understanding of what the trial's linguistic practices are for two reasons. First, it is consistent with important ideals surrounding the common law trial. Factual accuracy is essential if any of the values surrounding the rule of law are to be achieved. If factual determinations cannot be made accurately, then citizens have no assurance that law-abiding behavior will protect them from the intrusive action of state officials. Their autonomy is so threatened. It is likewise threatened within this perspective if there is no manner in which the underlying fact can be understood in a manner that does not smuggle in norms that are inconsistent with the preannounced rules in the substantive law. Thus, the trial's linguistic practices serve to strip away from the factual account norms that may contaminate the decision of the case solely by the norms embedded in the instructions and so ultimately in the substantive law. Second, the very practical utopians who have constituted the Anglo-American bar have been convinced enough of the ideals underlying "the rule of law as the law of rules" actually to cultivate, as judges and advocates, trial practices consistent with them.

How the Jury Knows the Law of Rules Within the Received View

In Justice Scalia's expressive phrase, within the received view, the rule of law means the hegemony of the "law of rules" (Scalia, 1989). Law is equivalent to the meanings expressed in legal rules. Now it is true that even this Spartan notion of law immediately gets complicated as we try to understand what this notion means in a common law context (where "the law" exists in the force field created by a never completely resolved tension among facts, results, stated rules, and stated rationales). Or ponder the relationship between the meaning of a rule and legislative purpose or intent. But we can put aside those complexities for the moment.

The most obvious place where the jury learns of the law is through the jury instructions. The statement of the law in the instructions is inevitably formulaic and completely in the language of rules. The jury knows nothing of the facts, results, and rationales of the cases through which those rules were developed. Most jurisdictions and some federal circuits have standard jury instructions, drafted by committees and approved by the court, which must be used when germane to disputed issues in the case. In each individual case, the instructions are normally worked out in a conference that usually occurs after all the evidence has been presented but before the closing arguments of the lawyers.[3] At this conference, lawyers will propose instructions and must object to the instructions offered by the opponent or proposed by the court to preserve the issue for appeal. These instructions must contain all the relevant qualifications that make them an "accurate" statement of the law that emerges from the earlier decisions of the appellate courts. Thus, they tend to be complex and sometimes practically incomprehensible. They are normally read orally to the jury, and sometimes they may be taken by the jury into the jury room. There is some variation from jurisdiction to jurisdiction about how lawyers may use the instruction in argument, but in most places, lawyers may say something like, "In a few minutes, the court will instruct you as to the law that you have sworn to follow in deciding this case. I think he will tell you that . . ." The lawyer may then offer common-sense arguments as to why the narrative that the jury ought to construct from the evidence in the case[4] falls fairly within the authoritative categories embedded in the instructions.

In bench trials, by contrast, judges can come to know the law through the same professionally prescribed ways as they can before trial. Lawyers quite regularly file trial briefs and orally argue both the facts of the case and the legal significance of those facts. They may engage in genuine common law reasoning in those arguments, and the judge is in a position to evaluate those arguments by analogy to earlier cases. If the common law is a never completely resolved tension among the stated facts of the case (usually at a highly conclusory level), the result, the stated rule, and the court's rationale, the judge will be able to continue the process by which legal doctrine is determined.

How Judges Know the Law of Rules in Their Policing Function Within the Received View

The trial judge's obligations to the law of rules go beyond formulating legally correct instructions. He or she also has a policing function in determining which cases will go to the jury at all, what I call the judge's *policing function* at trial. Lawyers contemplating bringing a lawsuit must anticipate how the judge will exercise this policing function should the case get to trial, and so its effect is felt well before the trial begins. In the case of lawyers in private practice, their determinations will, of course, be affected by the opportunity costs of their filing the cases and an economic calculus of their remuneration in the possible case. Lawyers in prosecutors' offices and civil public interest lawyers will be affected by judgments about the consistency of the case with their own professional norms, as they are partially constrained by predictions about the likelihood of adverse summary disposition. Prosecutors are likely to be constrained by legal judgments, integrated in quite different ways in different offices, about their professional obligations not to bring cases if there is no probable cause or if they believe a jury will not convict at trial or, in some parts of the country, if they don't subjectively believe that the defendant is guilty under the statutory definitions. Lawyers in civil matters will be constrained by professional judgments that prohibit the filing of frivolous cases. That, of course, will require a judgment of the legal merit of a particular case. A case can be the basis of professional discipline against the lawyer and other sanctions imposed by the court if it is "frivolous" or defective as to law or fact or filed for an improper "purpose" under Rule 11 of the Federal Rules of Civil Procedure or its state law analogues. There is a good deal of authority for the proposition that a case that survives dispositive motions at trial is a case inappropriate for such sanctions, another indication of the convergence of different sorts of professionally sanctioned understandings of what the law of rules means. Thus, professionally acceptable modes of legal interpretation in a case are in play long before the case reaches the courthouse. At the margin, a lawyer will have to deploy these professionally acceptable norms of interpretation to determine whether a novel case can be supported by a "good faith argument for an extension, modification, or reversal of existing law."[5] If so, he or she may proceed.[6]

This initial determination by a lawyer is thus the first time the "rule of law as the law of rules" makes its effect felt. In the American context, it requires the deployment of the ordinary principles for the interpretation of constitutional provisions, statutes, and the case law interpreting them, themselves embodied in more or less legally normative principles for legal interpretation. They follow a shifting and informal set logic based on the semantic meaning of the legal rules and the ways in which the situation may be fairly given a description and the relationship between them, supplemented by notions of the "purposes" of various enactments (Eisenberg, 1988).

The criminal defendant is here formally privileged because his or her lawyer may always "defend the proceeding so as to require that every element of the case be established" even when the defense involves, through a general denial, denials of assertions of fact that would be frivolous if made by a defendant in a civil case. This is the first recognition that criminal prosecutions involve the direction of state power against an individual so as to raise distinctively political issues. "He who punishes the criminal is the real master of society" (Tocqueville, 1945, 293). Similarly, there is no summary procedure by which the prosecution may obtain a judgment of conviction in a criminal case.[7] A prosecutor may never obtain a conviction "as a matter of law" based solely on undisputed facts. The political context of the criminal case, the deployment of state power against an individual, changes the normative terrain surrounding the defense lawyer's general duties of candor to the tribunal.[8]

But the criminal defendant is not wholly immune from the judge's professional determinations within the rhetoric of the law of rules. An American judge in a criminal case may not direct the jury to find any fact against the criminal defendant, regardless of how overwhelming the evidence on the point is and even if there exists a general evidentiary presumption that would, in a civil case, require the court to direct a verdict on at least that one issue. However, a criminal trial judge may refuse to give a jury instruction on a lesser included offense if he or she deems that a jury could not reasonably conclude that the evidence supports a conviction on that lesser offense as defined by the law of rules. For example, in a homicide case, a criminal trial judge may decline to give an instruction on involuntary or voluntary manslaughter under circumstances where he or she concludes that the homicide could not but be intentional. Thus, a criminal jury would be presented with an either–or decision on a murder conviction or an acquittal. The jury would be deprived of the opportunity to resolve normative issues suggesting the real, but qualified, blameworthiness or responsibility of the defendant through a conviction on a lesser offense. Such a determination increases the likelihood that the norms in the law of rules, and only they, will determine the outcome.

Criminal and civil defendants may obtain a favorable summary disposition before trial by convincing the judge that the opposing party does not propose (or in the case of summary judgment and criminal arraignment, does not *plausibly* propose) to prove the facts that fall within the scope of the legal categories that would generate a civil judgment or criminal conviction. Likewise, a civil plaintiff may obtain judgment based solely on the admissions in the Answer ("Judgment on the Pleadings") or summary judgment (no *substantial* issue of *material* fact) based on sworn affidavits and depositions. In all these cases, the judge may make a determination based solely on the "law of rules." Now these rules are certainly different depending on whether they are constitutional, statutory, or common law. There exists a set of legally authoritative commonplaces available to judges for the interpretation of constitutions, statutes, and case law. As Llewellyn demonstrated some time ago, these sources hardly impose a geometric necessity on the court but provide at least a set of canonical justifications that can be offered more or less artfully to justify a particular subsumption of the facts expressed in the civil context often as a set of written conclusions (as in a complaint) and rules (Llewellyn, 1960). Further, there exist "rules of recognition" that determine which rules are authoritative. Authoritative rules are brought into conjunction with written factual conclusions, not disputed in any way that the court deems legally significant, to decide the case in summary fashion. Of course, this form of decision making does not exclude questions of policy, purpose, or context, but the semantic meaning of legal rules is at the center of at least the rhetoric of the court's decision making. As usual, there is a continuum here. Sometimes virtually all judges would agree that summary disposition is appropriate. In other cases, it appears that a particular judge's moral or political sensibility is decisive.

In exercising this function, the court screens out certain cases from going to trial at all. There are, of course, doctrinal standards for summary disposition. They are thought to support the rule of law as the law of rules. To an extent greater than exists at trial, the semantic meanings of legal rules are in play in this screening function. The social function of this screening function is, I suspect, to identify those cases that threaten basic and relatively abstract features of the basic structure of society that are thought to be too important to be thrown into competition with other norms that inhabit the society's life world and may effectively compete with the norms embedded in the semantic meanings of the rules. Rawls's notion that the "precepts of justice" are subordinate to the principles informing the basic structure is a normative expression of this view (Rawls, 1971, 303–310). Formalism and "mechanical jurisprudence" have their natural homes here. By deliberately depriving the decision maker of a large range of the personal, dramatic, and normatively charged particulars that would emerge at trial, the law may appear as a structure whose rigidity itself is appealing, which maintains a "stable worldly structure" (Arendt) that is the condition for planning and concrete freedom (Hart).

A Summary Phenomenology of Trial Practices

The foregoing account of how we know in the trial court is an abstract and theoretically driven account of how a certain philosophy of law understands the institution: as a set of practices for imposing the law of rules in situations when there are disputes of fact. It does touch down in the reality of actual trial languages and practices for the reason I gave: that philosophy of law has been and is embraced by legal actors committed to maintaining institutions consistent with it. Additionally, it is consistent with the assumptions underlying much doctrinal *and* empirical investigation of the trial so that those assumptions are imported into the conclusions of the investigation (Constable, 1994, 49–66).

There are many aspects of our actual practices at trial with which it is inconsistent (Burns, 1999, 26–33). The general verdict entered by juries in most civil and all criminal trials affords no assurance that the jury has actually decided the case in a manner consistent with the received view. The rule against "impeaching the verdict" prohibits inquiry into the mental processes and internal deliberation of jurors. Aspects of trial rhetoric inevitably invoke norms that emerge not from the law of rules but from the jury's life world. Liberalized pleading rules make access to the jury relatively easy. Appellate reviews of jury findings are very relaxed. There has been a strong drift in the law of evidence since the mid-1970s toward admissibility, and review of the trial judge's evidentiary determinations is permissive. (The law of evidence is, as we have seen, designed to keep the inquiry at trial focused on the issue determined by the law of rules.) And even errors in the trial judge's jury instructions, the holy of holies of the law of rules, are now often held to be harmless.

Further, one of the consistent findings of social scientific study of the trial is that juror comprehension of jury instructions is quite low (Charrow and Charrow, 1979). This is not surprising, given the focus of the lawyers who draft them on accurately reflecting the often very finely qualified generalizations in the legal doctrine. Appellate courts review jury instructions on a demanding *de novo* standard, and so trial courts are pressured into sacrificing clarity to be completely fair to all the qualifications that may inhabit the legal doctrine. This skeptical view of the extent to which the jury knows the law of rules embedded in the instructions is of a piece with the most consistent conclusions of the social science investigation of jury trials: Juries approach the evidence in an equitable rather than a rule-based manner; they are insensitive to many of the distinctions the law makes; their life-world values affect even the fact-finding process; the norms implicit in the narrative structure of the trial are of greater significance than the rules embedded in the instructions. Given that the jury is exposed to an intense and dramatic event often lasting weeks, can it be surprising that a half-hour of legal jargon will have relatively little effect on their verdicts (Burns, 1999, 141–154)?

It turns out, then, that even a compressed account of what actually happens at trial suggests that this received view commits the fallacy of misplaced concreteness that confuses one set of abstractions for a concrete reality. To understand how the law knows in the trial court, it is essential that we begin not with what a particular legal philosophy says about how the jury should know the facts and law but with the actual linguistic practices that prevail there. Then we can ask about the form of awareness that those practices are likely to occasion. *Then* we can ask whether that form of awareness can be called "knowledge." This is both a circular and a normative process, and our understanding of what knowledge is may well be modified by careful attention to the practices by which we achieve it. That means, of course, that I cannot really provide a detailed account here, something I have tried to do elsewhere (Burns, 1999). The summary I will now provide can be of limited use.

The trial does not begin with bits of circumstantial evidence relayed to the jury through testimony in the language of perception from which it inductively reaches a value-free factual conclusion that awaits the stamp of the law of rules. It begins with the opening statements of the lawyers. These complex narrative performances depend on construction of a double helix of norms drawn from strictly legal rules but also from common-sense morality, an "ethics already realized" in social institutions and practices. These narratives present to the jury "what the evidence will show" (not what the evidence will *be*). They express the lawyer's "theory of the case"—a simple, plausible, coherent, legally sufficient narrative that can easily be integrated with a moral theme. The battle for the jury's imagination that begins with the opening statement radiates through the case. Furthermore, the narratives have been chosen by the lawyers to effect the purposes of their clients to the extent that those purposes can be "narrativized." It follows, as John Dewey put it approvingly, an "experimental and flexible logic" that is "relative to consequences rather than to antecedents" (Dewey, 1924). A lawyer representing a competent but mentally ill criminal defendant who prefers an eight-year sentence for voluntary manslaughter to a not guilty by reason of insanity verdict followed by an indefinite psychiatric hospitalization will tell the defendant's story differently in opening statement, will tell the jury that "the evidence will show" something different about the defendant's state of mind than would the opening for the defendant who prefers the hospitalization.

This process of narrativization by which, as Hanna Pitkin put it, "I want" becomes "I am entitled to," is not seamless. It involves a mediation, a narrative resolution of tensions between the party's purposes and the community's norms, norms that are embedded in narrative form. Because opening statements are promises as well as stories, promises about what the evidence will show, the opening involves the resolution of tensions among the client's purposes, the legal norms, the common-sense morality of the community, *and* the evidence as it will be presented at trial. It is true that, as trial lawyers say, each bit of evidence "has two faces"—can be interpreted in different ways. (Does the fact that the defendant had four beers before the shooting mean that she didn't have the dexterity to fire the fatal shot or that she had the lowered inhibitions to do the deed? Does the very high level of certainty the witness shows about his identification of the defendant mean that his testimony is accurate or was the result of prejudice or other motives?) But evidence is not *infinitely* plastic. To borrow from Henry James, the evidence will be a kind of indeterminate pudding, but a "lumpy" pudding. And so no lawyer wants to "break the promise" made in opening by promising to show what the evidence fails to show.

Thus, the opening statements themselves, limited by the law of professional responsibility, embody the resolution, before the trial event starts, of an important tension—that between the purposes of the litigants and the stories that can fairly be told about the problematic situation that has led to the trial. Facts are not purposes, but stories can be told that are fair to facts and stretch out toward human purposes. One may say fairly that the trial is pragmatic "all the way down" in that the ultimate versions of events proposed by the litigants are constructed to effect purposes. However, the trial is not exclusively a *political* forum in that those purposes must be presented through *constrained* narratives that appeal to our common moral sentiments if "I want" is to be transformed into "I am entitled to." As Aristotle noted, narrative is the medium of forensic, not political, rhetoric.

Thankfully, not one opening statement is made, but two. This immediately relativizes each narrativization and alerts the jury to the gap between "what is told and the telling of it." On the other hand, it is usually impossible for the jury to compare the two accounts in openings to "the evidence" for the reasons alluded to earlier, that what the evidence is, even down to the most basic bare narrative, will be largely determined by the narrative within which the jury is persuaded to see it. And the narratives of opening statement will be relatively appealing for a number of different reasons. One or the other may be more internally coherent, more consistent with common sense (understood as a set of coping skills as well as a storehouse of empirical generalizations), more comprehensive in that it can interpret plausibly a larger range of the evidence to be presented, and invokes more important moral or political norms.

The trial is not, however, only about deft storytelling. The trial can achieve a truth *beyond* storytelling because of the severe tensions that are built up between the relatively comprehensive and "diplomatic" opening statements and the often jagged and idiosyncratic direct testimony of witnesses who are often uninterested in whether or not their accounts are easily subsumed within either theory of the case. If the openings appeal to common sense, the testimony provided in the language of perception serves as a critique of common sense. The jury cannot but see that things do not fall nicely into the ordinary "scripts" to which the lawyers appealed in the beginning. The cross-examinations of those same witnesses will be trying to tug them back toward each lawyer's theory of the case, an effort that witnesses may more or less successfully resist. The cross-examinations will also invoke fifteen or so modes of "impeachment" of the witness to suggest to the jury that they should not credit the witness's account, that it is the result of misperception, failures of memory, emotional allegiance to the adverse party, antipathy to the client, or some interest the witness may have in the outcome of the suit or in the continued affection of the adverse party. Cross may suggest as well that the trial account is not consistent, in blatant or more subtle ways, with earlier accounts the witness has given, that the witness is a known liar, or has run afoul of the law in ways that suggest untruthfulness. Each of these rhetorical commonplaces may be understood to rely on an empirical generalization that has the same "generally and for the most part" structure as do the generalizations that support the factual theory of the case itself. And each of these generalizations concerning credibility will be strengthened ("... especially when ...") or weakened ("... but not when ...") in the same kind of mutually determining manner as functions with regard to the factual theory of the case that I described earlier. Witness follows witness, and case follows case. Consider the vastness of those mutually conditioning probabilities as the case moves toward conclusion: requiring the resolution of "the cumulations of probabilities ... too fine to avail separately, too subtle and circuitous to be convertible into syllogisms" (Newman, 1930, 288).

But more than the simple complexity of the assumed calculation suggests that the trial is something other than a theoretical probabilistic exercise. Recall that the opening statements have moral and political force and that they suggest the appropriate mode of social ordering for the case. Recall as well that the determination (in the strong sense) of each bit of evidence depends on the narrative within which the jury ultimately comes to, chooses to, see it. Consider the never completely resolved tensions that the trial creates. Openings create tensions among factual theories and moral-political themes that pervade the case. Both sides will experience tensions between the diplomatic storytelling of opening and the extremely particular accounts of the individual witnesses. There are often unresolved tensions between the assertions of direct examination and the deconstructive methods of cross. There are important tensions, dramatized in the dialogic encounters between lawyer and witness, between what a witness wants to say and what the witness can say. There are tensions between what the lawyer wants the witness to say and what that witness refuses to say, a tension, by the way, that can cut in either direction.

There are harsh tensions between the roles of judge and lawyer and witness. The jury feels these dialogic tensions, and they are meaningful. The jury has a kind of prepredicative intuition of what these interpersonal encounters show about the actors and about the case. Ideally, and it is an ideal that is regularly realized, there the trial's structured hybrid of performances and languages will be an appropriate lens and metaphor to realize justice in the case. A strong case should allow lawyers and witnesses to engage in tension-filled encounters that "ring true" in the holistic perception that jurors have of the evidence. Performing the case makes that assessment possible. On the factual level, they will, of course be within the hermeneutical circle in which the parts and the whole are mutually determining. But they will also be within a practical circle of which "practical holism" gives the best account. The best course of action in the case and the jury's understanding of the case will also be mutually determining so that the patches of narrative necessary to sustain the best course also fall into place as that course becomes apparent.

There is a corollary about the nature of law. "True law," to use an older language, is precisely the intelligent performance of a jury or judge responding to the "discipline of the evidence" of a well-tried case. The latter, I believe, represents a considered judgment of justice embedded in our institutions and practices. In the language of analytical jurisprudence, the norms embedded in the practices of the jury's life world and its political identity, refined and disciplined by the linguistic performance of the trial, are intrinsic to law. Just as Dworkin maintains that "principles" identified by a normative philosophy of law that seeks to see law in its best light are intrinsic to law, I maintain that the norms embedded in all of the practices of the trial court are likewise intrinsic to law. To anticipate, this is what maintains law's distinctiveness in contrast to bureaucratic rule. But the phenomenology of the contemporary trial reveals that the law of rules, understood positivistically, *does* have a place in what I think is a fuller understanding of the trial. The instructions have some normative force. The lawyers must be concerned about the possibility of a directed verdict. The normative context of the trial is thus hybrid, and hence, it requires of the jury a highly contextual judgment of relative importance.

How the Trial Knows the Law of Rules

The jury also knows the rules in a way other than their jumbled announcement at the end of the trial. Ethical and evidentiary doctrines tend to encourage the lawyers to cluster the evidence they present around the rules. A lawyer must always be concerned about the possibility that the judge will direct a verdict if there is insufficient evidence on those issues that the substantive rules make central in the case. A judge may try to embarrass a lawyer who, in argument or the presentation of evidence, strays too far from what the law of rules interpreted by professional practices would justify. One of the standards of the double helix of norms mentioned earlier is formed by the norms explicit in the legal rules. The extreme consequences of a possible directed verdict will tend to cause evidence to accumulate around those rule-based norms.

The evidentiary doctrine of materiality is likely to have the same effect. All evidence must be linked by its proponent to an issue created by the law of rules to be "of consequence" to the case. The *factum probandum*—the factual conclusion to which each bit of evidence must be linked by a common-sense or occasionally scientific generalization approved by the judge—must be warranted by the specific norms embedded in the law of rules. As is so often true, the law of evidence here pulls in two directions. On the one hand, the judge is entitled to exclude a bit of evidence offered by an imaginative advocate that *does* meet the basic materiality threshold if its "probative value" judged by the standard that the law of rules is "substantially outweighed" by the danger, *inter alia*, of "unfair prejudice." Unfair prejudice occurs when the evidence is likely to evoke norms that are not embedded in the law of rules and may be in tension with them—for example "second-level" moral precepts about the goodness of persons, putatively irrelevant to legal decision making in the liberal state, or distributive norms about which party is best able to bear the burdens of social cooperation and interaction. Consider a case for defamation by a household employee against a wealthy householder who has accused the employee of stealing jewelry. The householder claims a defense of truth and urges that the household employee's nervousness on the morning in question is evidence of her guilt. Assume that the householder had recently violently shaken another maid who had inadvertently spilled coffee on him, and the household employee offers the incident as a "logically relevant" explanation for her demeanor on the crucial morning. The law of evidence would provide an argument that evidence of the incident should be excluded because, though relevant, it is likely to be considered for an improper purpose—to punish the householder for his past bullying of a sympathetic victim.

On the other hand, the law of evidence tilts toward admissibility in that the unfair prejudice in a potentially offending bit of evidence must *substantially* outweigh the probative effect to exclude the evidence. Once the evidence meets that threshold, its "weight" is a matter for jury consideration. Given the inevitably holistic and equitable modes of jury decision making, such evidence is likely to evoke consideration of the complete universe of jury norms and turn the issue before the jury to a determination of *which* norms are more important in the *particular* situation that the case presents.

In the trial court, the oral medium has a momentum of its own, an "autopoietic" quality. What is talked about is likely to be what is important. To an extent about which our practice is itself ambivalent, the doctrine of evidentiary materiality will tend to make the problematic situation that finds its way into the court *about* the issues that the law of rules dictates.

Why the Law Knows the Law of Rules in the Trial Court

How should we understand this "intrusion" of the law of rules into a forum whose phenomenology suggests cognitive operations in tension with rule-based decision making? There are a number of possibilities, generally quite compatible with one another. Both formalists and positivists will generally stress the importance of realizing the sovereign will of the people, as expressed in constitutional provisions and statutes. For a strictly formalist or positivist view of law, it is a deep misfortune that the fact-value and the fact-law distinctions are extremely provisional. Procedural rules can only cabin and never avoid the resolution of normative issues in the course of jury fact-finding. It is in the nature of things and language that "man cannot see by another's eye, nor hear by another's ear; no more can a man conclude or infer the thing to be resolved by another's understanding or reasoning. . . . [Juries] resolve both law and fact complicatively, and not the fact by itself."[9] The values underlying formalism and positivism are stability, predictability, and so effective planning and autonomy, control of officialdom, and realization of popular will at least insofar as the latter is currently realized through legislative action. They are not wholly illusory, though strict construction of constitutions and statutes often needs support from the moral, professional, and political sensibilities of the judge, which will generally be quite reliably consistent with regime values, to achieve those values. Unfortunately for the formalist, there are inevitably disputes of fact, and so we need an institution to institutionalize the law of rules in cases where such disputes exist. Because of the weakness of the fact-law distinction on the ground, we need special conventions that attempt to screen out the contamination of the trial with norms that do not have the proper pedigree. The received view of the trial has rightly pointed out that we employ procedural and evidentiary conventions at trial to serve that function.

A Blackstonian version of natural law theory provides a traditional justification for the place of the law of rules in the trial court. Here the notion is that constitutional interpretation and common law as corrected by statute embody normative judgments that are superior to the common-sense judgments that even an attentive and sincere jury is likely to reach. This notion leads in somewhat the same direction as the positivist-formalist perspective. Here again, the factual material in which the natural law will be "individuated" should have the qualities of that good Aristotelian principle of individuation, "prime matter." Evidence should be plastic to the imprint of the higher norms embedded in the natural law and so should bring with it as few popular life-world norms as possible. The hope here is that justice can be achieved at a level of generality consistent with the rather abstract accounts of the facts of previous cases and that "the facts" of the particular case fairly quickly reach a level of detail that is legally (and morally) irrelevant. The more contextual morality is, the more difficult this becomes.

Another understanding of the intrusion of the law of rules into the trial court in modern law would connect it with distinctions between the life world and the systems world. Large swaths of modern life are organized by systems that have "steering mechanisms" that do not touch down in the life-world common-sense moral intuitions. Theorists argue about the relative independence of these systems from the normative sources of the culture and the nature of the norms that may be applicable to structure and limit the systems worlds. The qualified role of the law of rules in the trial courts reflects one version of these disputes (Deflem, 1996).

The presence of the law of rules in the trial court may be understood from any of the foregoing perspectives. The law of rules in the trial court functions to give legal positivism and the values attendant to it their due. Likewise, they may reflect the place of the more basic and settled convictions that are embedded in the society's fundamental law. Finally, they may serve to preserve for the systems world the efficiencies that derive from highly abstract steering mechanisms. Of course, there are major disputes of all kinds that rage around those assertions, but some mixture of those accounts seems inevitable to explain our current practices.

How the Trial Can Know the Practical Truth of What Is

And so, does the law know at trial? The jury understands by relying on different levels of *constrained* narrative to build the ladder toward their understanding of the case. To the extent that narrative captures the reality of human action and is not an epiphenomenon, an "as if" added on, to the extent that stories are lived before they are told, to that extent will the jury know at trial. To the extent that the critical devices of the trial, cross and argument and rebuttal cases, are able to refine the limitations that inevitably inhabit the common sense that underlies the stories that seem most plausible to us, to that extent will the jury know in the trial court. They will know a truth beyond storytelling. Not that they will be able to represent or picture that truth to themselves because it will, once again, be consistent in a literally unimaginable grasp of facts, norms, and possibilities for action. That grasp allows them to go forward with practical wisdom.

To the extent that those same critical and deconstructive devices can sharpen the inevitably overgeneralized moral maxims and empirical generalizations as they are brought to bear through the "discipline of the evidence," to that extent will the jury know in the trial court. To the extent that the jury can dwell in the discursively irresolvable tensions that the trial creates and see the way forward, to that extent will the jury know at trial. To the extent that fundamentally interpretive methods can reveal the practical truth of a human situation, to that extent will the jury know at trial. To the extent that the devices of the trial illuminate the competing modes of social ordering available to the court and allow the jury to determine which is the most important, not in general but under the circumstances of the particular case, will the trial achieve the practical truth of the situation. This latter is crucial for us who have divided our social world into many competing spheres and whose "task is less to create constantly new forms of life than to creatively renew actual forms by taking advantage of their internal multiplicity and tensions and their frictions with one another" (Kolb, 1986, 259).

If, as Stuart Hampshire has recently argued, justice *is* conflict, then a multivoiced adversarial-style set of linguistic practices may be precisely suited to allow us to know what is just in particular situations. If, as Hannah Arendt urged, political situations are fundamentally plural, not only complex, in that the multiple perspectives the participants bring can never be theoretically or morally unified, but some "illumination" of those situations is still possible, then some sort of adversarial presentation may be fairest to human events. If, as Alasdair MacIntyre has argued over several decades, living traditions are traditions of ongoing conflict and bureaucratic styles of speaking and acting are ideological devices to suppress healthy debate, then the decline of adversarial forums and bureaucratization of American law are signs of malaise, not the advent of the peaceable kingdom ushered in by lawyer "problem solving." If, as Marianne Constable has recently argued, what separates law from bureaucracy is law's constitutive concern for justice, then the adversarial conditions for the "construction" of truth in the trial court may be the ideal conditions for us to know "true law" once we kick aside the necessary ladder of legal rules, so we can see "the poem behind the poem" and "know" a practical truth about how to go forward, which cannot wholly correspond to a consistent set of propositions. And if, as James White has argued for decades, a purely propositional notion of truth and an instrumental concept of law dominate the legal academy, then the usual forms of legal scholarship will consistently fail to understand how it is that the law knows in the trial court.

The reference to Arendt suggests that one brief clarification by contrast seems appropriate. The law does not know bureaucratically in the trial court.[10] Insofar as we identify bureaucracy with the vices of officialdom, the lay jury will surely not think bureaucratically. Insofar as we identify bureaucracy with the mindless imposition of overgeneralized and formal rules and purely inferential reasoning, the trial as we have it will not easily be a bureaucratic instrument of the modern state. The jury's decision making integrates; inference is ancillary to integration, and its mode of decision is equitable, not rule based. There is a much sharper dialectic within the trial between doing justice in the individual case and the maintenance of institutions of justice—in other words, between "the simultaneous creation of justice and the enabling conventions of justice" (Luban, 1994, 380). Insofar as we identify bureaucracy with achieving predetermined goals through instrumental reasoning, the trial will not be bureaucratic. For the jury, the trial does not serve as an instrument by which to shape outcomes extrinsic to the evidence. Insofar as we identify bureaucracy as "rule by nobody," the abdication of personal responsibility, the trial will not be bureaucratic. All of the narrative, rhetorical, and dramatic devices of the trial tend to invite a response of the whole personality to the trial itself. And so the decision reached at trial is not "rule by nobody," as Arendt described bureaucratic decision making. The prominence of ordinary language and the dramatization of the two-story structure that pervades ordinary moral decision making tend to engage the jury and preclude the kind of Cartesian aloofness of the decision maker that may well be a condition of purely instrumental reasoning.

A Final Reflection on the Inevitability of Practical Knowledge at Trial

We have reached the point where we can see the relationship between the philosophical considerations with which we began and the nature of the trial as we have it. There is, in some of the political debate surrounding the trial, the notion that the lack of full certainty surrounding much of what it does is a defect stemming from failures in institutional design. In some of the polemics, the suggestion is that issues now addressed at trial should be transferred to other modes of social ordering, typically the market or bureaucracies, that can achieve higher levels of certainty. But something would definitely be lost in such a quest for certainty. That we cannot know with either intuitive or deductive certainty either the past or the future is an essential element of our humanity, that which corresponds directly to our finitude and the primacy of the practical, in the sense of the primacy of the ethical. "An intellect which creates its contents is no longer an intellect as we experience it, and a will which contemplates is no longer what we know as will; in neither case do we conceive what is meant by an intellect and will in God" (Kroner, 1956, 118). Or as MacIntyre puts it in his polemic against what he takes to be Promethean, and false, claims of some social scientists to eliminate true contingency from the social world:

> [O]mniscience excludes the making of decisions. If God knows everything that will occur, he confronts no as yet unmade decision. He has a single will . . . It is precisely insofar as we differ from God that unpredictability invades our lives. This way of putting the point has one particular merit. It suggests precisely what project those who seek to eliminate unpredictability from the social world or to deny it may in fact be engaging in. (MacIntyre, 1984, 96–97)

Insofar as the trial is a practical enterprise and the ultimate determination the jury must make is a grasp of a constellation of facts, norms, and possibilities for action, it participates in this contingency. At the very least, the jury bears the responsibility of deciding how much uncertainty in a case is morally tolerable as a basis for the judgment they are asked to make. Their responsibility goes well beyond that. Responsibility for the consequences of trial decisions cannot ever be removed from jurors and placed in a mechanical process. That is one reason the trial is a rhetorical enterprise, for rhetoric rules where there must be decision under uncertainty. It relies on "the cumulative force of minute considerations" rather than rigorous deductive reasoning from a few premises. The truth it can hope to achieve bears some resemblance to Peirce's vision of philosophical argumentation, a thick cable that is strong though comprised of thousands of small and thin wires. "[I]t is mindful of logic, but more so of the incoherence and contradictoriness of experience" (Wolin, 1972, 44–45).

This kind of responsibility applies when one is trying to determine what has occurred in the past, a very important element of what occurs at trial. It is true that the notion that something determinate happened and that it is morally important to determine what it was serve a significant regulative function at trial. Again to quote MacIntyre, "man is in his actions and practice, as well as in his fictions, essentially a story-telling animal. He is not essentially, but becomes through his history, a teller of stories that aspire to truth" (MacIntyre, 1984, 216). But because we must approach the past through narrative, *we* cannot but accept responsibility for the accounts we give of the past. For outside a story, each fact about a human action is merely one of the "disjointed parts of some possible narrative" (MacIntyre, 1984, 215) and so quite incomprehensible.

As I mentioned earlier, *different* kinds of questions are asked at trial. The different sorts of stories, those of direct examination and of opening statements, for example, are answers to different sorts of questions. One question, the kind addressed by the narratives of direct examination, is, "What would you have seen had you been there?" Another is, "What do these human actions mean to us?" both morally and politically. Another is, "How should we respond to those actions as we understand them?" Narrative has the resources to address each of those kinds of questions, even the pragmatic ones. In the actual progress of the trial, the latter questions come first and the former questions later, usually to help adjudicate among competing narratives. But indeterminacy is often great even at the perceptual level, where enormously significant details conveyed to the court through the often watery medium of human memory are likely to be deeply in dispute. (What *exactly* did the defendant say? Where *precisely* was the victim standing?) The normatively characterized narratives come first in opening statement and begin the battle for the jury's imagination and judgment. There are multiple reasons for accepting one story rather than another, some of them normative. The whole is understood in light of the parts, and the parts in light of the whole. Both are understood in light of the possibilities for action that the jury has. And so, what each disjointed part is will be determined in part by its place within the more persuasive narrative. At the next level "above" determining what the contested details of the circumstantial evidence are, there is another level of indeterminacy. For each bit of circumstantial evidence[11] is connected with the bare narrative in which it has its place by a common-sense empirical generalization that has the form, "Generally and for the most part . . ." The inevitable question that follows is always, "Does the specific context of this particular case make that generalization more or less probable than it would be generally and for the most part?" But the existence and proper characterization of these additional "facts" that provide the context for the likelihood of primary fact have exactly the same relation to the primary fact, which provides part of the context for determining their probability. All circumstantial evidence is caught in this web of mutually determining probabilities often of enormous complexity and unique to the case at bar. This is the level at which Kalven and Zeisel's "liberation hypothesis" functions: The inevitability of fact indeterminacy at trial liberates the jury to follow its moral sentiments. Once again, this is not an accidental quality of our trial procedures but an inevitable aspect of our finitude as knowers. Commentators and judges who pretend this is not the case and suggest that "the law and the facts" dictate the result in any value-free logical sense are usually speaking ideologically.

Notes

1. Some thinkers argue that even pure science is intrinsically instrumental or "technological" insofar as its notion of truth is bound up with the successful modification of nature in theoretically driven experiments (see, e.g., Glazebrook, 2000).

2. In the twentieth century, the "linguistic turn" changed the preferred philosophical selection of terms from the human mind to human language, just as Kant's Copernican revolution had changed the preferred selection from the nature of things to the mind.

3. Various sets of reforms have been offered concerning the jury instructions. Some believe that rendering the law into simpler and clearer language is an important goal. Others believe that the timing of the instructions should be changed so that the jury hears the instructions at the beginning of the trial rather than at the end.

4. In a "triable" case, each lawyer should be able to offer plausible reasons to suggest that this narrative is mainly congruent with the story that he himself has told in opening statement along with the promise that this is indeed "what the evidence will show."

5. American Bar Association Model Rules of Professional Conduct (Model Rules), Rule 3.1.

6. Remember that I am describing the judge's function within the received view. I would not resist the notion that rulings on dispositive motions and on sanctions are determined by sources other than a formalist understanding of the semantic meanings of legal rules. Lawyers do consider the political perspectives of the bench and broader climates of opinion in deciding whether their cases expose them to Rule 11 sanctions. A higher level of predictability in the rulings of certain judges than of randomly selected juries would not prove that the predictability emerged from a more predictably *correct* interpretation of legal rules.

7. Of course, most criminal cases are disposed of through plea bargaining. The causes of this shift from public trial to private bargaining are themselves of great practical and theoretical importance (Fisher, 2003).

8. They do not by any means wholly eliminate the criminal defense lawyer's duty of candor to the tribunal. See Model Rules 3.3 and 3.4. On the other hand, Rule 3.1 provides

that the criminal defense lawyer may enter a general denial of the charges even on behalf of a client he knows to be "guilty."

9. Chief Justice Vaughn of the Court of Common Pleas in *Bushell's Case*, 6 How. St., Tr. 999, 1015.

10. I am using this term in an ideal-typical manner here. It may well be that even bureaucrats do not always know bureaucratically.

11. The law of evidence usually distinguishes between direct evidence and circumstantial evidence. Direct evidence, such as eyewitness testimony, merely has to be believed to be relevant. Circumstantial evidence has probative value because of links through chains of reasoning to some fact that is of consequence to the action. (Wigmore called these inferences "catenate" inferences, from the Latin *catena*, meaning "chain.") But since the probative value of direct evidence depends on the credibility of the witness, and credibility is inevitably determined circumstantially, the *probative value* of all evidence must be determined circumstantially.

Bibliography

Burns, Robert. *A Theory of the Trial* (Princeton, NJ: Princeton University Press, 1999).

———. "The Lawfulness of the American Trial," *American Criminal Law Review* 9, 2001, 205–239.

Charrow, R., and Charrow, V. "Making Legal Language Understandable: A Psycholinguistic Study of Jury Instructions," *Columbia Law Review*, 79, 1979, 1306–1374.

Constable, Marianne. *The Law of the Other: The Mixed Jury and Changing Conceptions of Citizenship, Law, and Knowledge* (Chicago: University of Chicago Press, 1994).

Deflem, Mathieu, ed. *Habermas, Modernity, and Law* (London: Sage Publications, 1996).

Dewey, John. "Logical Methods and the Law," *Cornell Law Quarterly* 10, 1924, 17–27.

Eisenberg, Melvin Aron. *The Nature of the Common Law* (Cambridge, MA: Harvard University Press, 1988).

Fisher, George. *Plea Bargaining's Triumph: A History of Plea Bargaining in America* (Stanford, CA: Stanford University Press, 2003).

Glazebrook, Trish. *Heidegger's Philosophy of Science* (New York: Fordham University Press, 2000).

Kisiel, Theodore. *The Genesis of Heidegger's "Being and Time"* (Berkeley: University of California Press, 1993).

Kolb, David. *The Critique of Pure Modernity: Hegel, Heidegger and After* (Chicago: University of Chicago Press, 1986).

Kroner, Richard. *Kant's Weltanschauung* (Chicago: University of Chicago Press, 1956).

Lieter, Brian. "Positivism, Formalism, Realism" *Columbia Law Review* 99, 1999, 1138–1364.

Llewellyn, Karl N. *The Common Law Tradition: Deciding Appeals* (Boston: Little, Brown, 1960).

Luban, David. *Legal Modernism: Law, Meaning, and Violence* (Ann Arbor: University of Michigan Press, 1994).

MacIntyre, Alasdair. *After Virtue*, 2nd ed. (Notre Dame, IN: University of Notre Dame Press, 1984).

Newman, John Henry. *An Essay in Aid of a Grammar of Assent* (London: Longmans, Green, 1930).

Rawls, John. *A Theory of Justice* (Cambridge, MA: Harvard University Press, 1971).

Scalia, Antonin. "The Rule of Law as a Law of Rules," *University of Chicago Law Review* 56, 1989, 1175–1188.

Sheehan, Thomas. "Reading a Life: Heidegger and Hard Times," in *The Cambridge Companion to Heidegger*, ed. Charles B. Guignon (Cambridge: Cambridge University Press, 1993).

Steinberger, Peter J. *The Concept of Political Judgment* (Chicago: University of Chicago Press, 1993).

Taylor, Charles. *Sources of the Self: The Making of the Modern Identity* (Cambridge, MA: Harvard University Press, 1989).

Tocqueville, Alexis de. *Democracy in America*, trans. Henry Reeve (New York: Vintage Books, 1945).

Warnke, Georgia. *Gadamer: Hermeneutics, Tradition and Reason* (Stanford, CA: Stanford University Press, 1987).

Wolin, S. "Political Theory as a Vocation," in *Machiavelli and the Nature of Political Thought*, ed. M. Fleisher (New York: Atheneum, 1972).

Fact-Finding in Constitutional Cases

DAVID L. FAIGMAN

The empirical world informs the Constitution's very meaning as well as its application to daily affairs. From its earliest opinions to today, the Supreme Court has consistently relied on facts to inform its constitutional jurisprudence.[1] Yet the Court has never developed an intelligible constitutional fact jurisprudence. No rules apply to courts' reception of constitutional fact-based evidence. Constitutional facts come to courts' attention through expert witnesses, legislative records, and briefs. Juries occasionally decide them, and at other times, judges do so. There has never been an attempt to set procedural rules for constitutional fact-finding. Burdens of proof are left, at best, implicit and are usually overlooked completely. Moreover, no general rules apply concerning the standard of appellate review of constitutional facts. Although a few scholars have weighed in on some of the issues presented by constitutional facts,[2] the subject remains adrift in an epistemological fog. This chapter seeks to give some direction to the subject of fact-finding in constitutional cases.

The theme of this book is *how law knows*, which raises the corollary issue of how the law "finds" and "constructs" facts. Fact-finding is one of the great silences in constitutional law. However large a role facts may play in actual constitutional cases, they have received little attention in constitutional jurisprudence. In attempting to redress this state of affairs, I can only offer a modest start here, for the task of establishing a coherent, much less a comprehensive, jurisprudence of constitutional facts is well beyond the pages accorded me in this book.[3] Instead, I seek to accomplish three principal tasks. In this first section, I provide a general introduction to the subject of constitutional facts. In the next section, I set forth a proposed taxonomy of constitutional facts that furnishes the foundation on which a coherent jurisprudence of constitutional facts might be built. In the final section, partly to demonstrate the solidity of the foundation constructed in the previous section, I address one of the most intractable issues of constitutional fact-finding—specifically, when, if ever, a lower court can distinguish (and thereby decline to follow) higher court precedent because the facts supporting that precedent have changed or our knowledge of them has changed.

Although it is a matter of some controversy, fact-finding is an essential component of both constitutional interpretation and constitutional adjudication. Historically, however, courts and commentators have sought to avoid this essential truth—and for good reason. Facts are highly indeterminate, and they inevitably destabilize the sought-after stability of fundamental constitutional values. For instance, many commentators were highly critical of the Supreme Court's seeming reliance on social science research in *Brown v. Board of Education*.[4] In concluding that segregated schools were "inherently unequal," the *Brown* Court cited the work of Kenneth Clark and others that indicated that blacks suffered psychological harm as a result of segregation.[5] Many prominent commentators challenged the Court's use of science on the basis that the findings were either obvious or largely irrelevant. Professor Ronald Dworkin, for example, beginning with a premise from another scholar, argued both of these together:

> "We don't need evidence for the proposition that segregation is an insult to the Black community—we know it; we know it the way we know that a cold causes snuffles." It is not that we don't need to know it nor that there isn't something there to know. There is a fact of the matter, namely that segregation is an insult, but we need no evidence for that fact—we just know it. It's an interpretive fact.[6]

Dworkin's term "interpretive fact" is a component of a legal theory he calls "creative" or "constructive" interpretation.[7] He analogizes constitutional interpretation to the writing of the latest chapter of a chain novel.[8] The interpreter fits his or her interpretations into the prior chapters and, at the same time, extends the overall work in the "best possible" direction. The theory contemplates first that the interpreter identify the "fit" between the interpretive history and the practice being interpreted and, second, that the interpreter impose a "purpose on an object or practice in order to make of it the best possible example of the form or genre to which it is taken to belong."[9] The difficulty in Dworkin's formulation, for present purposes, lies in understanding the role of science in this legal-interpretive discourse. Science certainly is used by the law as a means to accomplish certain objectives. But science, at least good science, does not permit any interpretation the interpreter desires, much less the "best possible." Although science cannot entirely divorce itself from its social context, sound science and reputable scientists have no preset agendas about the proper shape that the world should take. The law, in contrast, is primarily about setting such agendas. Whereas the insult associated with segregation may be plain legally (at least after 1954), just how plain it is as a matter of science depends on the data. How, then, should scientific interpretation be combined with legal interpretation? Although Dworkin has yet to address this specific issue, his chain of logic can be considered in regard to its application to the matter at hand.

If, as Dworkin apparently accepts, "there is a fact of the matter," even such a fact as the insult attributable to segregation, when is that "real-world" fact relevant and when is its interpretive cousin relevant? If all constitutional facts are repackaged under Dworkin's definition as merely interpretive facts, this solves one problem by creating another one. It solves the problem inherent in basing constitutional doctrine on indeterminate and changeable factual premises. Accordingly, in the *Brown* example, it would not matter what quantum of evidence might later be adduced to demonstrate the salutary attributes of state-sponsored segregation. If the fact is interpretive, no amount of data could ever disprove the "fact" that segregation is insulting. It is so, like other constitutional matters, because the Court says so. The problem this fact-finding by fiat creates, however, is the almost certain erosion of the legitimacy of Court pronouncements. Despite the elegance of Dworkin's efforts, the empirical world still exists outside the Court's dictates. Facts are what they are, and the Court's insistence otherwise will sometimes make it appear, at best, didactic and, at worst, dogmatic.

Dworkin's approach relies on an expansive notion of "facts." In his view, facts are elastic enough to be able to serve the normative needs of the Constitution. But the question is: Can we make facts mean whatever we want them to mean? Dworkin seems to vacillate between describing constitutional facts as a function of normative judgment and believing them to be a matter of common-sense experience. But the former—"normative facts"—are reminiscent of the practices of the sixteenth-century Catholic Church, and the latter resemble a caricatured version of the seventeenth-century inductive methods of Francis Bacon. We may know, as Dworkin argues we should know "interpretively," "that a cold causes snuffles." But surely, if the "interpretive" judgment is accurate, valid scientific studies should corroborate that judgment. Science is not irrelevant for demonstrating what everyone believes to be the case, though courts might wish to relegate studies corroborating the relationship between a cold and snuffles to a footnote. And some day, to our surprise, it might turn out that a malady only associated with colds causes snuffles and that we were wrong the whole time. Certainly, researchers should not be discouraged from studying the question on the basis that we know it to be true because we know it to be true.

In practice, of course, so-called "interpretive facts" play a steadying role. This utility is their virtue. Seen as an interpretive fact, the deleterious effects of segregation are not open to reexamination. An interpretive fact thus corresponds neatly with traditional notions of constitutional doctrine in that neither need change except by dictate of the Court. Real facts, in contrast, are mercurial. Given their proclivity for change, either because our knowledge of the facts improves over time or the facts themselves change, they provide, depending on your view, a healthily evolving or a disturbingly unsteady foundation for constitutional doctrine. Described as a factual matter, therefore, the holding in *Brown* that blacks are disadvantaged by segregation would appear vulnerable to refutation by well-designed studies that indicate that blacks are not disadvantaged or even are better off with this practice. This is probably not an occurrence to which the Court gave much thought in writing the *Brown* opinion. Almost certainly, the justices would have agreed with the gist of Dworkin's argument that changing facts regarding segregation's insult did not undermine the continuing validity of *Brown*. This proposition, however, was eventually tested in a courtroom in Savannah-Chatham, Georgia.

In 1963, in *Stell v. Savannah-Chatham*,[10] the county defended its segregated schools on the basis that black children in that locale, unlike in the cities involved in the *Brown* litigation, were not psychologically harmed by attending segregated schools. The plaintiffs argued that the district court had no discretion to reopen this factual question. According to the plaintiffs, it had been conclusively determined by the Supreme Court in *Brown* that segregation harmed black children. The trial court in *Stell* disagreed. The court explained that the lower court in *Brown* had found that "'segregation with the sanction of law . . . has a tendency to (retard) the educational and mental development of Negro children and to deprive them of some of the benefits they would receive in a racial[ly] integrated school system.'"[11] The judge stated, "[t]hese are facts, not law," explaining:

> Whether Negroes in Kansas believed that separate schooling denoted inferiority, whether a sense of inferiority affected their motivation to learn was increased or diminished by segregation was a question requiring evidence for decision. That was as much a subject for scientific inquiry as the braking distance required to stop a two-ton truck moving at ten miles an hour on dry concrete.[12]

Based on the expert testimony introduced in the case, the trial court concluded that "prejudices, whether ethnic, religious or racial, increase rather than decrease in proportion to the degree of non-voluntary contact between separately identifiable groups."[13] The court said that this "is a psychological phenomenon which was noted in the time of Periclean Greece."[14] Moreover, modern "studies made of actual intermixing of groups in classrooms confirm the predicted result that an increase in cross-group contacts increases pre-existing racial hostility rather than ameliorates it."[15]

On appeal, the Fifth Circuit summarily reversed the *Stell* district court. The appellate court admonished that "no inferior federal court may refrain from acting as required by [the *Brown*] decision even if such a court should conclude that the Supreme Court erred either as to its facts or as to the law."[16] Moreover, the circuit court discounted the importance of the social science evidence for the *Brown* result. "We do not read the major premise of the decision of the Supreme Court in the first *Brown* case as being limited to the facts of the cases there presented. We read it as proscribing segregation in the public education process on the stated ground that separate but equal schools for the races were inherently unequal."[17]

The Fifth Circuit effectively understood *Brown* "interpretively," in that the facts set forth in 1954 had become established law a decade later.[18] This creative approach to constitutional facts can be found in many cases.[19] Typically, the Court's first entry into a particular constitutional arena involves an ostensibly serious evaluation of the relevant factual underpinnings of the eventual holding. Subsequently, however, the precedent hardens into established constitutional doctrine, and as a consequence, the factual premises petrify.[20] If the relevant facts were not "interpretive" at the start, they become so once the case has entered the lexicon of settled law.

Treating facts interpretively solves the problem of having changeable constitutional standards due to a changing understanding of the empirical world. The factual premises are "interpreted" in conformance with the constitutional outcome, notwithstanding evidence to the contrary. But this stability comes at a cost. A rule that has outlived its reasons for being is correctly seen as illegitimate. As various justices have lamented, advancing technology threatens the stability of established precedent in a multitude of constitutional contexts.[21] If, for example, the right of reproductive choice is based on the medical concept of viability—the time after which a fetus is likely to survive outside the womb—the Court's failure to follow advancing technology will undermine the cogency of the precedent. The rule in *Roe v. Wade*[22] provides that states cannot prohibit abortions previability, a point in time of around twenty-four to twenty-eight weeks in 1973 and closer to twenty-two to twenty-four weeks today. However unlikely it might appear to be, a technological revolution in this area could move viability considerably closer to conception.[23] If a woman's basic right of choice is truly based on the values associated with viability, then the right should change as technology changes. Such a changeable constitutional jurisprudence could be derided as illegitimate.[24] Dworkin's interpretive fact approach ingeniously resolves this dilemma because interpretive facts are as solid as the doctrine demands or as flexible as they need to be to allow the doctrine to evolve. Under this approach, because constitutional facts are "interpreted" and not "found," justices can employ them with little fear that future researchers might call into question the premises of their handiwork.

Yet, the world does not always cooperate with the wishes of the justices or constitutional scholars. At least on occasion, scientists will demonstrate the errors in the Court's factual premises with enough certainty to engender doubt over the soundness of the Court's logic. Indeed, this can be expected to occur with increasing frequency as basic scientific methods improve or the Court finds facts that are amenable to more definitive proof. Opinions that employ facts interpretively are more reminiscent of Holy Writ than reasoned and informed legal judgment. But there is no inherent contradiction between enlightened factual investigation and a cogent constitutional jurisprudence. Constitutional doctrine should be informed by contemporary understandings of the empirical world. By necessity, such an approach would take into account the dynamic nature of fact-finding and science, albeit in combination with the paramount need for some measure of steadiness in constitutional doctrine.

The Configuration of Constitutional Facts

Any practical jurisprudence of constitutional fact-finding must have at its base a workable correspondence between the outside world and the task assumed by constitutional lawmakers. The Constitution was intended, and is generally considered, to be an eminently pragmatic document, so legal rules and decisions springing from it should be informed by the best evidence available. Facts, whether they are the function of decades of Nobel-level research or the anecdotal observations of a police officer, come to the legal system in a wide variety of ways. Constitutional facts arrive in court through expert testimony at trial, congressional (or other legislative) hearing testimony, amicus briefs, a court's own research, and many others. There would be little practical benefit in defining a comprehensive and rigid scheme for the reception of constitutional facts. A more salutary approach is to determine who within the judiciary will be the principal decision makers, who will be the ultimate decision makers, and most important, the dynamic between them.[25] This dynamic, in turn, depends on the kinds of factual matters that the Constitution makes relevant. Whether the empirical consequences of segregation by race are relevant, for instance, is a matter of constitutional interpretation. Moreover, whether the focus is on the consequences at a particular school in a particular city or on those effects more generally is also a matter of constitutional interpretation. In this section, I describe a framework by which the full range of constitutional facts can be classified. Only once they have been sorted can an intelligible jurisprudence be applied to them.

A Taxonomy of Constitutional Facts

In a landmark article, Professor Kenneth Culp Davis identified two basic kinds of facts having evidentiary significance.[26] The first he termed *legislative facts*, and the second he called *adjudicative facts*. According to Davis, legislative facts are those facts that have relevance to legal reasoning and the fashioning of legal rules.[27] In a later text, Davis explained, "[a]djudicative facts usually answer the questions of who did what, where, when, how, why, with what motive or intent. . . . Legislative facts do not usually concern the immediate parties but are general facts which help the tribunal decide questions of law and policy and discretion."[28] Judges typically decide questions of legislative fact. Adjudicative facts, on the other hand, because they are facts particular to the dispute,[29] are usually within the province of the trier of fact (the jury or, if there is no jury, the judge) to decide.[30]

A key distinguishing feature between legislative and adjudicative facts is the level of decision making at which the asserted facts are relevant. Whereas legislative facts ordinarily relate to matters that transcend individual disputes and would likely recur in different cases involving similar subjects, adjudicative facts ordinarily are peculiar to a particular case.[31] In *McCleskey v. Kemp*,[32] for example, the petitioner claimed that Georgia's capital sentencing system discriminated on the basis of the race of the victim. This allegation was based on an extensive and sophisticated study conducted by David Baldus and his colleagues. Among other things,

Baldus concluded that, all things being equal, "defendants charged with killing white victims were 4.3 times as likely to receive a death sentence as defendants charged with killing blacks."[33] This discrimination claim was based on legislative facts in that it was directed at the Georgia system as a whole and McCleskey did not allege that he personally was a victim of discrimination. As Justice Powell, writing for the Court, pointed out, "[e]ven Professor Baldus does not contend that his statistics prove . . . that race was a factor in McCleskey's particular case."[34] Indeed, of great concern for the Court was that "McCleskey's claim, taken to its logical conclusion, throws into serious question the principles that underlie our entire criminal justice system."[35] Legislative facts, as their name connotes, typically have broad impact across large areas of the law.

How the constitutionally relevant inquiry is described, therefore, as being at either the adjudicative or legislative level, obviously is of great importance. In principle, the Constitution itself establishes what sorts of facts are relevant under its dictates. In other words, the description of the relevant factual inquiry under a particular provision of the Constitution is an interpretive exercise. In the cases leading up to *McCleskey*, for instance, the Court had indicated that substantial evidence of *systemic* discrimination would constitute an Eighth Amendment violation.[36] The relevant facts under this earlier interpretation of the Eighth Amendment, then, were legislative in character. In *McCleskey*, however, the Court stepped away from this precedent. In its new interpretation of the Eighth Amendment, the Court redefined the level of relevant fact-finding. The *McCleskey* Court said that the relevant facts under the Eighth Amendment were case specific, or adjudicative, and held that claims of systemic discrimination were insufficient to sustain a cause of action. Under both the Eighth and Fourteenth Amendments, according to the Court, claimants had to demonstrate individualized discrimination. McCleskey was thus required to show that the jury, prosecutor, or judge had intentionally discriminated against him.

Davis's dichotomy generally describes the kind of fact-finding that occurs in constitutional cases, and it has become the established vocabulary for describing the kinds of facts that are relevant to legal discourse.[37] My approach roughly parallels Davis's, though the constitutional arena requires refinement of his approach. Davis's legislative fact category can usefully be distilled in the constitutional context into two subcategories, "constitutional rule-facts" and "constitutional review-facts."[38] This revision turns out to have special relevance for constructing procedural rules in constitutional cases.[39]

Constitutional rule-facts are advanced to substantiate a particular interpretation of the Constitution. Constitutional rule-facts join, and sometimes are a component of, the traditional sources of authority—the text, original intent, constitutional structure, precedent, scholarship, and contemporary values—in establishing the *meaning* of the Constitution.[40] Indeed, one of the most common bases for constitutional interpretation, original intent, is almost wholly fact-based. Most debates over original intent resolve down to disagreements over historical facts, such as whether the drafters of the Fourteenth Amendment expected it to invalidate segregated public schools or whether the Free Speech Clause was intended to cover obscenity. In addition, many arguments based on constitutional structure depend either implicitly or explicitly on hypotheses that might be the subject of political science or sociology. John Marshall's assertion in *Marbury v. Madison*,[41] for instance, that legislators are less likely than judges to be bound by a written constitution is a rule-fact of this sort.[42] Rule-facts, therefore, are employed to determine or justify the development of rules or standards that apply to all similarly situated cases. Constitutional doctrine, of course, is replete with examples of such rules and standards, including tiered-scrutiny in due process and equal protection, the *Miller* test for obscenity, *Brandenburg*'s incitement test, *Crawford*'s test of testimonial evidence under the Confrontation Clause, and so on. Many of these were based, in part, on empirical arguments. Moreover, virtually all of them establish constitutional inquiries that are answerable only by the other two kinds of constitutional facts—review-facts and adjudicative-facts.

Constitutional review-facts embody the more generally recognized function of legislative fact-finding in constitutional cases. Courts examine constitutional review-facts under the pertinent constitutional rule or standard to determine the constitutionality of the state's action. Review-facts transcend particular disputes and thus can recur in identical form in different cases and varying jurisdictions. Under the Commerce Clause, for instance, the applicable standard asks, among other things, whether the federal law "substantially affects interstate commerce."[43] A good example comes from *Gonzales v. Raich*,[44] in which the Court determined whether Congress had the authority under the Commerce Clause to regulate the home production of marijuana. Under the applicable standard, the Court had to consider whether Congress had a rational basis for concluding that home production of marijuana substantially affects price and national market conditions for marijuana.[45] The Court noted, initially, that "at least nine states . . . authorize the use of marijuana for medicinal purposes."[46] The question presented, therefore, implicated facts that transcended a particular dispute and thus involved constitutional review-facts. After reviewing the record and Congress's reasons for regulating, the Court concluded that "the regulation is squarely within Congress' commerce power because production of [marijuana] . . . has a substantial effect on supply and demand in the national market for that commodity."[47] The Court explained that "[o]ne need not have a degree in economics to understand why a nationwide exemption for the vast quantity of marijuana . . . locally cultivated for personal use (which presumably would include use by friends, neighbors, and family members) may have a substantial impact on the interstate market for this extraordinarily popular substance."[48] The Court concluded that "Congress' judgment is not only rational, but 'visible to the naked eye,' under any commonsense appraisal of the probable consequences of such an open-ended exemption."[49]

Constitutional rule-facts and constitutional review-facts refer to factual determinations that transcend particular cases and that are relevant to either the formation of a constitutional rule or the application of a rule to similarly occurring cases, respectively. *Constitutional adjudicative-facts*, in contrast, refer to factual determinations that are relevant to the application of constitutional rules in particular cases. For example, whether a police department "intentionally discriminated" against black police officers when it relied on an exam for making promotion decisions on which whites received significantly higher scores is a constitutional adjudicative-fact. Similarly, the likely consequence of Nazis marching through a predominantly Jewish neighborhood in Skokie, Illinois, would be a constitutional adjudicative-fact.

Unfortunately, no bright lines mark the boundaries between different kinds of constitutional facts. Because the procedural standards developed later in the chapter depend on these categorizations, however, ambiguity in this area is a matter of some consequence. More problematic still, uncertainty surrounding categorization arises across the entire spectrum of constitutional facts. The process of determining what facts are constitutionally relevant and what category they fall into must be determined on a case-by-case, or constitutional-provision-by-constitutional-provision, basis.

Classifying Constitutional Facts

Constitutional rule-facts are marked by their relevance to the formation or justification of constitutional rules or standards. Recognizing a constitutional rule-fact as such is often fairly straightforward. One of the most famous examples of a constitutional rule-fact comes from the litigation of *Brown v. Board of Education.*

The case was first heard during the Court's 1952–1953 term. Led by Chief Justice Vinson, a divided Court decided to hold the case over to the following term. The Court issued a series of questions for the parties to answer upon reargument. Several of these were directed at the historical question of whether the drafters of the Fourteenth Amendment had intended to invalidate segregated public schools by guaranteeing the equal protection of the laws.[50] In the opinion, Warren found that the historical materials were "not enough to resolve the problem with which we are faced. At best, they are inconclusive."[51] The historical fact of the drafters' and ratifiers' intentions regarding the scope of the Fourteenth Amendment was thus ostensibly relevant to the meaning it was to be given, though in the end the Court believed that these facts were known with too little certainty to be relied on. Other authorities would have to be used.

Frequently, however, the line between constitutional rule-facts and constitutional review-facts is indistinct. The more controversial factual issue in *Brown* involved the Court's citation to research indicating the negative effects of segregation on black schoolchildren. But was this evidence used to support a categorical rule prohibiting segregation by race, or was it proof that was relevant under a different rule, one that queried whether the state had a sufficient justification for its discriminatory treatment? The cases decided immediately after *Brown* suggest the former interpretation, that the research was employed in service of a new per se rule prohibiting segregation by race. After all, following *Brown*, the Court invalidated discrimination in a wide variety of public contexts and, along the way, never again mentioned social science data. Under this interpretation, the social science of *Brown*, to the extent that it had any value at all,[52] was merely employed to justify a new rule of law.

With the benefit of hindsight, however, it appears that the constitutional issue of segregation's effects is a review-fact and not a rule-fact.[53] The modern rule provides that discrimination by race (or segregation) is unconstitutional unless the state's scheme is justified by a compelling objective and the means used are closely tied to achieving that end. If Michigan, for example, were to create an all-black high school in Detroit that emphasized an African American curriculum, the state's means and ends would be strictly scrutinized rather than invalidated under some per se rule emanating from *Brown* and its progeny. Presumably, any defense of this segregation policy would be based largely on social science research regarding the benefits that would accrue to black students from a segregated high school education. The rule of *Brown* and its progeny seems to be that segregation by race is highly suspect but that it may be possible for a state to justify such disparate treatment if its reasons are sufficiently compelling. But admittedly, the matter is not free of all ambiguity. Nothing inherent in a particular constitutional fact dictates whether it is a rule-fact or review-fact. Categorization depends on how a particular court employs the fact, and this might only be determined in particular constitutional contexts by subsequent case law.[54]

The line distinguishing constitutional adjudicative-facts from other constitutional facts can also be elusive. In principle, adjudicative-facts should be readily recognizable. Constitutional adjudicative-facts involve only the case before the respective court, and their resolution should have little or no precedential value. Under the *Miller* test, for instance, one of three necessary findings of fact involves whether the allegedly offending materials appeal to the prurient interest.[55] This fact is determined on a case-by-case basis in light of local community standards. A finding in a Lexington, Virginia, court that a particular Mapplethorpe photograph is obscene, therefore, does not bind a court in Richmond, Virginia, that might be evaluating the same photograph. Similarly, in a libel action under *New York Times v. Sullivan*,[56] the question whether a false statement was made with "actual malice" will be unique to that particular case. Categorizing a fact as adjudicative or legislative will often be a straightforward exercise.

On occasion, however, determining whether a particular constitutional fact is adjudicative in character will not be obvious. Another component of the *Miller* test illustrates this very point. The third prong of the test requires, for a finding of obscenity, that "the work, taken as a whole, lacks serious literary, artistic, political, or scientific value."[57] Although this fact is to be determined in individual cases for specific materials in dispute, the question involves matters that transcend particular cases. Whether Nabokov's *Lolita*, for instance, has serious literary or artistic value is a fact of general import that is not readily classified into either the review-fact or adjudicative-fact bins. In the end, the decision whether to label a particular fact as adjudicative or otherwise may depend on what procedural path the court wants the fact to walk.[58]

The very act of classifying a fact as a rule-, review-, or adjudicative-fact is an interpretive exercise. A good example of the freedom inherent in classifying constitutional facts, and the policy ramifications that follow from such classifications, comes from the Court's standard for reviewing the constitutionality of abortion regulations. In *Planned Parenthood of Southeastern Pennsylvania v. Casey*,[59] the Court ruled that regulations that impose an undue burden on the exercise of the right to a previability abortion are unconstitutional. The undue burden standard was operationally defined to include any regulation that created a "substantial obstacle" to the exercise of the right. In *Casey*, the Court invalidated the spousal notification provision of the disputed law applying this rule. The opinion for the Court, written by Justices O'Connor, Kennedy, and Souter, treated the issue as a review-fact and itself found that research indicated that domestic violence might occur in a small percentage of cases as a result of this notification requirement. There was no suggestion that the claimants before the Court had experienced, or were in danger of suffering, violence due to the spousal notification requirement. Yet the prospect of such violence in the class of possible complainants, even if it constituted only a small percentage of cases, was enough to invalidate the law in all cases.

At the same time, the *Casey* Court upheld the twenty-four-hour waiting provision, finding the proof inadequate to conclude that such requirements unduly burden the right. But is this issue a review-fact or an adjudicative-fact, and if the former, was the appropriate domain the nation or the state? In *Woman's Choice-East Side Women's Clinic v. Newman*,[60] the Seventh Circuit offered a confusing, if not confused, answer to this question. The district court had enjoined Indiana's informed consent law shortly after it was enacted on the basis that it would constitute an undue burden. Under the Indiana law, women had to wait at least twenty-four hours after receiving information regarding the risks of the abortion procedure, thus necessitating two visits to the abortion provider. The lower court enjoined this specific provision on the basis of empirical studies conducted in Mississippi and Utah that indicated that the higher costs it imposed would reduce the number of abortions performed in those states by 10% to 13%. Yet, as pointed out by the Seventh Circuit, no research was available regarding the effect that the present requirement would have in Indiana, and the researchers had not compared the experience of Mississippi and Utah to Indiana. At the same time, however, depending on how the legal question was defined, the research might not have to apply specifically to Indiana at all for the Indiana law to be invalidated on the basis of that research. In other cases, the Court had employed a national scope for determining when abortion regulations constituted undue burdens. In *Casey* itself, the Court struck down the spousal notification provision based on general research and did not inquire regarding statewide experience under the challenged Pennsylvania law. In *Stenberg v. Carhart*,[61] the Court similarly used a national focus when it invalidated a Nebraska law that prohibited the use of "intact dilation and extraction," or what critics have dubbed "partial-birth abortion." In subsequent litigation over this issue, in particular involving congressional legislation on the subject, courts have routinely considered the relevant level of analysis to be at the review-fact stage.[62]

In cases like *Casey* and *Stenberg*, the national approach served the strong jurisprudential value of ensuring consistent constitutional outcomes from state to state.[63] The *Newman* court explained the Supreme Court's approach:

> [C]onstitutionality must be assessed at the level of legislative fact, rather than adjudicative fact determined by more than 650 district judges. Only treating the matter as one of legislative fact produces the nationally uniform approach that *Stenberg* demands.[64]

The Seventh Circuit, however, after setting forth this sound explication of why the relevant fact is a national legislative fact, devoted the lion's share of its opinion to evaluating the applicability of the research to the operation of the challenged provision *in Indiana*. The court observed that "because the undue-burden approach does not prescribe a choice between the legislative-fact and adjudicative-fact approaches, we think it appropriate to review the evidence in this record and the inferences that properly may be drawn at the pre-enforcement stage."[65] Based on this analysis—what essentially constituted a state-level review-fact analysis—the Seventh Circuit reversed the district court's ruling:

> Indiana is entitled to an opportunity to have its law evaluated in light of experience *in Indiana*. . . . [I]t is an abuse of discretion for a district judge to issue a pre-enforcement injunction while the effects of the law (and reasons for those effects) are open to debate. What happened in Mississippi and Utah does not imply that the effects in Indiana are *bound to be* unconstitutional, so Indiana . . . is entitled to put its law into effect and have that law judged by its own consequences.[66]

The logic of the Seventh Circuit's *Newman* decision is not obvious. If, indeed, *Stenberg* specifically, and this area of the law more generally, "demands" the application of a "uniform approach," then the "experience in Indiana" is not particularly relevant to the ultimate determination. It may very well be that the Mississippi and Utah studies were not sufficiently valid or persuasive to conclude that, on a national scale, informed consent provisions like Indiana's unduly burden the abortion right. But that is a very different determination than saying that the research does not apply in Indiana. Indiana's particular experience is largely irrelevant under *Casey*'s and *Stenberg*'s apparent interpretation of the relevant level of factual inquiry.

As already emphasized, the issue of what level of factual inquiry should be employed in a particular constitutional context (i.e., adjudicative-, review-, or rule-fact) is an interpretive matter. Both *Casey* and *Stenberg* appear to treat the applicable inquiry under the undue burden standard as a nationally defined review-fact. It is possible, however, to distinguish the twenty-four-hour waiting provision from the *Casey* and *Stenberg* subjects of spousal notification and late-term abortion. Whereas the *Casey* and *Stenberg* subjects do not vary from place to place, a twenty-four-hour waiting provision might be more or less burdensome depending on the state in which it operates. Waiting twenty-four hours might be a very substantial obstacle in Oklahoma or Utah, but not particularly burdensome in Rhode Island or Delaware, because of the respective distances some women might have to travel to obtain abortion services. Regardless, whatever the judgment regarding the level of fact that is relevant under a particular constitutional provision, it should be an explicit part of the constitutional analysis.

Although sorting constitutional facts into their respective categories appears somewhat haphazard, certain conclusions can be offered in regard to this process. First of all, the distinction between adjudicative-facts and review- and rule-facts in constitutional cases is mainly clear in theory, though not always in practice. Adjudicative-facts pertain to specific cases and have little or no precedential force, whereas review- and rule-facts are general in nature and usually have import as a matter of precedent. These general facts will sometimes be relevant to the definition of the constitutional rule itself (i.e., constitutional rule-facts) or, more often, will be relevant when some rule is applied to a set of general facts (i.e., constitutional review-facts). Second, the decision whether the relevant fact under a particular constitutional rule falls into one category or another is an interpretive judgment; and it is a judgment that should always be made explicitly. Under *Casey*'s undue burden standard, as discussed earlier, the determination whether a twenty-four-hour waiting provision constitutes a "substantial obstacle" could be an adjudicative-fact or a review-fact. Indeed, at the review-fact level, the pertinent scope for fact-finding could be national, statewide, or the respective court's jurisdiction. What measure of fact-finding is ultimately deemed appropriate must depend on the constitutional principles or values at stake. Finally, the choice made regarding what kinds of facts are relevant under a particular constitutional provision will affect the process by which those facts are found. The sort of evidence used to prove adjudicative-facts typically differs markedly from the sort of evidence used to prove review-facts.

Defining the kinds of facts that are relevant under particular constitutional provisions is an essential prerequisite to establishing the processes by which these facts are found or the precedential force of having found them. As noted earlier, a court's finding, for instance, that a particular book "appeals to the prurient interest" in Lexington, Virginia, has no precedential force in an obscenity case arising in Richmond, Virginia. As a consequence, it would be unsurprising for the U.S. Court of Appeals for the Fourth Circuit to affirm a civil verdict *against* the publisher in Lexington but *for* the publisher in Richmond based on this prong of the *Miller* test. Constitutional review-facts, in contrast, present considerably more challenging issues because, by definition, they transcend individual disputes. For instance, if defined as a constitutional review-fact, the Fourth Circuit's ruling that *Lolita* has redeeming literary value would presumably be binding on district courts in that circuit. The next section takes up these issues and considers the particularly vexing question of whether a lower court should have the power to reconsider higher court authority when the facts on which that precedent was established have changed.

Lower Court Review of Higher Court Fact-Finding

General Considerations

It goes without saying that the judiciary is structured hierarchically. Higher court legal judgments are binding on lower courts. This would appear especially so in the constitutional arena. After all, it was John Marshall who famously declared that it was his Court's duty to "say what the law is."[67] But what happens when settled law relies on changeable facts? If the underlying predicate facts of a higher court's holding should change, should lower courts subsequently be allowed to revisit the holding taking into account this new information? The answer may well depend on an assortment of considerations. Indeed, this subject implicates certain foundational premises of the American constitutional system. Given the richness of the subject and the large role facts play in constitutional decision making, it is surprising that the Court has given so little attention to this matter.

Perhaps the only time that the issue was squarely presented regarding a lower court's power to distinguish precedent because predicate facts had changed was in *Roper v. Simmons*.[68] The principal issue in *Roper* was the constitutionality of imposing the death penalty on convicted killers who were sixteen or seventeen years of age when they committed their crimes. In 1989, in *Stanford v. Kentucky*,[69] the Court had held that this practice did not offend the Constitution. In 2003, however, the Missouri Supreme Court distinguished *Stanford* on the basis that the predicate facts on which that decision rested had changed and ruled that executing those who had committed their crimes when they were under eighteen years of age violated the Eighth Amendment's prohibition of cruel and unusual punishment. In particular, the Missouri court found a shift in national public sentiment indicating that such punishment now ran afoul of contemporary standards of decency.[70] The Supreme Court granted certiorari on two questions. The first was the constitutionality of executing those who had committed their crimes as juveniles. The second concerned the question at issue here: "Once this Court holds that a particular punishment is not 'cruel and unusual' and thus barred by the Eighth and Fourteenth Amendments, can a lower court reach a contrary decision based on its own analysis of evolving standards?"[71]

Justice Kennedy's opinion for the Court, however, did not mention, or even allude to, this question. The Court, instead, limited its analysis to the principal question presented—the constitutionality of executing minors. Affirming the Missouri decision, the Court held that imposing capital punishment on juveniles violated the Eighth Amendment's ban on cruel and unusual punishment. The Court relied on three grounds for its holding, all of which involved statements of scientific or social scientific fact. First, based on surveys of state practice, the Court agreed with the Missouri court that, in the period of time since *Stanford*, the national consensus had shifted sufficiently to cast doubt on the premise that executing juveniles met modern "civilized standards of decency."[72] Second, the Court found that juveniles were distinguishable from adults in three ways that indicated that they "cannot with reliability be classified among the worst offenders."[73] These grounds include juveniles' (1) underdeveloped sense of responsibility and general immaturity as compared to adults, (2) susceptibility to outside influence and peer pressure, and (3) lack of fully formed characters. These three characteristics indicated juveniles' diminished culpability which, according to the Court, meant "that the penological justifications for the death penalty apply to them with lesser force than to adults."[74] The final argument advanced by the Court to support its holding was "the stark reality that the United States is the only country in the world that continues to give official sanction to the juvenile death penalty."[75]

Although the majority opinion ignored the question of a lower court's power to find facts contrary to higher court authority, the separate dissents of Justices O'Connor and Scalia did not. Both justices took extreme umbrage at the lower court's temerity. O'Connor wrote that she took "issue with the Court's failure to reprove, or even to acknowledge, the Supreme Court of Missouri's unabashed refusal to follow our controlling decision in *Stanford*."[76] She conceded that the Eighth Amendment rule calling for a contemporary assessment of "evolving standards of decency" meant that "significant changes in societal mores over time may require us to reevaluate a prior decision."[77] But, she emphasized, "it remains '*this* Court's prerogative *alone* to overrule one of its precedents.'"[78] Finally, she warned, "[b]y affirming the lower court's judgment without so much as a slap on the hand, today's decision threatens to invite frequent and disruptive reassessments of our Eighth Amendment precedents."[79]

Justice Scalia similarly found the behavior of the lower court intolerable. As an initial matter, he rejected the entire premise that the Eighth Amendment's meaning changes with evolving standards of decency.[80] Scalia said that it "add[s] insult to injury" that the "Court affirms the Missouri Supreme Court without even admonishing that court for its flagrant disregard of our precedent in *Stanford*."[81] The lower court's insolence, according to Scalia, was a product of a jurisprudence that permitted the Constitution's meaning to change as circumstances changed. He observed as follows:

> The Court has purported to make of the Eighth Amendment . . . a mirror of the passing and changing sentiment of American society regarding penology. The lower courts can look into that mirror as well as we can; and what we saw 15 years ago bears no necessary relationship to what they see today. Since they are not looking at the same text, but at a different scene, why should our earlier decision control their judgment?[82]

In addition, Scalia noted that this danger was not limited to any "special character" of the Eighth Amendment. "Nothing in the text reflects such a distinctive character—and we have certainly applied the 'maturing values' rationale to give brave new meaning to other provisions of the Constitution, such as the Due Process Clause and the Equal Protection Clause."[83] Left unchecked, Scalia warned, the majority's permissiveness would allow lower courts to reinterpret the Constitution "whenever they decide enough time has passed for a new snap shot."[84] This outcome "leaves this Court's decisions without any force," a result that "crown[s] arbitrariness with chaos."[85]

Possibly the starkest example of the nightmare Justice Scalia envisions, and one that might unsettle the more liberal-minded justices as well, comes from *Stell v. Savannah-Chatham*, discussed earlier in the chapter. The *Stell* district court distinguished *Brown v. Board of Education* on the basis that black children in its locale, unlike those in Topeka, were not psychologically harmed by attending segregated schools. The trial court concluded, therefore, that whatever the state of the facts existing in 1954 in Topeka, the weight of the evidence indicated that in 1963 in Savannah-Chatham County, black and white children would mutually benefit from separate schooling.

In summarily reversing the *Stell* district court, the Fifth Circuit stated that "no inferior federal court may refrain from acting as required by [the *Brown*] decision even if such a court should conclude that the Supreme Court erred as to its facts or as to the law."[86] Further, the circuit court discounted the importance of the social science evidence for the *Brown* result. "We do not read the major premise of the decision of the Supreme Court in the first *Brown* case as being limited to the facts of the cases there presented. We read it," the court observed, "as proscribing segregation in the public education process on the stated ground that separate but equal schools for the races were inherently unequal."[87]

The Fifth Circuit, therefore, made two arguments for why the *Stell* trial court had erred. The first was that a lower court was bound by the factual findings and legal conclusions of a higher court, and the second was that the holding in *Brown* had not depended on the factual findings set forth in the opinion. The latter argument was not controversial in itself because it simply concerned the appellate court's assertion that the trial court had misinterpreted the *Brown* decision. Whereas the trial court had believed that *Brown* was premised on the fact-based psychological consequences of segregation, the Fifth Circuit held that it rested on the legal principle of equality. No one seriously believes that a lower court should have the power to reassess a higher court's *legal* judgments. If this legal assessment had been the full extent of the Fifth Circuit's decision, it would have been unremarkable.

The Fifth Circuit's former statement—that the trial court had inappropriately reconsidered factual findings previously made by a higher court—is considerably more open to question. The Fifth Circuit essentially held that lower courts do not have the power to reconsider the predicate facts of otherwise binding precedent. But the court did not explain the basis for this conclusion. It simply assumed that it was obviously correct, much as Justices O'Connor and Scalia assumed the obviousness of this conclusion in *Roper*. The conclusion that lower courts cannot revisit constitutional facts—and in due course, higher court constitutional precedent—is not at all obvious. This statement of the law is too broad, for it fails to consider the different kinds of constitutional facts that percolate up and trickle down the hierarchy of the courts. This principle of deference might be obviously correct regarding some kinds of constitutional facts, but it is not with regard to all kinds of constitutional facts. The three basic kinds of fact—rule, review, and adjudicative—present very different issues regarding their place in the lexicon of constitutional doctrine.

Specific Considerations

A basic argument of this chapter is that facts should be taken seriously when they are offered as a component of constitutional decision making. Implicit in this argument is the assumption that "facts" are out there to be found. I don't mean to suggest, however, that constitutional facts—of whatever variety—can always be found with a high degree of certainty or without a good deal of baggage associated with the socially constructed worlds of their finders. Facts, whether they concern the question of when a fetus has the lung capacity to survive outside the womb or the question of the empirical consequences of locating adult-entertainment establishments in particular neighborhoods, are known with more or less certainty. The potential for error associated with virtually all fact-finding means that, as a normative matter, the law must allocate the risks associated with making a mistake. The law primarily accomplishes this through procedural devices such as burdens of proof and presumptions. In criminal cases, for instance, where the consequences of making an error of guilt ("false positive") are substantial, the "beyond a reasonable doubt" rule is used; in civil cases, in which similar errors of inclusion have less gravity, the more lenient "preponderance of the evidence" standard is employed. In constitutional fact-finding, the prospect of error (whether of the false positive or false negative variety) should be a key element in the development of rules of procedure. As a consequence, therefore, the issue of how well the fact must be known is a legal determination. Viability, for example, is actually a statistical prediction of fetus survivability. Whether the probability of survival must be 10% or 90%, estimates that directly correspond with gestational age, must be resolved as a matter of law. What the probability of survival is at, say, twenty-seven weeks, on the other hand, is a constitutional review-fact.

An additional, and fundamental, consideration in devising rules of procedure for constitutional facts is the variety of players who might be involved in the fact-finding process. For present purposes, the principal actors in this drama range from jurors to Supreme Court justices, with trial and appellate judges in between. Any workable procedural scheme will have to be tailored to the respective roles these participants are assigned to play under the Constitution. In general, for instance, jurors are limited to deciding facts in particular cases, while judges are obligated to say what the law is, a task that includes, at the least, finding rule- and review-facts. But the realities of this seemingly simple division of authority are rather more complicated in practice. Procedural rules must account for this complexity, and they create a rational dynamic between the respective finders of fact at every level of constitutional process. The rationality of this dynamic must be found in the Constitution itself.

Professor Davis's original division between legislative- and adjudicative-facts was based largely on the identity of the fact-finder deciding the fact rather than the legal relevance of the fact. If the fact was found by lawmakers, it was legislative, and if found by the trier of fact (jury or, if none, judge), it was adjudicative. There was thus a degree of circularity in his taxonomy. The very same fact might be described as adjudicative because it was part of a jury's deliberations and as legislative because a lawmaker used it to form or interpret the law. To a large extent, I turn Davis's scheme on its head. In my taxonomy, facts are classified on the basis of the demands of constitutional doctrine. What facts are material to the resolution of a constitutional dispute, therefore, depend on a reading of the Constitution. Thus, for example, whether the issue of the factual consequences of a spousal notification provision, as presented in *Casey*, is a review-fact or an adjudicative-fact depends on the values inherent in the Due Process Clause. As a general matter, very different consequences follow depending on what type of constitutional fact is involved. The costs and benefits associated with those consequences are a matter of constitutional import. The following sections consider some of those costs and benefits in regard to the single issue of whether a lower court should have the authority to reconsider higher court precedent when the facts on which that precedent depend have changed.

Constitutional Rule-Facts. Constitutional rule-facts are relevant to the definition of, or establish the foundation for, a constitutional rule or standard. Although the line between rule- and review-facts can sometimes be blurry, in most cases the distinction is clear. The distinction is based on the difference between interpreting the Constitution and applying it. In *Roe v. Wade*, for instance, the Court established the end of the second trimester—viability—as the point in time when the state's interests were sufficiently compelling to justify prohibitions of abortion, subject to exceptions for the health of the mother. In *Casey*, the Court reaffirmed this rule, calling it the "central holding" of *Roe*. The selection of viability was based on a host of arguments, including historical practices, the nature of the doctor–patient relationship, precedent, and in the end, the Court's assessment of the strength of the state's interest in preserving the potential life of the fetus. The Court balanced the nature of the right against the strength of the state's interest and established a standard that was fastened to the point at which a fetus was likely to survive outside the womb. Viability thus became the rule to be applied in subsequent cases.

Describing viability as the rule to be applied suggests that if medical technology were to change, the contour of the "right" would change as well. Indeed, this is one of the principal features of employing rules that depend on possibly different circumstances occurring from those that existed when the rule was first defined. It could be argued that the compromise point—viability—was really chosen for certain unstated reasons, such as giving the pregnant woman sufficient time to exercise her right to an abortion. Under this interpretation of *Roe*, the "rule" is not viability at all but rather the end of the second trimester—twenty-four weeks—approximately the time at which viability occurred in 1973. Of course, changes in technology or medical science would not affect the twenty-four-weeks rule. But the Court never said that the rule was twenty-four weeks; it said, and thereafter has maintained, that the rule is "viability"—presumably whenever that should occur.

The issue of what the "rule" is in *Roe* is reminiscent of the debate following *Brown v. Board of Education* as to whether the holding in that case depended on the factual question of segregation's effects or on the inherent inequality of separate schooling. If the former, subsequent research could result in different outcomes, and segregated education might pass constitutional muster. This, of course, was the *Stell* district court's reading of *Brown*. If the latter, the rule would be that segregated schools are per se unconstitutional, the Fifth Circuit's reading of the case. Given the modern test of strict scrutiny, it appears that the district court's interpretation of *Brown* was more accurate and that, at least if the state's interests were compelling enough, segregated public schools would be constitutionally permissible. If this interpretation is correct, then the *Stell* court's attempt to distinguish *Brown* based on different factual circumstances was wrong because it got the facts wrong, not because it should have refrained from any reconsideration of how the equality rule of *Brown* should be applied when the factual circumstances have changed.[88]

Similarly, subsequent precedent should reveal whether the rule in *Roe* was viability or twenty-four weeks. If the former, changing technology should lead the Court to contemplate an alteration in the twenty-four-week point in time, whereas if the latter, twenty-four weeks should remain inviolate, subject always to the possibility of it being replaced with another rule. The answer seemed to come from *Webster v. Reproductive Health Services.*[89] In *Webster*, the Court upheld a Missouri law that, among other things, required physicians to use medically appropriate tests to determine whether a fetus was viable at twenty or more weeks of gestational age.[90] Although the Court did not discuss the issue explicitly, it effectively accepted the Missouri scheme of treating viability as a constitutional adjudicative-fact. After twenty weeks, the viability of every fetus was to be measured individually. In contrast, if *Roe* had stood for an inviolate rule of twenty-four weeks, the Missouri viability testing provision would have been invalid as a matter of law. Under *Roe*, therefore, at least as it is presently applied, viability is the rule and, in some situations, will be applied on a case-by-case basis.

But the decision to adopt a rule employing the medical concept of viability also depended partly on factual arguments. In particular, Justice Blackmun cited extensive historical sources regarding both ancient and more contemporary abortion practices. Indeed, justices contemptuous of *Roe*'s holding have long expressed particular disdain for this historical analysis.[91] What if, then, a lower court had access to a new and definitive examination of the historical issues surveyed in *Roe*? Should that Court have the authority to reconsider the rule of viability? Or suppose that a treasure trove of historical documents was discovered that indicated unequivocally that the drafters and ratifiers of the Fourteenth Amendment uniformly believed that adoption of the Equal Protection Clause would not result in integrated public schools. Would a lower court have the power to employ these new facts to reassess the continuing validity of the holding in *Brown*?

The answer to these and similar questions is no. Lower courts cannot have the authority to reevaluate the empirical bases for constitutional rules or standards. An essential question raised in these sorts of cases is whether the rule would be different if the facts were to change. Any procedure that would allow lower courts to distinguish higher court precedent and come to a different conclusion about the Constitution's meaning would have to be able to answer this question in the affirmative. By their nature, however, constitutional rule-facts are almost invariably set forth as part of a litany of premises offered to support a rule or standard. Rarely do they stand alone, and when they do, they are often considered—at the time or later—as proxies for normative principles or values. The historical premises underlying conclusions regarding original intent are routinely buttressed by arguments from the text, precedent, and constitutional structure. The Constitution's meaning is stitched together from a patchwork of authorities, and a change in the understanding of one or two will not necessarily undermine the soundness of the rule.

As a practical matter, therefore, the boundary between fact and value is nearly impossible to ascertain when a doctrine is premised on constitutional rule-facts and other considerations. Given the entangled relationship between values and facts in interpreting the Constitution's meaning, this would be impossible in the vast majority, if not in all, cases. The authorities that the Court relies on to discern the Constitution's meaning tend to be a mixture of normative and empirical. In most cases, it would be impossible for a lower court to disentangle the empirical from the normative or be able to say whether the Constitution would mean something different if the facts were to change or our knowledge of them changed.

Constitutional Adjudicative-Facts. Adjudicative-facts occupy the opposite pole from that of rule-facts in constitutional cases. Whereas rule-facts affect whole areas of law and are an inextricable component of lawmaking, adjudicative-facts have minimal impact outside the immediate litigation in which they are found.[92] Because constitutional adjudicative-facts are unique to particular cases, they appear to present little difficulty on the question of lower court power to reconsider higher court precedent. And this will be true in most situations mainly because there will be no higher court rulings on the specific factual question. In a defamation case, for instance, the application of the *New York Times v. Sullivan* "actual malice" test will be highly context specific. The question of whether a statement was made "with knowledge or reckless disregard of its falsity" will have to be determined on a case-by-case basis.[93] At the same time, however, two aspects of constitutional adjudicative fact-finding implicate principles that transcend individual cases. The first involves the obvious one that the initial definition of the applicable test is a matter of law. The choice of the "actual malice" standard itself, then, is a rule that could only be reconsidered by the Supreme Court. The second aspect of constitutional adjudicative-facts is a component of the first but worthy of separate consideration. The burden of proof that must be met in constitutional cases is set as a matter of law.

The subject of burdens of proof is considerably more complex than the usual discussions among legal practitioners would indicate. There is little question that the "ultimate" burden of proof must be set as a matter of law and is binding on lower courts. For example, in *Addington v. Texas*,[94] the Court held that the state must meet the "clear and convincing" evidence standard to civilly commit an allegedly mentally ill and dangerous person. But this seemingly straightforward requirement hides a fair amount of empirical complexity. In particular, consider the element of "dangerousness" that, together with mental illness, must be demonstrated by the state. Most recently, this issue has been discussed in the subclass of potential committees popularly referred to as "sexually violent predators" (SVPs).

In SVP cases, the Court has held that the state must prove that the defendant is both mentally abnormal[95] and dangerous. The Court, however, has yet to say how dangerous an alleged SVP must be to satisfy the second prong of the test, though it is likely to be at least by clear and convincing evidence and possibly by a stricter standard yet. If clear and convincing evidence is estimated as approximately a 75% likelihood, and proof beyond a reasonable doubt as exceeding a 90% likelihood, very few alleged SVPs would in fact qualify for commitment. The level of social scientific technology is not sophisticated enough to permit predictions with this level of certainty.[96] But if these levels of proof mean something different, then the state might be able to meet its evidentiary burdens with today's technology.

Although the Supreme Court has yet to consider the issue of what quantum of proof of future violence is constitutionally mandated in SVP cases, state courts have weighed in on the matter. In *People v. Ghilotti*,[97] for instance, the California Supreme Court interpreted a California statute that provided for the commitment of a person who has a "diagnosed mental disorder so that he or she is likely to engage in acts of sexual violence without appropriate treatment and custody."[98] The state argued that "likely" does not mean "probable" or "more likely than not." The state urged that "likely" meant "a significant chance, not minimal; something less than 'more likely than not' and more than merely 'possible.'"[99] The defendant, in contrast, argued that "likely" meant "highly likely" or at least "more likely than not."[100] The California court sided with the state and found that "'likely to engage in acts of sexual violence' does not mean the risk of reoffense must be higher than 50 percent."[101] The court stated as follows:

> [T]he phrase requires a determination that, as the result of a current mental disorder which predisposes the person to commit violent sex offenses, he or she presents a substantial danger—that is, a serious and well-founded risk of reoffending in this way if free.[102]

Under California law, therefore, the *kind* of proof required is the substantial danger test.[103] Yet the burden of proof under the applicable statute is the beyond a reasonable doubt standard. The court found no incongruity in asking juries to determine whether, by proof beyond a reasonable doubt, the defendant "presents a serious and well-founded risk of committing new acts of criminal sexual violence."[104] In effect, the California test asks the jury to determine with near certainty ("beyond a reasonable doubt") that there is a significant probability (something less than 50%) that the defendant will be violent. And indeed, when it comes to scientific statements of fact, it is not unusual to speak in these terms. It would not be incongruous, for instance, for a meteorologist to express 95% confidence that the chance of rain tomorrow is 60%. In the same way, as *Ghilotti* arguably requires in California, juries must determine by proof beyond a reasonable doubt (90% to 95%?) that the defendant is likely (25% to 30%?) to be sexually violent.

Constitutional Review-Facts. So far, there has been little of great controversy in my elucidation of constitutional facts in this section in that I have concluded that rule-facts should be decided as matters of law and adjudicative-facts should largely be subject to ordinary fact-finding rules. Although most judges and scholars have given little attention to these issues, if they had, virtually all would agree with at least the broad outlines of my analysis to this point. But such agreement likely ends here. By far the most difficult situation is presented by constitutional review-facts, a category that includes the vast majority of facts in constitutional cases. Review-facts are relevant under a particular interpretation of the Constitution (i.e., some constitutional rule or standard), and by definition, their resolution has precedential import in other cases. There is no shortage of examples, including some of the better known being the point at which the fetus becomes viable,[105] the effects of segregation on black schoolchildren,[106] the general and specific consequences of child pornography,[107] the group dynamics associated with jury size,[108] the effects of spousal notification provisions,[109] and so on.[110] As regards these sorts of facts, lower courts should have the authority to distinguish higher court rulings when there is substantial proof that the facts themselves have changed or our knowledge of the facts have changed, as long as those facts were necessary and sufficient for the earlier ruling.

In *Casey*, for example, the Court set forth the "undue burden" standard, which in turn established the relevance of the factual issue of whether a challenged regulation poses a "substantial obstacle" to the exercise of the abortion right. In *Casey* itself, the Court invalidated the Pennsylvania spousal notification provision primarily on the basis of research indicating its potentially burdensome nature, at least in a small percentage of cases. The Court, however, refused to invalidate the twenty-four-hour waiting provision, with the Joint Opinion observing that the research had yet to demonstrate that this waiting requirement posed a substantial obstacle to the exercise of the abortion right. Presumably, the Court understood that research might someday demonstrate this fact and, moreover, that other regulations might be challenged as being unduly burdensome. Lower courts should have the latitude, indeed the obligation, to review the evidence to determine whether the regulation passes muster under the *Casey* standard.

The power to review the predicate facts of precedent would not, however, give lower courts carte blanche to challenge higher court authority with which they disagree. When assessing the continuing validity of a precedent, lower courts would have to resolve two issues in a satisfactory and unequivocal way. First, the court would have to determine that the changed fact was necessary and sufficient for the earlier ruling; and second, it would have to put forward sufficient proof to support the new findings of fact.

The first consideration, whether the review-facts were necessary and sufficient for the earlier ruling, will sometimes be a delicate task. This assessment is easiest, of course, when essentially only one review-fact is offered to support an outcome. In *Ballew v. Georgia*, for example, the single basis for the outcome was the empirical assertion that juries are less effective when their numbers fall below a certain total, with six-member panels somewhat arbitrarily chosen as minimally required under the Constitution. Similarly, viability is based on a fairly concrete and unitary empirical proposition—the point in time when a fetus can survive outside the womb. In *Roper v. Simmons*, discussed in the first main section, in contrast, the empirical arguments were somewhat more complex. The Court listed three factual bases for concluding that those who kill as juveniles cannot be subject to capital punishment under the Eighth Amendment. These included surveys of state law indicating acceptance or renunciation of such punishments, the physiological and psychological developmental differences between children and adults, and a survey of international practice and opinion. Suppose, after some period of time, the evidence for one of these three premises indicates a changed empirical landscape. Should a lower court be entitled to rely on that basis alone to distinguish the *Roper* precedent? The answer is that there is no definite answer. Like virtually all aspects of constitutional law, there is no formula applicable under such circumstances. The lower court would have to determine to the best of its capacity whether the fact that has changed was the central premise for the otherwise controlling precedent. It might be, for instance, that a changed landscape with regard to state death penalty practices would be enough, but not if the changed landscape concerns international standards. But this is a judgment call.

Moreover, before challenging an established precedent, a lower court would also have to find that the research data are substantial enough to support the new empirical conclusion. The question for courts in subsequent cases would be whether research conducted after the earlier decision was sufficient to warrant reaching a different conclusion than was reached in the earlier case. In the situation of the twenty-four-hour waiting provision, for example, lower courts would not be able to reassess the research data that had been available to the Court in 1992 when *Casey* was decided. A court's assessment of an existing body of research data should be binding on lower courts. In fact, lower courts should act in this realm only when the research data are very robust and largely unambiguous. This is especially so when a Supreme Court precedent is in issue. Given the gravity of distinguishing a Supreme Court decision on a factual basis, lower courts should, and can be expected to, tread carefully over the new research terrain.

There is an assortment of significant advantages that come from adopting a procedural rule by which lower courts can reevaluate precedent when research data clearly indicate that predicate constitutional review-facts have substantially changed. First of all, it advances the legitimacy of constitutional lawmaking by keeping it in line with contemporary knowledge of the facts underlying constitutional decisions. As Oliver Wendell Holmes Jr. put it, "It is revolting to have no better reason for a rule of law than that so it was laid down in the time of Henry IV. It is still more revolting if the grounds upon which it was laid down have vanished long since, and the rule simply persists from blind imitation of the past."[111] When a constitutional rule is applied to a stated set of facts, the legitimacy of the outcome is undermined to the extent that those facts are not what the court says they are. The rule should fit the facts as they are known today.

In addition, giving lower courts authority to reconsider constitutional review-facts will have a salutary effect on the Supreme Court's sometimes harum-scarum reliance on such facts in its jurisprudence. Just the knowledge that lower courts might revisit factual premises for their holdings should lead the justices to be more careful in explaining the reasons for their decisions. In *Brown*, for example, few, if any, constitutional scholars believe that the social science research was anything more than a makeweight for an outcome reached on other grounds. But what were those other grounds, and why didn't the Court simply cite them instead? The truth is that in the early 1950s none of the other authorities unambiguously supported the outcome. The text itself was ambiguous, the precedent was weak or contrary, and original intent was inconclusive. Social scientific authority provided a seemingly neutral basis for the outcome, though in retrospect it was not seriously relied on. Similarly, in *Roe*, it appears fairly clear that Justice Blackmun used "viability" as a convenient placeholder for a sensible compromise between the fundamental right of women to control their bodies and the compelling interests of the state. Although *Webster* might suggest otherwise, I suspect that few constitutional scholars (or justices) believe that if viability were to move, say, to ten weeks, the abortion right would follow suit. By giving lower courts the authority to reconsider precedents based on outmoded review-fact premises, the Court should hesitate before expounding empirical reasons that are not real reasons for the outcome.

It might be argued, however, that taking away the Court's ability to find facts "normatively" or "interpretively" will limit the Court's flexibility to achieve outcomes it wishes to reach. Only if facts are understood interpretively can they be used rhetorically to support whatever outcome is sought. Especially when the Court operates at the vanguard of societal evolution, as it did in *Brown* and *Roe*, when traditional authorities militate against the "enlightened" path the Court has chosen, interpretive facts might play an essential rhetorical role. And indeed, one should be reluctant to advocate any jurisprudential approach that would have made deciding *Brown* more difficult.

Although I am sympathetic to the argument that the Court sometimes needs the latitude interpretive fact-finding gives it, I ultimately find it unpersuasive. The principal reason the Court relies on scientific arguments, as in *Brown* and *Roe*, is that the usual so-called neutral principles of interpretation are not available. The Court, ever solicitous of its legitimacy, which has been historically associated with restraint and reliance on neutral principles, is sometimes reluctant to give the true reason for its decisions. It was easier to say in *Brown* that social science revealed the inequality that was inherent in segregation than to say that the Court had reached the moral conclusion that segregation was wrong under virtually all circumstances, despite an ambiguous text, contrary precedent, and original intent that was, under only the most generous historical view, inconclusive. The argument from a moral basis makes the justices seem platonic guardians. Similarly, in *Roe*, viability as a scientific concept sounded more neutral than an opinion that instituted an "arbitrary" line at twenty-four weeks on the basis of little more than that at least five justices agreed that it was a reasonable compromise between two fundamental and irreconcilable principles.

The approach proposed here would thus take an important rhetorical arrow out of the Court's quiver. It might also weaken the Court's legitimacy to the extent anyone paying attention continues to believe that members of the Court actually adhere exclusively to nonsubjective neutral principles for their constitutional opinions. To the extent that taking facts seriously will accomplish anything, it is hoped that it will lead the Court to be more plainspoken about the reasons for what it does. This might pierce the judicial veil, but it will contribute in one very salutary way more generally. In the United States, the people are the ultimate sovereign. The people, therefore, should be fully engaged in the dialogue that takes place every time the Court decides a constitutional case. If the bases for decision are hidden beneath a scientific façade, and the true reasons are not made plain, then meaningful dialogue cannot occur. The Court, perhaps, has no greater obligation than giving reasons for its decisions. It should be candid about those reasons. Anything less and its legitimacy should be jeopardized.

Another significant advantage of giving lower courts the authority to reevaluate constitutional review-facts is that it will facilitate the introduction of new information into the law. Although discovery of constitutional review-facts is not limited to the adversarial process—since they can be brought to the attention of courts through amicus briefs or even independent research—they are likely to be developed most fully if first put into issue at the trial court level. The multiple layers of the trial and appellate process are well suited to the full exploration and development of the empirical record upon which disputed constitutional review-facts rest. Moreover, the courts' taking constitutional facts seriously sends an important message to researchers. Good research will be valued and potentially relied on whenever it is done. Previous decisions relying on early research data, therefore, do not foreclose reconsideration in light of the publication of substantial new data.

One striking change that would follow from a jurisprudence that permits lower courts to reconsider constitutional review-facts would be on the Supreme Court's control over its own docket. By distinguishing a controlling precedent on the basis of changed constitutional review-facts, a federal appellate court or a state's highest court could effectively force the Supreme Court to grant certiorari.[112] The Court uses its control over its docket partly to manage the timing of constitutional decisions, sometimes waiting considerable time for an issue to mature in the lower courts. The rule proposed here would give lower courts some leverage in forcing the High Court to enter a field (or return to a field) when, perhaps, the justices would have preferred to avoid the issue altogether.

Although loss of full control of its docket is a danger of the proposed rule, it is not one of great consequence. Even when the Supreme Court feels its hand has been forced, it need not issue an opinion that resolves the dispute on the merits. In the most extreme instances, the Court could reverse the lower court summarily, simply as being contrary to controlling precedent, and provide no further explanation. This is not likely to happen often, however, because the Court may feel compelled to explain why the changed factual situation does not alter the application of the constitutional rule. It might also be argued that the Court's loss of some control over its docket could itself be a salutary event. There is nothing sacred about the Court's certiorari power, and indeed, such absolute control is a relatively recent phenomenon. The proposed rule injects a measure of democracy into the High Court's docket, an outcome that might increase its responsiveness to the pressing and most dynamic issues of the day.

Finally, it is worth emphasizing that lower courts are unlikely to exercise their power to distinguish higher court precedent very frequently. They are likely to do so only when they have enough empirical ammunition to overwhelm the opposing precedent. This will not occur often. In most of the areas in which the Court employs empirical arguments, there are limited amounts of research available, and much of it tends to be fairly soft social science. Even a considerable number of research studies on many social science subjects will not be enough to sustain a court's reconsideration of a higher court's holding in a particular review-fact context. Also, many of the empirical questions the Court resolves concern highly complex matters that even the best efforts of mainstream scientists will not soon conquer. In *Kansas v. Crane*, for instance, the Court discussed the scientific research involved in defining "lack of volitional control," the principal component of the mental abnormality requirement in the commitment of sexually violent predators. Psychologists, psychiatrists, and neuroscientists are some distance from obtaining a good understanding of this construct. Many of the facts the Court employs share this level of complexity. Once the Court has weighed in with a review of the evidence and has provided an answer based on contemporary research, a lower court should be disinclined to revisit any particular constitutional review-fact without substantial research data supporting its holding. As Holmes, quoting Emerson, said, "When you strike at a king, you must kill him."[113]

Conclusion

The basic theme of this chapter could be that courts should take constitutional facts seriously. The first section outlined an alternative conception, one in which facts are found "interpretively," such that they serve the interpretive outcomes of constitutional adjudication. Facts under this view have a normative function and are used rhetorically to buttress a conclusion largely reached on other grounds. Accordingly, the deleterious consequences of segregation are put forth to support the conclusion that segregated schools are "inherently unequal." Any research offered subsequently to demonstrate the benefits of segregation is irrelevant under this conception because the empirical accuracy of the data was never intended to be taken seriously. As discussed in the first section, however, such fact-finding by fiat suffers serious limitations. Principal among these is the threat to the Court's legitimacy when the facts upon which it bases its rulings are demonstrated to be wrong.

The second section set forth a taxonomy by which the variety of constitutional fact-finding could be understood. I identified three basic types of constitutional facts: rule-facts, review-facts, and adjudicative-facts. Constitutional rule-facts are relevant to the definition of a rule or standard to be applied in a set of cases. These facts are instrumental in the process of *interpreting* the Constitution's meaning and are typically used in conjunction with, and are sometimes a component of, traditional constitutional authorities, such as the text, precedent, original intent, and constitutional structure. Perhaps the best-known type of constitutional rule-facts is historical facts used to determine "original intent." In contrast, the remaining two categories of facts are associated with the *application* of constitutional rules or standards. Constitutional review-facts involve facts that are relevant under a particular interpretation of the Constitution and that transcend individual cases. Constitutional adjudicative-facts similarly involve the application of the Constitution, but they are peculiar to individual cases.

The third section considered the operation of these three kinds of facts in regard to a seemingly intractable issue in constitutional fact-finding. Specifically, this section considered the issue of whether lower courts should have the power to distinguish (and thereby ignore) higher court precedent when the facts on which that precedent is based have changed or our knowledge of them has changed. The answers I provide to this question vary depending on the type of fact involved.

Constitutional rule-facts are employed in the service of interpreting the Constitution and, therefore, are ordinarily combined with an assortment of textual, normative, and structural considerations. In practice, it would be virtually impossible for lower courts to disentangle the importance of fact-finding to the development of a particular rule, and thus, lower courts cannot have the power to revisit rule making, even when the facts on which a rule is based have demonstrably changed. It is not that these facts should not be taken seriously but that their reconsideration upon a new record must be carried out by the level of court that found them originally. On the other end of the spectrum are constitutional adjudicative-facts. Because these facts are particular to the case, they generally recur in different form and thus, by their very nature, will be considered *de novo* by lower courts. Adjudicative-facts are invariably taken seriously because they ordinarily are highly disputed between the parties. Lying in the middle ground, with attributes of both rule-facts and adjudicative-facts, are constitutional review-facts. Taken seriously, these facts present the most controversial answer to the question of whether lower courts can revisit higher court authority when the facts have changed. I conclude that they should, as long as the review-facts were necessary and sufficient for the earlier ruling and substantial new research is available that unambiguously indicates that the facts have changed or our knowledge of them has changed.

In *Abrams v. United States*,[114] Justice Holmes, in a dissenting opinion, hypothesized "that the best test of truth is the power of the thought to get itself accepted in the competition of the market."[115] He added, somewhat laconically: "That at any rate is the theory of our Constitution. It is an experiment, as all life is an experiment."[116] Holmes, as perhaps the first legal realist, well understood the interaction between the Constitution's words and societal consequences. The Constitution may promulgate theories, but only life provides an experimental test. A well-functioning Constitution must be fully grounded in the empirical world and responsive to empirical demands. A Constitution is measured by its practical consequences. Constitutional provisions divorced from the world in which they operate are destined to become empty articles of faith, their legitimacy resting on repetition rather than reason. Our Constitution was "intended to endure for ages to come" and, as a consequence, must "be adapted to the various crises of human affairs."[117] Only through a candid and realistic constitutional fact jurisprudence will this intention be met.

Acknowledgments

I would like to thank the many people who read and commented on various drafts of this chapter. Of particular assistance were the faculty workshops at which I presented the main themes developed here. I am deeply indebted to the participants of the workshops at Arizona State University, University of California, Berkeley (The Center for the Study of Law and Society—Boalt Hall), Washington & Lee University, University of California, Irvine (Social Ecology), University of Texas, and University of California, San Diego (Psychology). Many individuals as well provided invaluable feedback and were very generous with ideas and suggestions. I would like to thank, in particular, John Monahan, Michael Saks, Chris Slobogin, Scott Sundby, John Robertson, and Wendy Wagner. I also want to thank my wife, Lisa, whose sharp editorial eye improved the quality of my writing and saved me from many embarrassing errors. Finally, I want to extend an especially heartfelt thank you to Austin Sarat and his very talented colleagues at Amherst College both for inviting me to participate in this speaker series and for their insightful comments and enthusiastic response to my talk.

Notes

1. See David L. Faigman, *Laboratory of Justice: The Supreme Court's 200-Year Struggle to Integrate Science and the Law* (New York: Henry Holt, 2004).

2. The corpus of scholarship on the immense subject of constitutional fact-finding is relatively small, though the subject has interested some better known scholars. See Kenneth Karst, "Legislative Facts in Constitutional Litigation," *Sup. Ct. Rev.* (1960): 75; Laurence H. Tribe, "Seven Deadly Sins of Straining the Constitution Through a Pseudo-Scientific Sieve," *Hastings L. J*. 36 (1984): 155; Henry P. Monaghan, "Constitutional Fact Review," *Colum. L. Rev.* 85 (1985): 229; see also Stuart Minor Benjamin, "Stepping into the Same River Twice: Rapidly Changing Facts and the Appellate Process," 78 *Tex. L. Rev.* 269 (1999); Rachel N. Pine, "Speculation and Reality: The Role of Facts in Judicial Protection of Fundamental Rights," *U. Pa. L. Rev.* 136 (1988): 655; Dean M. Hashimoto, "Science as Mythology in Constitutional Law," *Or. L. Rev.* 76 (1997): 111; Adam Hoffman, Note, "Corralling Constitutional Fact: De Novo Fact Review in the Federal Appellate Courts," *Duke L. J.* 50 (2001): 1427; Frank R. Strong, "The Persistent Doctrine of 'Constitutional Fact,'" *N.C. L. Rev.* 46 (1968); Frank R. Strong, "Dilemma Aspects of the Doctrine of 'Constitutional Fact,'" *N.C. L. Rev.* 47 (1969): 311; Jeffrey M. Shaman, "Constitutional Fact: The Perception of Reality by the Supreme Court," *U. Fla. L. Rev.* 35 (1983): 236; Ann Woolhandler, "Rethinking the Judicial Reception of Legislative Facts," *Vand. L. Rev.* 41 (1988): 111.

3. Given the range of issues raised by the topic of constitutional facts and the necessary page limitations imposed on participants in this book, this chapter is only an initial explora-

tion of the subject. I consider this general topic more comprehensively in *Our Empirical Constitution: The Science, Art, and Process of Finding Facts in Constitutional Cases* (forthcoming, 2007).

4. 347 U.S. 433 (1954). See, e.g., Edmund Cahn, "Jurisprudence," *N.Y.U. L. Rev.* 30 (1955): 150, 157–158: "I would not have the constitutional rights of Negroes—or of other Americans—rest on any such flimsy foundation as some of the scientific demonstrations in these records."

5. *Brown*, 347 U.S., 494, n. 11.

6. Ronald Dworkin, "Social Sciences and Constitutional Rights—The Consequences of Uncertainty," *J. L. & Educ.*, 6 (1977): 3, 5, quoting Cahn, *Jurisprudence*, 157–158 (emphasis added).

7. A second component of Dworkin's notion of interpretive facts is his belief that the social sciences are not sufficiently valid to support constitutional rulings. For example, Dworkin argues that "[w]hile in physics it is now thought to be an unsound judgment that rests merely on correlation between observable events unsupported by some notion of the mechanics that translate the cause to the effect, social science is only able to provide correlations without the mechanics." Ibid. Dworkin's criticism displays an unhealthy amount of "physics envy." Today, in fact, many scientific disciplines operate in a methodological world that is essentially based on correlational designs. Indeed, many applied sciences, such as epidemiology, meteorology, cosmology, and ecology, are largely unable to describe the sort of "mechanics" that Dworkin longs for. Dworkin's model of science is more Newtonian than Einsteinian. I agree that very often social science research is not valid, but sometimes it is, and there is no inherent reason it cannot be conducted in a rigorous manner. See David L. Faigman, "To Have and Have Not: Assessing the Value of Social Science to the Law as Science and Policy," *Emory L. J.* 38 (1989): 1005.

8. Ronald Dworkin, *Law's Empire* (Cambridge, MA: Harvard Univ. Press, 1986). See also Ronald Dworkin, "Law as Interpretation," *60 Tex. L. Rev.* 527 (1982): 540–546. For an analysis of the chain novel metaphor, see Stanley Fish, "'Working on the Chain Gang': Interpretation in Law and Literature," *Tex. L. Rev.* 60 (1982): 551.

9. Dworkin (1986), *Law's Empire*, 52.

10. 220 F.Supp. 667 (S.D.Ga. 1963).

11. Ibid., 677–678.

12. Ibid., 678.

13. Ibid., 674.

14. Ibid.

15. Ibid.

16. 333 F.2d 55, 61 (5th Cir. 1964).

17. Ibid.

18. The latter argument—that the major premise of *Brown* depended on the normative proposition that segregated schools were "inherently unequal"—effectively reads the

factual dispute out of the decision. This strategy boils down to a later court saying that despite an earlier opinion's stated reliance on a factual proposition, it was really based on a normative judgment. For all intents and purposes, this is the essence of Dworkin's notion of interpretive facts. The Fifth Circuit's first argument—that lower courts cannot reconsider earlier holdings even if the facts on which they were based have changed—raises a host of other issues. These issues are the principal subject of the third section of this chapter.

19. See generally, David L. Faigman, "'Normative Constitutional Fact-Finding': Exploring the Empirical Component of Constitutional Interpretation," 139 *U. Pa. L. Rev.* 541 (1991).

20. See, e.g., *Akron v. Akron Center for Reproductive Health*, 462 U.S. 458 (1983): Despite changes in medical technology that permitted abortions in 1983 to be performed more safely than childbirth through at least week sixteen, the Court held that "[t]he *Roe* trimester standard . . . continues to provide a reasonable legal framework for limiting a State's authority to regulate abortions."; *United States v. Salerno,* 481 U.S. 739, 751 (1987): "[T]here is nothing inherently unattainable about a prediction of future criminal conduct," quoting *Schall v. Martin,* 467 U.S. 253, 276 (1984).

21. See, e.g., *Ashcroft v. ACLU*, 124 S.Ct. 2783 (2004).

22. 410 U.S. 113 (1973).

23. See generally Laurence H. Tribe, *Abortion* (1990).

24. See *Washington v. Glucksberg*, 521 U.S. 702, 754 (1997) (Souter, J., concurring), discussing the need to avoid establishing constitutional standards on factual premises that might change as more research is done.

25. To some extent, of course, determining who must decide a constitutional fact will determine how evidence of that fact is received. For example, if a jury is the principal decision maker, evidence regarding constitutional facts will rarely, if ever, be introduced through amicus briefs or independent research.

26. Kenneth Culp Davis, "An Approach to Problems of Evidence in the Administrative Process," *Harv. L. Rev.* 55 (1942): 364, 402–403.

27. See *Fed. R. Evid.* 201(a) advisory committee's note: "Legislative facts . . . are those which have relevance to legal reasoning and the lawmaking process, whether in the formulation of a legal principle or ruling by a judge or court or in the enactment of a legislative body."

28. Kenneth Culp Davis, *Administrative Law Text* (3rd ed., 1972), § 7.03, 160.

29. See ibid.; see also Davis, "An Approach to Problems of Evidence," 402, noting that the rules of evidence for finding facts that form the basis for creation of law and policy should differ from the rules for finding facts specific to parties in a particular case.

30. Professors John Monahan and Laurens Walker expanded upon the Davis dichotomy by adding a third category that they call "social frameworks." Laurens Walker and John Monahan, "Social Frameworks: A New Use of Social Science in Law," *Va. L. Rev.* 73 (1987): 559, 563–570. The term *social framework* refers to the use of general conclusions from social

science research in determining factual issues in specific cases. Ibid., 570. A social framework consists of facts that in part transcend the particular dispute and in part pertain to that dispute. For example, a doctor might be called upon to testify that cigarette smoking has been linked to lung cancer and also be asked to testify that the plaintiff's lung cancer was caused by smoking cigarettes. The former fact is similar to Davis's legislative fact category in that it transcends particular cases, so that the fact question should have the same answer in every case in which it is asked. In contrast, the latter fact, whether the plaintiff's lung cancer is attributable to smoking, is akin to Davis's adjudicative-fact category. Monahan and Walker argue that the judge should decide and instruct the trier of fact regarding facts that transcend the litigation, and the jury should hear evidence on the facts peculiar to the dispute. Ibid., 592–596.

The social framework concept principally has evidentiary significance and generally falls within the constitutional-adjudicative category in my analysis. The Monahan and Walker thesis initiates a significant debate over the role of the judge versus that of the jury in finding adjudicative-facts. Monahan and Walker would give the judge responsibility for finding all facts that transcend the litigation, whether legislative or adjudicative. In contrast, under both Davis's dichotomy and traditional rules of evidence, adjudicative-facts of general import are determined by the jury. Thus, for example, the issue of whether defendant's substance X caused the plaintiff's illness Y would be answered by the jury, even though one part of the question—does substance X cause illness Y—is true or false as a general matter and transcends any one piece of litigation. Although Monahan and Walker did not apply their analysis to constitutional cases, it turns out that it works well in that context. At bottom, however, my interest is very different from, and broader than, Monahan and Walker's. They focused on the evidentiary practices that surround the reception of data and the resolution of disputes concerning the meaning of those data. Although these issues do arise in the constitutional cases I discuss, my concern involves how responsibility should be apportioned throughout the governing framework for deciding relevant factual issues under the Constitution. Therefore, although evidentiary issues are central to my enterprise, they comprise just one part. The taxonomy developed here would also be relevant to issues such as the judiciary's obligations vis-à-vis congressional fact-finding, standards of appellate review, and so on.

31. The reason I say "ordinarily" is that there is a basic ambiguity inherent in Davis's categories. His division of facts into legislative and adjudicative categories is based on how the fact-finder employs the particular fact. If the fact is used to resolve a particular litigation, it is, by definition, "adjudicative." This is so even though the factual issue may transcend a particular dispute, such as whether secondhand smoke causes lung cancer or silicone implants cause autoimmune disorders. Similarly, if a legislature points to a particular case to support its lawmaking—as occurred in the "right-to-die" controversy involving Terri Schiavo in 2005—this particularized fact is, by definition, "legislative." The scheme I develop in this section for the constitutional arena largely avoids this ambiguity because

the generality or specificity of the factual inquiry operates as a definitional feature of my framework.

32. 481 U.S. 279 (1987).

33. Ibid., 321.

34. Ibid., 308.

35. Ibid., 314–315.

36. Ibid., 323 (Brennan, J., dissenting): "A constitutional violation is established if a plaintiff demonstrates a 'pattern of arbitrary and capricious sentencing,'" quoting *Gregg v. Georgia*, 428 U.S. 195, n. 46 (1976).

37. In addition to the Monahan and Walker taxonomy of fact, Judge Robert Keeton has suggested the use of the term "premise facts" to describe any facts that support a reasoned decision of law or policy. Robert E. Keeton, "Legislative Facts and Similar Things: Deciding Disputed Premise Facts," *Minn. L. Rev.* 73 (1988) 1, 11.

38. See David L. Faigman, "'Normative Constitutional Fact-Finding': Exploring the Empirical Component of Constitutional Interpretation," *U. Pa. L. Rev.* 139 (1991): 541, 552–554.

39. See the following section, which discusses different standards for when lower courts should have the authority to reconsider constitutional legislative facts depending on whether they are rule-facts or review-facts.

40. See ibid.

41. 5 U.S. 137 (1803).

42. Ibid., 137: "The powers of the legislature are defined, and limited; and that those limits may not be mistaken, or forgotten, the Constitution is written."

43. *Wickard v. Filburn*, 317 U.S. 111, 128–129 (1942).

44. 125 S.Ct. 2195 (2005).

45. Ibid., 2197.

46. Ibid., 2198.

47. Ibid., 2197.

48. Ibid., 2212.

49. Ibid., quoting *Lopez*, 514 U.S. at 563.

50. Historians have since discovered that the Court was never particularly interested in the answer to this question because, even before reargument, a majority supported invalidating segregation on other grounds. See Richard Kluger, *Simple Justice* (New York: Vintage, 1975). But the year delay had monumental consequences. Chief Justice Vinson died that summer and was replaced by Earl Warren. Chief Justice Warren orchestrated a unanimous opinion in the case that has come to symbolize the inception of modern constitutional jurisprudence.

51. *Brown*, 347 U.S. at 489. Chief Justice Warren further observed: "The most avid proponents of the post-War Amendments undoubtedly intended them to remove all legal distinctions among 'all persons born or naturalized in the United States.' Their opponents,

just as certainly, were antagonistic to both the letter and the spirit of the amendments and wished them to have the most limited effect. What others in Congress and the state legislatures had in mind cannot be determined with any degree of certainty. Ibid.

52. The question whether the social science cited in *Brown* was truly relied on by the Court has been debated ever since the opinion was announced. Most commentators have concluded that the studies were a makeweight for a holding reached on other grounds. Elsewhere, I argue that the studies were important to the rhetoric of the decision and permitted the Court to reach a controversial legal judgment under cover of science. See Faigman, *Laboratory of Justice* (2004), 199–204. Long term, however, in regard to the cause of desegregation, the social science research had little consequence.

53. At oral argument in *Brown*, there was some confusion regarding whether segregation's effect was an adjudicative-fact or a legislative-fact. In the trials below, the petitioners had produced evidence on both issues, introducing general social science research conducted years earlier and also litigation-generated research in which students in the respective jurisdiction were tested using Kenneth Clark's notorious doll tests. At the argument, the NAACP's Robert Carter asked the Court to abide by the *Topeka* case's finding of fact that segregation had deleterious psychological consequences. He told the Court that the district judge's factual findings make a reversal "necessary." He argued, "[i]f there [are inequalities] in fact, that educational opportunities cannot be equal in law." Justice Hugo Black asked him whether that was "'a general finding or do you state that for the State of Kansas, City of Topeka?" Surprisingly, Carter's initial answer was the same as the *Stell* district court reached a decade later. Carter told the justices that "the finding refers to the State of Kansas and to these appellants and to Topeka, Kansas." He added, "I think that the findings were made in this specific case referring to this specific case." Black was troubled by the ramifications of limiting the empirical lesson to the single case of Topeka and asked whether this meant that "then you would have different rulings with respect to the places to which this applies, is that true?" Carter quickly realized his error, although in his haste to backtrack, he too readily abandoned the general social science available. He argued, "[n]ow, of course, under our theory, you do not have to reach the finding of fact or a fact at all in reaching the decision because of the fact that we maintain that this is an unconstitutional classification being based upon race and, therefore, it is arbitrary." Mark Whitman, ed., *Removing a Badge of Slavery* (Princeton, NJ: Markus Wiener Publishers, 1993), 131–132.

54. The sometimes ambiguous character of constitutional facts complicates the task of establishing a rational constitutional-fact jurisprudence, but it is not fatal to that effort, and this level of uncertainty is not unknown in constitutional cases. Consider, for example, the longstanding debate over whether the *Miranda* rule was constitutionally mandated or a judicially enacted remedy that could be revisited by legislative majorities. This ambiguity remained in the law for more than thirty years. Compare *Miranda v. Arizona*, 384 U.S. 436 (1966), setting forth the now-famous "Miranda warning" but leaving open the question whether it was constitutionally based, with *Dickerson v. United States*, 530 U.S. 428, 444

(2000): "Miranda announced a constitutional rule that Congress may not supersede legislatively." At the same time, however, because I prescribe very different rules of procedure for the different kinds of constitutional facts, any ambiguity over what kind of facts are at stake will increase the uncertainty endemic to the process.

55. *Miller v. California*, 413 U.S. 15 (1973).

56. 376 U.S. 254 (1964).

57. *Miller*, 413 U.S. at 15.

58. This is the lesson that Ronald Allen and Michael Pardo draw—and advocate—in their excellent article on the law—fact distinction. Ronald J. Allen and Michael S. Pardo, "The Myth of the Law-Fact Distinction," *Nw. U. L. Rev.* 97 (2003): 1769.

59. 505 U.S. 833 (1992).

60. 305 F.3d 684 (7th Cir. 2002).

61. 530 U.S. 914 (2000).

62. See *Hope Clinic v. Ryan*, 195 F.3d 857, 884 (7th Cir. 1999) (Posner, J., dissenting): "The health effects of partial birth abortion should indeed be treated as a legislative fact, rather than an adjudicative fact, in order to avoid inconsistent results arising from the reactions of different district judges . . . to different records," *vacated* 530 U.S. 1271 (2000). Early in the most recent litigation on so-called partial birth abortions, the Department of Justice sought the medical records of the plaintiff doctors on the theory that a review of these records would help answer the question of whether a health exception was necessary to a ban on the procedure. See *National Abortion Federation v. Ashcroft*, 330 F.Supp.2d 436 (S.D.N.Y. 2004). But these records would provide nothing more than anecdotal evidence and would not have been any more constitutionally relevant or empirically valid than any other group of records that could have been selected. In fact, they would have been less useful because they would not have been selected randomly.

63. *Newman*, 305 F.3d at 688: "*Stenberg* shows that the undue-burden standard must be applied at the level of logic, and to the nation as a whole, rather than one state at a time."

64. Ibid. See also *Majorek v. Armstrong*, 520 U.S. 968 (1997), holding that statute preventing nonphysician from performing abortions is not unconstitutional, without factual determination whether other medical professionals could perform the operation as safely or the costs of the rule are unduly burdensome.

65. *Newman*, 305 F.3d at 688–689.

66. Ibid., 693 (emphasis in original).

67. *Marbury v. Madison*, 5 U.S. 137 (1803).

68. 125 S.Ct. 1183 (2005).

69. 492 U.S. 361 (1989).

70. *State ex. rel. Simmons v. Roper*, 112 S.W.3d 397 (Mo. 2003).

71. *Roper v. Simmons*, Questions Presented for Review, Supreme Court of the United States (2005), http://www.supremecourtus.gov/qp/03-00633qp.pdf.

72. Ibid., 1190.

73. Ibid., 1195.

74. Ibid., 1196. The Court rejected the possibility of evaluating each juvenile defendant's level of maturity on a case-by-case basis. "The differences between juvenile and adult offenders are too marked and well understood to risk allowing a youthful person to receive the death penalty despite insufficient culpability." Ibid., 1197. In effect, the Court resolved juveniles' physiological and psychological capacities as a constitutional review-fact rather than a constitutional adjudicative-fact.

75. Ibid., 1187.

76. Ibid., 1209 (O'Connor, J., dissenting).

77. Ibid.

78. Ibid., quoting *State Oil Co. v. Khan*, 522 U.S. 3, 20 (1997) (emphasis in original).

79. Ibid., 1209–1210.

80. Ibid., 1217 (Scalia, J., dissenting): "What a mockery today's opinion makes of Hamilton's expectation [that the judiciary will be the least dangerous branch], announcing the Court's conclusion that the meaning of our Constitution has changed over the past 15 years—not, mind you, that this Court's decision 15 years ago was wrong, but that the Constitution *has changed*" (emphasis added).

81. Ibid., 1229.

82. Ibid., 1229–1230.

83. Ibid., 1228, n. 9, citing *Laurence v. Texas*, 539 U.S. 558, 571–573 (2003), *United States v. Virginia*, 518 U.S. 515, 532–534 (1996), *Planned Parenthood of Southeastern Pa. v. Casey*, 505 U.S. 833, 847–850 (1992).

84. Ibid., 1230.

85. Ibid.

86. 333 F.2d at 61.

87. Ibid.

88. *Stell* also got it wrong because it interpreted *Brown* to create an adjudicative-fact question, since it thought the issue was the consequences of segregation in its locale. Pretty clearly, however, the Court had cited the research at a general level, and thus, if the *Stell* Court were to make the argument, it would have had to have been as a changed review-fact.

89. 492 U.S. 490 (1989).

90. Ibid., 526. The statute provided that a twenty-week-old fetus was presumed valid so that viability testing effectively placed the burden of proof on the woman to disprove viability.

91. See, e.g., *Roe v. Wade*, 410 U.S. 113, 174–175 (Rehnquist, J., dissenting): "As early as 1821, the first state law dealing directly with abortion was enacted by the Connecticut Legislature. . . . By the time of the adoption of the Fourteenth Amendment in 1868, there were at least 36 laws enacted by state or territorial legislatures limiting abortion."

92. Constitutional adjudicative-facts have somewhat greater impact than ordinary adjudicative-facts simply because of their constitutional genesis. Although their resolution might not have any direct consequences for other cases, there may be substantial indirect consequences. For example, in the area of free speech, an adjudication that certain materials are obscene in one locale could chill their dissemination in other areas, even though the materials might not be deemed obscene in those areas.

93. A higher court, of course, retains the power to independently review a trial court's findings of fact. If the case were remanded, the lower court would be obligated to act in accordance with the directions of the higher court—both as to the facts and the law. But the specific facts of the case are not likely to recur exactly in any other case, and so lower courts are not bound to adjudicative fact-finding done by higher courts in other cases.

94. 441 U.S. 418 (1979).

95. In *Kansas v. Hendricks*, 521 U.S. 346 (1997), the Court held that civil commitments of sexually violent predators were not constitutionally limited to those who suffered mental *illness*. "Mental abnormality" would suffice, together with "dangerousness," as a basis for commitment.

96. David L. Faigman, David H. Kaye, Michael J. Saks, and Joseph Sanders, *Modern Scientific Evidence: The Law and Science of Expert Testimony* (2005).

97. 44 P.3d 949 (Ca. 2002).

98. Ibid., 915.

99. Ibid., 916.

100. Ibid., 915–916.

101. Ibid., 916.

102. Ibid. Oddly, the court sought support for its definition of the word *likely* from thesauruses rather than dictionaries. As Justice Werdegar pointed out in dissent, "[o]ne should look to a dictionary, rather than a thesaurus, for a definitive statement of a word's meaning." Ibid., 931, n. 3 (Werdegar, J., dissenting). She found that such a search supported a "more likely than not" meaning for the word "likely." Ibid.

103. Ibid., 923, n. 14. Examples of contrary authority include, *In re Leon G.*, 26 P.3d 481, 488–489 (Ariz. 2001), "likely" means "highly probable"; *Commonwealth v. Reese,* 2001 WL 359954 *15 (Mass.Super.Ct. April 5, 2001), "Likely" means "at least more likely than not"; *Matter of Linehan,* 557 N.W.2d 171, 180 (Minn. 1996), "likely" means "highly likely"; *In re Commitment of W.Z.,* 801 A.2d 205, 216 (N.J. 2002): "An individual may be considered to pose a threat to the health and safety of others if he or she were found, by clear and convincing evidence, to have serious difficulty in controlling his or her harmful behavior such that it is highly likely that the individual will not control his or her sexually violent behavior and will reoffend"; *State v. Ward,* 720 N.E.2d 603, 609 (Ohio App. 1999), "Likely" requires "a firm belief of conviction that an offender will more likely than not commit another sex offense in the future."

104. Ibid., 924, n. 15. Under the law, the jury would also have to find beyond a reasonable doubt that the defendant "(1) previously was convicted of qualifying violent sex crimes, [and] (2) has a mental disorder which seriously impairs volitional control of violent sexual impulses." Ibid.

105. *Roe*, 410 U.S. at 113; *Casey*, 505 U.S. at 833.

106. *Brown*, 347 U.S. at 483.

107. *New York v. Ferber*, 458 U.S. 747 (1982).

108. *Ballew*, 435 U.S. at 223.

109. *Casey*, 505 U.S. at 833.

110. See generally, Faigman, *Laboratory of Justice.*

111. Oliver Wendell Holmes Jr., "The Path of the Law," *Harv. L. Rev.* 10 (1897): 457, 469.

112. Federal district courts and intermediate state courts, of course, could also reevaluate constitutional review-facts, but superior courts short of the U.S. Supreme Court could check any unrestrained enthusiasm in this regard.

113. *Bartlett's Familiar Quotations* (16th ed.), ed. Justin Kaplan (1992) 433: 30, quoting "Recollected by Oliver Wendell Holmes, Jr. from Max Lerner," *The Mind and Faith of Justice Holmes* (1943).

114. 250 U.S. 616 (1919).

115. Ibid., 630.

116. Ibid.

117. *McCulloch v. Maryland*, 17 U.S. 316, 515 (1819).

Index

Aberdeen, John: on arrest, 63*n*14
abortion, 160–161, 167–170, 176–178, 191*n*20; nonphysicians performing, 195*n*64; partial-birth abortion, 169, 195*n*62; undue-burden approach, 169, 170, 181–182; waiting period requirement (24-hours), 168, 170, 177–178, 184–185
Accu-Tek, Hamilton v., 105
actor network theory (ANT), 73–74, 79–82, 90–91; supplementation of insights, 83
"actual malice" standard, 179
Addington v. Texas, 179–180
admissibility of evidence, 146–147
affect, 98
African Americans: segregation. *See Brown v. Board of Education*; segregation
"after the fact," 27
alethes, 133
Amar, Akhil, 111
American Revolution, 75
American trial court. *See* trial court, U.S.
anonymous allusion, 84–86
ANT. *See* actor network theory (ANT)
Arendt, Hannah, 131, 149–150
Aretinus, 32
Aristotle, 148; rhetorical tradition, 28
Arizona, Miranda v., 194*n*54
arrest: suspicion and, 32–33, 63*n*13
Arte of Rhetorique (Wilson), 33–35
autopoeisis, 73, 83–84

Bacon, Francis: beyond reasonable doubt, 48; history, fact and, 53; inductive methods, 158; natural science, fact and, 57, 70*n*113; on suspicion, 63*n*13
balancing tests, 74
Ballew, 182
Barbones Parliament, 64*n*32
"before the fact," 27
belief: formation, 98; truth and, 27
belief beyond reasonable doubt. *See* beyond reasonable doubt
bench trials, 137
Best, William, 69*n*98
beyond reasonable doubt: belief beyond reasonable doubt phrase, 50; constitutional cases, 175, 181; development of concept, 26; jury trial, history, 48–50; sexually violent predators, 181
biased assimilation, 99
Bible. *See* New Testament; Old Testament; Scripture
binary, 79–82
Black, Justice Hugo, 194*n*53
black letter law, 74, 78
Blackmun, Justice Harry, 184
Blackstone, William, 148
Blandy, Mary, 47
Blasphemy Act of 1697, 64*n*33
Board of Education, Brown v. See Brown v. Board of Education
Boston Massacre Trials, 50
Bowles, Edward, 65*n*42
Boyle, Robert, 58
Bracton, Henry de: on circumstantial evidence, 43; on suspicion, 32, 35, 63*n*13
Bradley, Thomas, 65*n*42; *A Sermon Preached at the Assizes*, 65*n*47
Brady, Robert, 54
Brandeis, 125*n*105
Brandenburg incitement test, 164

Brown v. Board of Education, 177, 193*nn*50–52; classifying constitutional facts, 165–167; constitutional adjudicative-facts, 196*n*91; interpretive understanding of, 160; premise of, 190–191*n*18; social science research, 157, 183–184; *Stell*, distinguished, 174; validity of holding, 178; writing of opinion, 159
Bush, George H. W., 107
Butler, Bishop, 46

California: sexually violent predators (SVPs), 180; substantial danger test, 180–181, 197*n*103
Campbell, George: *Philosophy of Rhetoric*, 51
Campion, Jesuit Edmund, 45–46
Canada: epistemological sidelining, 87
candor, duty of defense lawyer, 138, 153–154*n*8
capital sentencing: race and, 162–163
Carhart, Stenberg v., 168–170
Carter, Jimmy, 107
Carter, Robert, 194*n*53
Casey, Planned Parenthood of Southeastern Pennsylvania v., 167–170, 176–177, 181–183
catenate inferences, 154*n*11
Catholic Church, 158
Chamberlain, Richard: *Complete Justice, The*, 37, 38
Chilotti, People v., 180, 181
Cicero, Marcus Tullius: pretrial examination, 33, 34; rhetorical tradition, 28–29; suspicion, 32
circumstances, 43, 66–67*n*65. *See also* circumstantial evidence
circumstantial evidence: history of jury trial, 42–48; jury trial, 134; manslaughter, 45; murder, 45–47; poisoning, 47; probative value of, 154*n*11; treason, 45–46, 66*nn*61, 63; witchcraft trials, 44
city councils, 88–89
Clark, Kenneth, 157, 194*n*53
Clarus, 32
clear and convincing evidence standard, 180
cognition, cultural, 94, 95
cognitive-dissonance avoidance, 98–100
coherence-based reasoning, 99–100
Coke, Sir Edward, 35; on presumptions, 44; witnesses, oaths and credibility, 66–67*n*65
Commerce Clause, 164
common-sense justice, 104, 121*n*5
Common Sense school, 51–52
Complete Justice, The (Chamberlain), 37, 38
concurrent circumstances, 51
confession: Renaissance rhetoric, 34
conflict: and cultural cognition, 100–101
conscience, 49; and belief, 50; "law of conscience," 67–68*n*83
Conseil d'État, 79, 82
constitutional adjudicative-facts, 165, 167, 170, 176, 196*n*91; free speech, 196–197*n*92; lower court review of higher court fact-finding, 179–181
constitutional cases, fact-finding, 156–198; abortion, 167–170, 176–178; ambiguous character of facts, 194*n*54; beyond reasonable doubt, 175; classification of constitutional facts, 165–171; configuration of constitutional facts, 161–171; constitutional adjudicative-facts, 165, 167, 170, 176, 179–181, 196*n*91; constitutional review-facts, 163, 164–165, 170, 181–186; constitutional rule-facts, 163, 164, 170, 176–179; corpus of scholarship, 189*n*2; general considerations, 171–175; interpretation, 157–160, 190*nn*7–8; lower court review of higher court fact-finding, 171–186, 181–186; normative facts, 158; right-to-die controversy, 192*n*31; social frameworks, 191–192*n*30; specific considerations, 175–186; taxonomy of, 162–165
constitutional review-facts, 163–165, 170; lower court review of higher court fact-finding, 181–186
constitutional rule-facts, 163, 164, 170; lower court review of higher court fact-finding, 176–179
Country Justice, The (Dalton), 35, 44

Crane, Kansas v., 186
Creation (Bible), 55–56
criminal prosecution, 138–139; duty of candor of defense lawyer, 138, 153–154*n*8; plea bargaining, 153*n*7
Crompton, 35
crude politics theory of law, 93, 101, 110
cruel and unusual punishment, 172
culpable causation, 104
cultural cognition, legal realism and, 94–101; affect, 98; belief formation, 98; biased assimilation, 99; cognitive-dissonance avoidance, 98–100; coherence-based reasoning, 99–100; conflict, 100–101; culturally threatening evidence, impotence of, 99; culture war thesis, 100; end of ideology thesis, 100; generally, 114–115; interpersonal trust, 98–99; interpretive method, 110–111; judges, 106–110; juries, 103; legal philosophy, 111–112; mechanics of cultural cognition, 98–101; naïve realism, 99; reactive devaluation, 99; risk, cultural theory of, 97
culturally threatening evidence, impotence of, 99
cultural realism, legal realism as, 93–125
cultural theory: internalization of social relations, 117*n*12
culture war thesis, 100, 101

Dalton, Michael: *Country Justice, The*, 35, 44; jury trial, 37; oaths, on, 65*n*49
dangerousness, 197*n*95
Davis, Kenneth Culp, 162–163, 176, 191–192*nn*30–31
death penalty: jurors, imposition by, 121–122*n*59; juveniles, 172, 195–196*n*74
De Copia (Erasmus), 33
defendants: civil defendants, 139; criminal defendants, 138–139
De Inventione (Cicero), 29
deontological reasoning, 76
Dewey, John, 133
DNA evidence, 127
doctrine of materiality, 146
doll tests, 194*n*53
Donellan, John, 48
drinking and driving cases, 89
Due Process Clause, 173, 176
Durantis, William, 31, 32
Dworkin, Ronald, 157–158, 190*nn*7–8

egalitarians, 124*n*94
egalitarianism, 97
Eighth Amendment, 163, 172–173, 182
Eirenarcha (Lambarde), 34
Emerson, Ralph Waldo, 186, 198*n*113
end of ideology thesis, 100
English/American law: pragmatism, 75–76
environmental law issues: judges, cultural cognition, 108, 122*n*64
epistemological sidelining, 86–88
Equal Protection Clause, 173, 178
Erasmus, Desiderius, 33, 43, 63*n*16
ESP, 100
Essays upon the Law of Evidence (Morgan), 51
Establishment Clause, 122*n*68
ethnic diversity: jurors, 105, 121*n*58
evidence: admissibility of evidence, 146–147; circumstantial. *See* circumstantial; clear and convincing evidence standard, 180; culturally threatening evidence, impotence of, 99; DNA, 127; individuation and, 148; law of, 135; probative value of, 154*n*11; treatise tradition and, 51
exemplary excerpting, 85–86
experience, 77, 85
expert witness: anonymous allusion, 84; reliance on, 105

fact, proof of, 25–71; arrest, 32–33; beyond reasonable doubt, 26, 48–50; fact, generally, 27–35; full and half proofs, 31; full proof of the fact, 52; historical study of, 26; jury, studies of, 26; jury trial, 35–50; medieval developments, 30–32; pretrial examination, Renaissance rhetoric, 33–35; rhetorical tradition, 28–30; scripture, 30; treatise tradition, 50–60
fact-finding: Common Sense school, 51; constitutional cases. *See* constitutional cases, fact-finding

factum probandum, 146
false positive, 175
Federal Rules of Civil Procedure, 138
firearms control. *See* gun control
First Amendment, 89
Fisher, John, Bishop of Rochester, 37, 63*n*26
formalism, 74, 95, 140, 147
Fortescue, Sir John, 36
Fourteenth Amendment, 164, 166, 172, 178
Frank, Jerome, 113, 125*n*101
"Frankification," 125*n*101
free speech, 164; constitutional adjudicative-facts, 196–197*n*92
frivolous cases, 138
full and half proofs, 31
Fuller, Thomas, 54

Gambier, James: *Guide to the Study of Moral Evidence, or of That Species of Reasoning that Relates to Matters of Fact and Practice*, 52
Gandinus, Albertus, 31
Garnett, Justice Henry, 66*n*61
gay marriage: opposition to, 96
generalizations, 134
genetics, 81
Georgia: capital sentencing, 162–163
Gilbert, Sir Geoffrey: *Law of Evidence, The*, 51, 68*n*92; treatise tradition, 51, 52; witnesses, oaths, and credibility, 39–41, 66–67*n*65
Glendon, Mary Anne, 125*n*105
Glennan, Andrew, Trial of, 68*n*87
"Glory of Historians," 54
Gonzales v. Raich, 164
grand jury: instructions as to nullifying powers, 120*n*39; oaths and witness credibility, 65*n*46
Greenleaf, Simon, 52–53
Guide to the Study of Moral Evidence, or of That Species of Reasoning that Relates to Matters of Fact and Practice (Gambier), 52
gun control, 112, 124–125*n*95
gun manufacturers: suits against, 105

Hale, Sir Matthew: beyond reasonable doubt, 49; jury trial, 37; religion and treatise tradition, 56; on suspicion, 35, 63*nn*13–14; witnesses, oaths and credibility, 39, 40
Hamilton v. Accu-Tek, 105
Hartley, David, 51
Hastie, Reid, 103, 120*nn*44, 48
Hawkins, William, 35, 63*n*13
Heidegger, Martin, 133
Hendricks, Kansas v., 197*n*95
Heylyn, Peter, 54
hierarchists, 124*n*94
History of the Pleas of the Crown (Hale), 63*n*13
Hobbes, Thomas: history, fact and, 53; natural science, fact and, 57
Holmes, Oliver Wendell Jr.: Emerson, quoting, 186, 198*n*113; "experience," 77; jurisdiction, transmuting into knowledge, 88; pragmatism, 74–78; rule of law, reasons, 183
Holt, Judge, 39
Hooke, Robert, 58–59
hung juries, 104, 105, 114
hypothesis: fact distinguished from, 71*n*122

idealism, 129
impeaching the verdict, rule against, 141
impeachment of witness, 144
imputed knowledge, responsibilization through, 89–90
incitement test, *Brandenburg*, 164
Indiana: abortion law, 168, 169
indicia indoubitata, 31
individualism, 97, 111, 124*n*94
individuation, 148
Institutes of the Orator (Quintilian), 29
interpersonal trust: cultural cognition and, 98–99
interpretation: Constitution, 157–160, 190*nn*7–8

James, Henry, 143
journalism, 86; legal realism, accounts of, 93

judges: adjudicative facts, 162; apolitical judiciary, demise of, 101; bench trials, 137; biases, 106; cultural cognition, overview, 106–110; decision-making, 103, 107, 109, 117*n*8, 123*n*85; environmental law issues, 108, 122*n*64; ideological involvement of, 116*n*4; individuality of, 118*n*14; interpretive method, 110–111; justice, sense of, 102; legal philosophy, 111–112; legal realism and, 93; meals of, influence on jurisprudence, 96, 118*n*17; minorities, members of, 122*n*67; morality and, 115*n*1; motivation of, 101–102; neutral principles and, 117*n*8; policing function, 137; political or moral tastes of, decisions based on, 118*n*16; political affiliation of, 109, 123*n*83; political behavior of, 116*n*2; politics of, 117*n*7; proxies, 108, 122*n*76; rules, knowledge of, 137–140; sentencing, criminal cases, 109; situation sense, 95

judicial statesmanship, 113, 125*n*105

juries and jurors: common-sense justice, 104, 121*n*5; comprehension of instructions, 141; constitutional facts and, 191*n*25; constrained narrative, 148–149; culpable causation, 104; cultural cognition, overview, 103–105; death penalty, imposition of, 121–122*n*59; decision-making, 103; disagreements of fact, 105; emotions of jurors, 116*n*3; ethnic diversity, 105, 121*n*58; expectations, 120–121*n*49; facts, knowledge of, 134–136; grand jury. *See* grand jury; hung juries, 104, 105, 114; instructions, reforms, 153*n*3; legal realism and, 93; memory, 120*n*48; motivation of, 101–102; narratives presented to, 142–143, 148–149, 152, 153*n*4; preconceptions, 120–121*n*49; prototypes used by, 120*n*47; recall, 103; rules, knowledge of, 136–137; situation sense, 95; verdicts, 140–141; verdict stories, 103, 120*n*48

jurisdiction: knowledge, transmuting into, 88–89

jury trial, history, 35–50; beyond reasonable doubt, 48–50; circumstantial evidence, 42–48; composition of jury, 35–36; credibility of witness, 38–42, 51; grand jury, oaths, 65*n*46; justices of peace, 64*n*36; manslaughter, circumstantial evidence, 45; "Matter of Fact," 38; murder, circumstantial evidence, 45–47; murder, witnesses, 64*n*33; murder of child, two-witness law and, 64*n*33; number of, 38, 64*n*31; oaths and credibility, 38–42; perjury, 38, 64*n*30; petty jurors, 36; poisoning, circumstantial evidence, 47; Royal Proclamation for Jurors, 63*n*23; studies of jury, 26; treason, 38, 45–46, 66*nn*61, 63; two-witness rule, 38, 64*nn*32–33; witchcraft trials, circumstantial evidence, 44; witnesses, 36–42, 51

justices of peace: jury trial, history, 64*n*36

juvenile death penalty, 172, 195–196*n*74

Kansas: segregation, 159–160, 173–174, 194*n*53, 196*n*88

Kansas v. Crane, 186

Kansas v. Hendricks, 197*n*95

Kant, 77, 131–132; Copernican revolution, 153*n*2

Keeton, Judge Robert, 193*n*37

Kemp, McCleskey v., 162–163

Kennedy, Justice, 168, 172

Kentucky, Stanford v., 171–173

Kierkegaard, Søren, 77

King, Rodney, 127

Kirwan, Richard, 51, 52

"know," described, 126–127

knowledge: described, 126–127; imputed knowledge, responsibilization through, 89–90

knowledge moves, 83; anonymous allusion, 84–85; dynamics of, 90–91; epistemological sidelining, 86–88; exemplary excerpting, 85–86; imputed knowledge, responsibilization through, 89–90; transmuting jurisdiction into knowledge, 88–89

Kozinski, Judge, 124*n*92

Labonte, U.S. v., 109
Lambarde, William: *Eirenarcha*, 34
language and legal realism, 124*n*92
law-and-society theories, 77–78
"law of conscience," 67–68*n*83
Law of Evidence, The (Gilbert), 51, 68*n*92
lawyers: civil matters, constraints, 137
left law-centered theories, 77
legal documents: interpretation of, rhetorical tradition and, 62*n*5
"legal factory," 79
legal knowledge practices, theoretical and methodological issues. *See* Theoretical and methodological issues
legal philosophy, cultural cognition and, 111–112; generally, 114–115
legal realism, 93–125; affect, 98; belief formation, 98; biased assimilation, 99; cognitive-dissonance avoidance, 98–100; coherence-based reasoning, 99; conflict and, 100–101; cultural cognition, 94–101; culturally threatening evidence, impotence of, 99; culture war thesis, 100; end of ideology thesis, 100; interpersonal trust, 98–99; interpretive method, 110–111; judges, 106–110; juries, 103; language and, 124*n*92; law, cultural cognition and, 101–112; legal philosophy, 111–112; mechanics of cultural cognition, 98–101; modern empirical legal realism, 112–114; naïve realism, 99; norms and, 94; reactive devaluation, 99; risk, cultural theory of, 97; values and, 94
legal texts, 79–82
Lexington, Virginia: obscenity case, 167, 171
liberation hypothesis, 153
likely, defined, 197*n*102
Lilburne, Leveller John, 64*n*32
linguistic practices, trial court, 135–136, 153*n*2
liquor inspections, 89
Locke, John, 37–38; beyond reasonable doubt, 49; "law of conscience," 67–68*n*83; treatise tradition and, 52; witnesses, oaths and credibility, 39
Lofft, Capel: and treatise tradition, 52
Lolita (Nabokov), 167
lower court review of higher court fact-finding. *See* constitutional cases, fact-finding

MacIntyre, Alasdair, 149, 152
Macmurry, John, 132
Madison, Marbury v., 164
Malleus Malificarum, 32
"manifest" crimes, 31
Mann, State v., 123–124*n*91
Manochius, Jacobus, 62*n*11
manslaughter, 45
Mapplethorpe photograph, obscenity and, 167
Marbury v. Madison, 164
Marian bail, 33
marijuana, 164–165
Marshall, John, 164, 171
Mascardus, 32
matter of fact, 38, 56, 57
Matthaeus, 32
McCleskey v. Kemp, 162–163
McDonald's, 90
McKinnon, Daniel: *Philosophy of Evidence, The*, 52
McNally, 52
mechanical jurisprudence, 140
medieval times: proof of fact, 30–32
mentally ill persons, 180, 197*nn*95, 102
methodology. *See* Theoretical and methodological issues
Mill, John Stuart: treatise tradition, 51
Miller test for obscenity, 164, 167, 171
minorities: judges as members of, 122*n*67
Miranda v. Arizona, 194*n*54
Miranda warning, 194*n*54
Mississippi: abortion law, 168
Missouri: abortion law, 178; cruel and unusual punishment, 172–173
modern empirical legal realism, 112–114
Monahan, John, 191–192*n*30
monetary awards for convictions, 48
moral certainty, 52
moral evidence, 50, 68*n*83

morality, 148
More, Sir Thomas: beyond reasonable doubt, 49; on circumstantial evidence, 43; treatise tradition, 53
Morgan, John: *Essays upon the Law of Evidence*, 51
motivation: individual consciousness of, 117*n*10
murder: child, two-witness law and, 64*n*33; circumstantial evidence, 45, 46–47; witnesses, 64*n*33

NAACP, 194*n*53
Nabokov, Vladimir, 167
naïve realism, 99
narrativization, 142–143, 152, 153*n*4; constrained narrative, 148–149
natural law theory, 148
natural science, fact and, 57–60
nature-nurture debate, 87
Nebraska: abortion law, 168–169
neighborhoods: concerns of, 85
New Haven colony: two-witness rule, 64*n*32
Newman, Woman's Choice-East Side Women's Clinic v., 168, 169
"New Philosophy," 57
New Testament, 55
New York Times v. Sullivan, 167, 179
Nixon, Richard, 123*n*89
norms, legal realism and, 94; cultural norms, 97
North, Francis, 40
North, Roger, 69*n*107
"notorious" crimes: medieval times, 31
nuclear power: utilization of, public opinion, 96

oaths, witness credibility and, 38–42; assize sermon (1663), 65*n*47; grand jury, 65*n*46; perjury, thoughts on, 65*n*42
obscenity: free speech and, 196–197*n*92; *Miller* test for, 164, 167, 171
O'Connor, Justice Sandra Day, 168, 172–174
Oklahoma: abortion law, 170
Old Bailey Trial, 47, 50, 68*n*87
Old Testament, 55; fact, proof of, 30
originalist modes of interpretation, 110

Paley, William, 48, 65*n*42; treatise tradition, 51
partial-birth abortion, 169, 195*n*62
Peake, Thomas, 52
Pennington, Nancy, 103, 120*nn*44, 48
People v. Ghilotti, 180, 181
perjury, 38, 64*n*30, 65*n*42
Philosophy of Evidence, The (McKinnon), 52
Philosophy of Rhetoric (Campbell), 51
Piperata, Thomas de, 31
Planned Parenthood of Southeastern Pennsylvania v. Casey, 167–170, 176–177, 181–183
Platonism, 132
plea bargaining, 153*n*7
poisoning, 47
politics: crude politics thesis, 93, 101, 110; or principle, 94
Popish Plot and Exclusion trials, 41
positivism, 147
Posner, Judge Richard, 111
Pound, Roscoe, 75
Powell, Justice Lewis F., 163
PowerPoint, 80
Practical Treatise on the Law of Evidence (Starkie), 52, 69*n*97
pragmatism, 74–78
prejudice, 147
presentist modes of interpretation, 110
presumptions of law: and circumstantial evidence, 43, 66–67*n*65; proof, as, 68*n*92; violent presumption, 47, 66*n*50
pretrial examination: Renaissance rhetoric, 33–35
probability, 51
Process and Reality (Whitehead), 132
Proof of Circumstances, 68*n*91
proof of fact. *See* Fact, proof of
proxies, 108, 122*n*76
psychological realism, legal realism as, 93–125
psycho-social fact, 132

public hearings on new law, 85–86
Pufendorf, Samuel, 68*n*83

Quintilian: pretrial examination, 33; rhetorical tradition, 28–29; suspicion, 32

race differences: capital sentencing, 162–163
race discrimination claims, 111
Raich, Gonzales v., 164
Raleigh, Sir Walter, 38
Ray, John: *Wisdom of Good Manifested in the Works of Creation, The*, 56
reactive devaluation, 99
Reagan, Ronald W.: judges appointed by, 107
realism. *See* legal realism
reality effect, 86
reasonableness: imputed knowledge, responsibilization through, 89–90
reasoning: coherence-based reasoning, 99–100
recall: jurors, 103
Rehnquist, William H., 123*n*89
Reid, Thomas, 51–52
religion, fact and: treatise tradition, 55–56
Renaissance rhetoric: pretrial examination, 33–35; revival of, 28
Reproductive Health Services, Webster v., 178
resistance, 81
responsibility, 151–152
responsibilization, 89–90
Rhetorica ad Herrenium, 28–30
rhetorical tradition, 28–30
right-to-die controversy, 192*n*31
risk: cultural theory of, 97; perceptions of, 118*n*23
Roe v. Wade, 160–161, 176–178; and social science research, 184
Romano-canon tradition, 32
Roper v. Simmons, 171, 174, 182
Royal Society, 57, 59
Ruffin, Justice Thomas, 111
Rule 11 sanctions, 153*n*6
rule by nobody, 150
rules of recognition, 139
Rye House Plot, 54

Savannah-Chatham, Stell v., 159–160, 173–174, 196*n*88
Scalia, Justice Antonin, 76, 111, 136, 172–174, 196*n*80
scallops, study of, 80
science: interpretation, 157–158; technological nature of, 153*n*1; treatise tradition, 57–60
scientific objects, biographies of, 82
Scripture: fact, proof of, 30, 55
secondhand smoke, 192*n*31
segregation, 157–160, 165–167, 177, 190–191*n*18. *See also Brown v. Board of Education*
sentencing: capital sentencing, 162–163; judges, cultural cognition, 109
A Sermon Preached at the Assizes (Bradley), 65*n*47
sex discrimination claims, 111
sexually violent predators (SVPs), 180, 181, 197*n*104, 197*nn*95, 104
sexual orientation, 87
Sherry, Richard, 43
Simmons, Roper v., 171, 174, 182
situated practical ideals, 126–134; history, intellectual, 131–134
situation sense, 95
slavery: slave owner shooting slave, case, 123–124*n*91
social, legal claims about, 83–90; anonymous allusion, 84–85; epistemological sidelining, 86–88; exemplary excerpting, 85–86; imputed knowledge, responsibilization through, 89–90; transmuting jurisdiction into knowledge, 88–89
social frameworks, 191–192*n*30
social ordering, 110
solidarists, 124*n*94
Souter, Justice David, 168
Sprat, Thomas: matter of fact, on, 57–58; treatise tradition, 54
standards of proof, 128
Stanford v. Kentucky, 171–173
Starkie, Thomas, 48; *Practical Treatise on the Law of Evidence*, 52, 69*n*97
State v. Mann, 123–124*n*91

Stell v. Savannah-Chatham, 159–160, 173–174, 196*n*88
Stenberg v. Carhart, 168–170
Stewart, Dugald, 51, 52
Stewart, Martha, 76
Stillingfleet, Edward: religion and treatise tradition, 55–56
Strafford, Earl of, 41
strict constructionist, 123*n*89
substantial danger test, 180–181, 197*n*103
Sullivan, New York Times v., 167, 179
Supreme Court: abortion, 169; certiorari, granting of, 185–186, 198*n*112; constitutional review-facts, 183; cruel and unusual punishment, 172; political nature of, 101
Susanna, Biblical story, 30, 35
suspicion: arrest and, 32–33, 63*n*13; Renaissance rhetoric, 33
SVPs. *See* sexually violent predators (SVPs)

Taft, 125*n*105
Tancred, 32
testimony vs. verdicts, 67*n*76
Texas, Addington v., 179–180
theoretical and methodological issues, 72–92; anonymous allusion, 84–86; binary, 79–82; Britain, 79; English/American law, 75–76; epistemological sidelining, 86–88; exemplary excerpting, 85–86; France, 79; imputed knowledge, responsibilization through, 89–90; knowledge moves, 83–90; legal texts, 79–82; North American scholarship, 79; pragmatism, 74–78; scope and method, 72–92; social, legal claims about, 83–90; transmuting jurisdiction into knowledge, 88–89
thief takers, 48
Thurmond, Senator Strom, 115*n*1
Timaeus (Plato), 132
Topeka, Kansas: segregation, 159–160, 173–174, 194*n*53, 196*n*88
tort law: responsibilization, 89–90
torture: medieval times, 31; Renaissance times, 33
treason, 38, 45–46, 66*nn*61, 63
Treatise of the Law of Evidence (Greenleaf), 52–53
Treatise of the Pleas of the Crown (Hawkins), 63*n*14
treatise tradition, 50–60; history, fact and, 53–55; matter of fact, 56, 57; natural science, fact and, 57–60; religion, fact and, 55–56
trial court, U.S., 126–155; admissibility of evidence, 146–147; doctrine of materiality, 146; facts and law, 134–140; factum probandum, 146; knowledge of facts by jury, 134–136; knowledge of law of rules by judges, 137–140; knowledge of rules by jury, 136–137; law of rules, 147–148; law of rules, knowledge of, 145–147; linguistic practices, 135–136, 153*n*2; practical knowledge, inevitability, 151–153; practical truth, knowledge of, 148–150; prejudice, 147; responsibility, 151–152; situated practical ideals, 126–134
"true law," 145
trust: interpersonal trust, cultural cognition and, 98–99
truth and belief, 27

"undoubted indicia," 31
undue-burden approach, abortion, 169, 170, 181–182
U.S. v. Labonte, 109
Utah: abortion law, 168–170

values: legal realism and, 94; voters, moral values as concerns of, 119*n*34
verdicts, 140–141; impeaching the verdict, rule against, 141; stories, jurors, 103, 120*n*48; testimony vs., 67*n*76
Vinson, Chief Justice Fred, 166, 193*n*50
violent presumption, 31, 47, 66*n*50
voters, moral values as concerns of, 119*n*34

Wade, Roe v., 160–161, 176–178; and social science research, 184
Walker, Laurens, 191–192*n*30
Wallis, John, 58–59
Warburton, Justice, 44, 46
Warren, Chief Justice Earl, 166, 193*nn*50–51

Waterhouse, Edward, 67*n*76
Watt, Isaac: treatise tradition, 51; witnesses, oaths and credibility, 39
Webster, John: *White Devil, The*, 44
Webster v. Reproductive Health Services, 178
Whately, Richard, 51
White, James, 150
White Devil, The (Webster), 44
Whitehead, Alfred North, 132
Wildavsky, Aaron, 117*n*12
Wilson, James, 51
Wilson, Sir Thomas: *Arte of Rhetorique*, 33–35; circumstantial evidence, on, 43
Winstanley, Digger Gerrard, 64*n*32
Wisdom of Good Manifested in the Works of Creation, The (Ray), 56
witchcraft statutes, 66*n*53
witnesses: credibility of witness, 38–42, 51; expert witness. *See* expert witness; impeachment of, 144; murder of child, two-witness law and, 64*n*33; number of, 38, 64*n*31; oaths and credibility, 38–42; perjury, 38, 64*n*30; two-witness rule, 38, 64*nn*32–33
Wittgenstein, Ludwig, 133
Woman's Choice-East Side Women's Clinic v. Newman, 168, 169

zoning, 85

The Amherst Series in Law, Jurisprudence, and Social Thought

EDITED BY

Austin Sarat, Lawrence Douglas, and Martha Merrill Umphrey

Law and the Sacred (2007)
How Law Knows (2007)
The Limits of Law (2005)
Law on the Screen (2005)